Jack
To a good &
and a kind "Regular"
Best Wishes
Roger Wagner

NO WORK
AND
ALL PLAY

NO WORK
AND
ALL PLAY
AUDACIOUS CHRONICLES OF A CASINO BOSS

ROGER WAGNER

Outskirts Press, Inc.
Denver, Colorado

Famous Quotes:

"I never did a day's work in my life. It was all fun."
-Thomas Edison

"Find a job you love and you will never have to work a day in your life."
-Jimmie Foxx

"I have never worked a day in my life. It's not work when you love what you are doing."
-David Shakarian

Almost Famous Quote:

"I never worked a day during my forty-five years in the casino business. It was all fun and games."
-Roger Wagner

Picture of Author and Jack Binion
courtesy of Michael Canoff, Chicago Photographer

Acknowledgments

I SPECIFICALLY WANT to dedicate this book to Jack and Phyllis Binion for giving me the opportunity to live a very comfortable life in retirement. Their trust and loyalty to me has been overwhelming and I will cherish that as much as the wonderful times I had being part of the leadership of their great company.

I also want to dedicate fifty percent of any royalties this book may generate to the UNLV College of Hotel Administration. Generally books of this type from unknown authors like me do not hit the Best Seller list, but if we get any traction on sales at all, fifty percent of the royalties will go to my alma mater. Without my introduction to the Dunes Hotel back in 1966 through the UNLV student center, I would never have considered working in a hotel casino in the first place. Certainly, the degree I received from the Hotel College at UNLV helped open the door for my first management position in Las Vegas. Who knows, maybe with this revenue opportunity, UNLV will make my book required reading for all new and prospective students considering hotel and/or casino management for their careers.

I also want to acknowledge Glenn Lillie, Jon Wolfe and my wife, Carolyn, for critiquing and suggesting worthwhile edits. I hope you enjoy the humorous stories of all the characters that made my life in the gaming industry so darn much fun.

Introduction

I FELT COMPELLED to provide my lifelong assessment of what I consider to be a "fairytale" profession worth pursuing by anyone who loves people, enjoys teamwork, values friendships and prefers never to really have to work in a mundane career position. This is not a story about me. Instead, it is really an actual chronicle of humorous episodes and the many interesting characters that crossed my path during my forty-five year career in the casino resort industry. These situations are typical of what any average individual can expect to experience if they should decide to step into the shoes of a management person in the gambling industry.

Over the course of my nearly five decades in the hotel and casino industry, I have been blessed with the opportunity to watch legal gambling evolve from the "sawdust" and syndicate controlled joints in Nevada to a multi-billion dollar industry controlled by big-money corporations and sovereign Native American tribal nations operating in forty-eight states and employing several hundred thousand people. I started in the business when African Americans were not permitted to rent hotel rooms on the Las Vegas Strip and women were prohibited from dealing table games in any Las Vegas casino south of Sahara Boulevard. Thankfully, today all that has changed and our industry is proudly comprised of almost half minorities and half female employees.

I grew up in Nevada back in the 1960s when Del Webb, the owner of the New York Yankees, was the biggest casino owner in Las Vegas. About the same time, I witnessed Howard Hughes purchase the 400-room Desert Inn and the 750-room Sands Hotel for less than $20,000,000 all together and where today in the exact locations stand the Wynn-Encore Resort and Venetian-Palazzo Casinos, whose combined value exceeds $20 billion dollars.

I had the opportunity to help develop and open the MGM Grand Hotel in Reno, which at the time was the largest gaming facility under one roof in the world, while simultaneously observing legalized gambling as it moved beyond Nevada with the opening of Resorts International Casino in Atlantic City back in 1978. As gambling became more and more accepted and perceived as legitimate adult recreation, gambling joints and palaces sprouted up in Laughlin, Nevada, Iowa, Biloxi and Tunica, Mississippi......and then all hell broke loose and casinos popped up everywhere. An industry that employed only 25,000 people in 1966 when I started my career now requires over three quarters of a million employees and managers.

Far too many careers are not fun. Most people make their living by performing services that ordinary people require to live their daily lives. Most businesses charge customers for fixing and repairing things that break in the home, the business, the car or in one's health. But the casino industry is different. We charge customers to have a good time and it's the one and only business where the customer has a chance to get the price of their admission back, if they are lucky.

For every thousand casino employees, there are about ten senior executive positions. These are the coveted jobs that only a few folks will achieve, but which provide a lifestyle both in and out of the workplace that is often the envy of even well-connected people in other professions, because we have so damn much fun. The best part about this career is the fact that while it looks like magic to run a casino, it is actually a business that is built on simple principles, lots of black and white arithmetic, financial accountability and sound employment practices.

I learned early on that to get the most out of a career in the casino business, there are special relationships you must nurture to ensure that when you show up at the workplace and advance through this exciting career, you never really have to work again. This book will identify real-life human beings who were important in my career. From the stories I will tell, you will see how they made me dream, set me straight and in many instances, made me laugh or cry.

These relationships formed the foundation and success of every movement I made throughout my career and they can be grouped into four categories. These are four relationships that will spur your potential to never have to work again:

1. Role models to inspire us:
   - These models set patterns for us to follow
   - They challenge us to dream
   - They also encourage us to take risks and change our paradigms

2. Mentors to teach us:
   - These are our coaches on the job
   - They become our personal counselors and trainers

3. Partners to assist us:
   - Partners are those co-workers and teammates who support each other
   - Partners provide mutual support
   - They form the informal workforce support network

4. Friends to support us:
   - They provide emotional support and intellectual stimulation
   - Friends are with us in the thick & thin
   - These individuals motivate us to make us do what we can do
   - They help us keep a humorous outlook on life
   - Friends enjoy life with us

As I wrote this book, I decided to divide it into seven sections that cover critical growth periods of my personal career path. Each of these sections is broken down into short chapters that describe some of the often humorous and sometimes bizarre events in which I found myself entangled. The various chapters also identify many of the key individuals and characters that formed my strategic relationships during each of these periods of time.

The seven sections cover many a character, some who became my role models, some my mentors, some my partners and many my friends. As you might expect, a few of these characters were all of the above.

Contents

Section 1

BEGINNING A SYNDICATED CAREER IN GAMING HOSPITALITY — MY FIRST DAYS AT THE DUNES
HOTEL AND COUNTRY CLUB WORKING FOR WELL CONNECTED BOSSES

"NO WORK AND all play." That is how my career ended but actually it did not start that way. My entry into the gaming industry came quite by accident. But luck, timing and fate are three key ingredients in the gambling business, so it is appropriate that I got my start that way.

While I grew up in Boulder City, Nevada just twenty-two miles from downtown Las Vegas, I had never contemplated a career in the gaming or hotel industry. During high school as I planned for college, I had focused all my efforts on studying to become an architect. I was good in art and I excelled in math during high school so I thought I would be a natural candidate for architectural school. I selected the University of Idaho for my undergraduate study because it was known for having a good solid program. But after my arrival at college in the fall of 1965, I discovered that I just could not comprehend calculus. While I faked my way through the final exams and squeaked out a passing grade, I recognized that I could not fake my way through a career that required calculus as a day-to-day tool. With money running short and my college goals shattered, I headed back home to Nevada to re-group.

In January, 1966 I enrolled at the Nevada Southern University (now known as the University of Nevada Las Vegas or UNLV) and began taking courses in general study, without any major in mind at the time. I was given an athletic scholarship for track and field which certainly helped defray the costs of college classes and books, but the general cost of living still required that I find a job to support my living expenses and extracurricular activities. This was before the advent of McDonalds or Burger King, but I was still able to secure a job as a fry cook in a small hamburger joint on the north end of the Las Vegas Strip for $1.25 per hour. But the hours were erratic and the overall paycheck always fell short of my needs. Labor laws in those days were weak and the owner of this fast food restaurant did not believe in paying overtime for extra-long work weeks or even straight time wages for the two hours it took to clean the kitchen every night after I clocked out. I had to do that as part of the job. Nonetheless, in 1966 jobs were tight for young people fresh out of high school, so while I spent much time reading the classified ads and visiting the Nevada Employment Center, the fry cook job was necessary to pay the bills. It was not much fun then but there was little time left over to play anyway, so I cannot say I was a dull boy.

Then one day in the summer of 1966 just before the next fall semester was going to begin, I was aimlessly wandering around the administrative offices of the university still trying to determine what I wanted to be when I grew up. At that time there were only four buildings at the Las Vegas campus, so it was difficult to get lost. The operation was small and run kind of by the seat of the pants, but the college employees in the administrative office were thoughtful and they were always on the lookout for employment opportunities for the students. They were well aware that Nevada Southern University (at that time called NSU for short) basically served the local community, and most of the students either lived at home or had to have a job of some kind to sustain their pursuit of a college education. Therefore, the clerks in the admissions office constantly polled local businesses for employment openings and prominently posted such openings on the bulletin board located next to their service window in the office.

Most of the available college jobs were in various service companies around Las Vegas. There were few openings in the casinos except during the summer when kids with prominent families might get a chance to be lifeguards at one of the resort's pools. In 1966, there were only fourteen major casino resorts operating on the strip of which at this writing, only four of the original brands remain: namely the Sahara, Riviera, Flamingo and the Tropicana. The other ten have all imploded and most have been replaced by the mega-structures we know Las Vegas to be comprised of today.

At that time in the mid-sixties, the then existing casino hotels on the strip seemed to be relatively large by comparative standards. It is hard to believe that The Wynn Resort with its Encore Tower has more hotel rooms in one entity today that all of these fourteen Casinos offered back in 1966. The location of the "Strip" started at Sahara Avenue and was never really part of Las Vegas. While the strip hotels south of Sahara Avenue all claim Las Vegas in their address, they reside in the unincorporated communities of Paradise and Winchester Townships with some overlap into the community of Enterprise, Nevada.

(Not counting motels, some which had a limited number of slot machines, the Strip at that time was comprised of the Sahara, Thunderbird, Riviera, Stardust, Desert Inn, Silver Slipper, Castaways, Sands, Flamingo, Dunes, Tallyho, Tropicana and Hacienda.

Caesars Palace opened in 1967, The International Hotel now known as the Las Vegas Hilton opened in 1969 and the MGM Grand, now operating as Bally's opened in 1973. Then for 16 years, no new major casinos were built on the Strip until Steve Wynn opened the Mirage Casino in 1989 on what had previously been the site of the Castaways Hotel.)

And this is where I caught my first break, finding a job that eventually led to a career of "all play and no work."

There, thumb tacked on the bulletin board, was a small card that read,

"WANTED, ROOM CLERK for the Dunes Hotel and Country Club. $300 per month salary. If interested please call Mr. Charles Gustin, General Manager at 734-4110 between 10:00 a.m. and 4:00 p.m. Monday through Friday"

CHAPTER **2**

WHILE IT WAS assumed by everybody I knew in Las Vegas that the big casinos were all run by mobsters, for this kind of pay check I could sell my soul to the mafia. Furthermore, while I didn't even know what a room clerk was or did, I figured out quickly that if I could snatch a job that paid $300 a month, it would solve my financial problems for certain, so it was well worth the call. I ran to the nearest pay phone there in Frasier Hall and with severe apprehension, I called Mr. Gustin at the telephone number on the card. I was passed through to a wonderful girl named Nancy, who professionally screened the call and then passed me on to talk with Mr. Gustin (By the way, I was fortunate to have Nancy become my secretary some seven years later).

Mr. Gustin, a soft spoken hotelier with his roots in Des Moines, Iowa, picked up the phone and was very jovial, thus making my first conversation with him very comfortable and unassuming. He hardly sounded like a mobster at all. "*Charlie*", as we all called him behind his back described the position that was open and that he was trying to support the students at the college by hiring as many of them for open positions at the Dunes Hotel as he could. He said that I sounded like I would fit in and he asked me to stop by the next day to fill out an employment application and meet with him personally. There I met his secretary, Nancy, and then at the end of my personal interview, Mr. Gustin said I could have the job as long as his two assistant managers concurred that I would fit in with the team. Therefore, before the job was mine to keep, I would still have to schedule one additional appointment to meet with the swing shift manager, Mr. James "Jimmie" Francis, because I would initially be working with Mr. Francis under his supervision.

Nancy set up an appointment for me to meet with Jimmie the next afternoon. As I sat waiting for our meeting in the small area behind the front desk at the Dunes that August evening, I noticed that most of the room clerks were considerably older than I and, in fact, I saw no one that I could tell was less than 30 years old around the front office. In those days 30 years old seemed quite old. For a minute, I started to get cold feet, wondering if I would fit in with their team. Later I learned that there were two or three people working the desk that were 25 years old and there was one guy, Bob Vannucci, who was a few months older than me, but after I hired on, he always referred to me as "the kid."

Anyway, to make a long story short, I met with Jimmie Francis and he let me know right away that I was being gently pushed into his department by Mr. Gustin, but that if I was going to survive in this job, I owed my allegiance to Jimmie. "And before you start, kid," Jimmie admonished me, " I want you to know that everyone working for me at this front desk understands up front, that we all live by the axiom: **The boss ain't always right, but the boss is always the boss and don't you ever forget it."**

Jimmie certainly sounded tough, but he didn't look like a mobster, either. I agreed to abide by his rules and he sent me on to the uniform shop with Bobby Vannucci to get fitted for work the following evening.

As I reflect back now, my first four personal acquaintances at the Dunes Hotel (Charlie, Nancy, Jimmie and Bobby) all became my role models, mentors, partners and friends. What a great start.

THE FIRST DAY on any job is always the toughest and this was no exception. Besides being the youngest employee on the staff, I knew nothing about how a hotel front desk worked, so I really felt stupid. On top of that, the atmosphere of the brand new expanded Dunes Hotel was so exquisite that I almost felt out of place with my $2.00 dress shirt and $5.00 shoes. I guess that is why they provided us uniforms; so we didn't look too backward to belong. There was so much to learn on that first day. Trying to remember the names and faces of fellow employees would take weeks. Then I found out that Mr. Gustin, the general manager, was not the real boss. He just ran the hotel. Now I had to remember the names and faces of the numerous owners, casino executives and other department heads on staff. I could never have imagined an organization this big. I was amazed to learn that the Dunes employed almost 1800 people. It was a city within a city and its population, including employees and customers in the rooms, was greater than little Boulder City, where I grew up.

Jimmie teamed me up with an old desk clerk named Vic Wilmot (who I later found out was an uncle of Jimmie's), and Vic tried to show me the ropes around the front desk. Vic was a good partner, but never was he a real role model or mentor. His friendship was shallow and it remained at the desk when we punched out. Little by little I started to catch on to the procedures and nomenclature used around a casino-hotel front office, but it was clear to me that I was an inconvenience to Vic and maybe I was a slower study than he was used to teaching. I will never know…..but what I do know is fate, luck and timing were all in the cards for me again.

About two weeks after I joined the company, the Dunes rehired a desk clerk who had taken a sabbatical for the summer in Mexico and now was returning to Las Vegas for the winter. This fellow was a charismatic young man about 26 years of age who could sell an icicle to an Eskimo. I didn't know his name but he was obviously legendary around the front desk and in other departments of the hotel where he had also previously worked, and everybody was anxious to have "Spike" back on duty.

Madison Seymour Cook was his real name, so it is easy to see why he preferred to be called Spike. He served in the role of philosopher and instigator at the Dunes Hotel front office for over 13 years. Anyway, Spike took a brotherly liking to me and saw that I was struggling to grasp some of the tougher aspects of the front desk procedures and he kindly took me under his wing to indoctrinate me on the nuances of hotel operations. He showed me short cuts and described in simple terms why certain things were done in order to comply with rules and to effectuate the best possible service for customers. Spike knew his way about the Dunes, but he was even more prone to excel outside the hotel on his personal time. A little more about that later.

But at any rate, Madison "Spike" Cook immediately became my role model both in and out of the hotel and he was the most involved mentor, partner and friend that I have encountered in my 45 years in the casino hotel business. Finally catching on to my role as a desk clerk and enjoying my first couple big paychecks that totaled over $120 take-home pay every two weeks, I was really starting to enjoy this line of work. Then disaster almost struck. I had only been working at the Dunes for about two months, when I was informed that there would be a seasonal layoff and, of course, the least senior employees would be let go first, which included me.

But good luck surfaced again. The night before I was to be discharged, the graveyard desk clerk got drunk and did not show up for work. Jimmie asked me to fill in for the missing employee and to my good fortune, the missing employee never returned. Consequently, I became the permanent "Graveyard" desk clerk, a position I held until I graduated from college three years later. The graveyard shift, which comprised the hours of midnight until 8:00 a.m. the following morning, permitted me the freedom to attend college and have a personal life during the daytime, while giving me time to learn the night audit procedures for a big hotel. Better still, this shift permitted me two hours to study for school on company time between 4:00 a.m. and 6:00 a.m. every morning.

The graveyard shift also enabled me to be my own boss, because my supervisor, Jimmie, ended his shift about 30 minutes after I arrived for duty every night, and the day shift manager, Frank, seldom showed up before I departed in the early morning. Being on this shift forced me to make the minor (and sometimes more major) management decisions usually deferred to the front desk supervisors by the day and swing shift clerks. Additionally, this late shift provided for my direct involvement with the owners of the casino that were constantly around on the graveyard shift, hosting the many premium customers who gambled during the wee hours of the night and early morning.

The more I learned about the hotel and casino business, the more I wanted to be involved with this industry as a career. The front desk of a hotel is the hub of the operation. Back in those days before computers, it was also the information center for the company. Room clerks had great discretion when assigning rooms and suites, processing upgrades and resolving guest grievances. With a stroke of the pen, a desk clerk can make or break a bellman. A case in point, shortly after I started at the Dunes, a snotty bellman started to harass me in a low-key way, but it was annoying. I soon realized that bellmen all lined up for their "fronts" in order, so whenever I saw this bellman ready for my next front, I would assign the next customer in line to room 1369 (or as close to room 1369 as I could find available).

Incidentally, 1369 was the longest walk from the front desk and the only way to get to room 1369 was by walking. After a while, this bell-man no longer harassed me.

More good luck followed. In 1967, Nevada Southern University introduced a new college to its curriculum so that enrolling students could earn a bachelor degree in Hotel Administration. I immediately focused my remaining college experience on course study that would enable me to pursue a degree and an eventual career in hotel management. In 1968, I became the first college intern at the newly opened Caesars Palace and life for me was beginning to move into the fast lane.

In 1969, Nevada changed the name of Nevada Southern University to UNLV, and I graduated fifth in my class from the University of Nevada, Las Vegas, in September of that year. I should note that while I graduated fifth in my class, there were only six people graduating that first year. With my degree behind me, I began looking for my first management position in the Las Vegas Resort arena.

To my dismay, the management people of the casino hotels in Las Vegas were less impressed with my college degree than I was. For the next five months I visited personnel offices and wrote letters and left resumes all over the Strip and downtown Las Vegas hotels soliciting an entry level management position. Management people in 1969 tended to be considerably older and less educated, and there was little reception for a 22-year-old graduate of UNLV to be hired into management off the street. It was customary then that managers were to be home grown through experience on the job. That is how it always had been and therefore always should be.

In the meantime, during my extended search for a management position, I moved on to the day shift from the graveyard shift at the Dunes to get my schedule back into a normal dimension. Young people have no patience and I was not an exception. I began to think that Las Vegas might not be my best avenue to pursue a hotel career and I began to look outside Las Vegas at some of the big hotel chains. As much as I did not want to leave the excitement or security of my home town in Nevada, I felt I had to exploit the college degree I had worked hard to earn.

Early on in my search with the big hotel chains, I received an opportunity to interview with the Western International Hotel Company for an entry level position at the newly opened Century Plaza Hotel in Los Angeles. It looked like an exciting hotel although quite boring in relationship to the Dunes casino. I felt comfortable during my interview and was well received by the recruiting manager at Western International Hotels (now know as Westin). At the conclusion of the interview, I was informed that they would make a determination for a potential entry level management job within two weeks.

As my continuing good luck would have it, when I returned to Las Vegas from my interview in Los Angeles, I received a call from Edward Zike, the resident hotel manager at the famous Sands Hotel in Las Vegas. My application for a management position had been referred to him, and he was interested in talking with me about a potential opportunity at the Sands Hotel.

I made an appointment and met up with Mr. Zike the following Monday morning. Mr. Zike, ("EZ" as we later referred to him) was a young 30-year-old hotel manager who had been promoted through his position as a desk clerk himself, and who also had a college degree, unlike so many of the other hotel managers in the town at the time. Mr. Zike liked my resume but was hesitant to engage me as a front desk manager at age 22, without seeing my abilities behind the desk. He made me a proposition that if I would come on to the Sands payroll as a desk clerk and prove my knowledge of hotel operations in that position, he would give me fair consideration for the position of assistant resident manager of the Sands Hotel within 120 days.

That same evening, I received a telephone call from the recruiter at the Century Plaza offering me an entry level supervisory position in their convention catering department, so now I had the dilemma of selecting my first career move. After consultation with my wife and my dear friend, Spike, I decided that my original passion for a hotel career was grounded by my introduction to the excitement of the gambling atmosphere at the Dunes Hotel, and therefore I should take a shot for the position at the Sands Hotel. The next morning I picked up the phone and called Mr. Zike, accepting his offer to become a desk clerk at his hotel, gambling that I would do a good enough job to impress him to promote me within my first 120 days of employment. A few minutes later, I reluctantly called the Century Plaza and informed them that I had accepted an alternative position. To this day, I have never regretted my decision. Before I leave this section, let me tell you some stories about the more interesting characters and memorable experiences I encountered working here.

CHAPTER **4**

THE DUNES WAS a microcosm of the many characters of the world. The most interesting of these characters were the owners themselves. While some of them may have resembled the mobsters you saw on the big screen, most of them looked like polished businessmen in expensive suits. I really never wanted to know exactly which one of these guys was really connected and which ones were merely of the connected. I never asked them and they didn't tell me. Nonetheless, they were characters that deserve a mention in this chapter.

Cool Owners:

- The primary real estate owner of the Dunes was a Chicago trucking company magnate, named Jake Gottlieb. A rotund man with terrible vision, he always came around the front desk looking for his messages and mail, holding them up to within one inch of his squinting eyes because he refused to wear reading glasses. The vision of this man hardly fit the stereotype of a mobster, either.

  Of all the Dunes owners, Mr. Gottlieb was no doubt the wealthiest and he lived in the best suite on the 22nd floor of the new Dunes Tower. While not involved in the day to day operations of the hotel or casino, he seemed to be the most respected of all the owners by everyone, including the other owners themselves. Mr. Gottlieb's wife had a small dog, and whenever Mrs. "G" called the front desk, you could usually hear the little dog yapping in the background. A little more about this dog later. Without a doubt, Jake Gottlieb was an early role model for me in that he demonstrated how a casino and trucking company entrepreneur could also be a caring and thoughtful employer.

■ Mr. Gottlieb had sold a small piece of the Dunes to a friend who became the official " Face of the Dunes Hotel" out in the Las Vegas community. He was a character by the name of Major Riddle. Also from Chicago, Mr. Riddle was not a General or a Colonel, nor was he a Major in the armed forces. "Major" was his name, and he appeared to watch over the administrative and financial aspects of the M&R Investment Company, the Holding Corporation of the Dunes. A spry fellow who was always courteous but fidgety when looking for his messages or mail at the front desk, the rumor was out all over the Dunes that he was the recipient of one of the country's first penile erection pumps. While humorous, it was an allegation that no one ever confirmed. I do remember that he occupied the suite one floor below Mr. Gottlieb on the 21st floor.

■ Another owner and key to the success of the Dunes Casino was Sidney Wyman. Mr. Wyman was the larger than life head of the Casino operations at the Dunes. This guy easily weighed in at 400 pounds and while rotund and soft, looked like he could have you killed in a minute if he wanted to. Mr. Wyman was the consummate host for customers of the Dunes, especially those from St. Louis from where he reigned. Unlike all the big casinos today, the Dunes had no big marketing staff.

Instead, its owners did all the marketing, managing and hosting, and Sid Wyman led that effort. Sid lived in suite 506-7-8 in the new tower and he spent much of his own personal recreational time in the Dunes poker room where he was also a consummate gambler himself.

The Dunes owners happened to also own the Royal Palms Motel, located next door to the Dunes. They always wanted to fill the Dunes rooms to the point that we had to frequently "farm" confirmed reservations next door to their motel. Inevitably, this policy would require the front desk to "walk" confirmed reservations next door quite often, especially on weekends when room availability in Las Vegas was always scarce. One of my favorite recollections of Mr. Wyman was that he would frequently "Fire" me in front of one of his customers that was being sent next door to the motel. He would rant and rave in front of the customer blaming me, the graveyard room clerk, as the scapegoat for giving up the customer's room reservation. My role was to walk away from the desk and begin removing my uniform jacket as if accepting my termination, while the disgruntled customer now was feeling better because I was fired for my indiscretion. Once the customer was satisfactorily relocated to the Royal Palms Motel next door, Mr. Wyman would always come into the office behind the front desk to where I had retreated, and would hand me a hundred dollar chip, and say "Thanks and buy yourself some books for college, son."

I was always impressed by the way Mr. Wyman catered to the customers. He was a gambler himself, so he knew well what made other gamblers tick, and he treated them like he would want to be treated.

Most of all, he valued his good employees. He loved it when

an employee would bring in their new born child and he usually had a monetary gift for the new parent. He also was very protective of his staff and he never let a customer abuse an employee. Case in point! One day as Mr. Wyman came strolling by the front desk he overheard a customer yelling at my co-worker, Spike Cook. The patron had arrived a day earlier than his confirmed reservation reflected and he was livid when he learned that no room was available for him. Refusing to accept an alternative room at the motel next door for the evening, he became more and more angry with Spike's inability to give him what he was demanding. At the height of the guest's anger, he threatened bodily harm to Spike. That's when Mr. Wyman steps in. He quietly said to the irate guest, "Make one more outburst like that and threaten my people, and you will depart this hotel in a pine box!" Employees really respected Mr. Wyman and you can see why.

- Robert Rice was a stately looking very tall and distinguished owner who handled the management of the hotel operations and who delved into the room inventory in great detail. Mr. and Mrs. Rice lived in a suite on the 18th floor of the Diamond of the Dunes Tower, and it was not uncommon for Mr. Rice to call the front desk directly at any time of the day or night in order to determine the room occupancy. I was always impressed that he knew exactly where the hotel inventory stood in a dynamic environment where nothing was ever static with check ins and check outs. Mr. Rice was always so serious and I never really remember any funny stories about him. Mr. Rice was from Providence and did not possess the countenance or demeanor of any mob stereotype.

- Charles "Kewpie" Rich was another owner from St. Louis and a close compatriot to Sid Wyman. Mr. Rich did not get involved in the day-to-day operations at the front desk. All he cared about was that there was always a room available if he called and needed one for a player. He was not happy when rooms were unavailable and he did not care for rooms at the Royal Palms Motel for his customers, even if he was an owner of the motel. My most vivid memory of Mr. Rich was an extreme concern for his personal hygiene, or so we thought. He would often call the desk and say. "Mr. Rich here! Hold a room out of order in the tower with a king bed for about thirty minutes so I can go up and wash my hands." This seemed like a strange request since he had a washroom in his executive office.

- Mr. Rich's son-in-law, George Duckworth, was a no-nonsense executive who looked at the cost side of the business and was always concerned about the costs and waste of sloppy comping. He suspected everyone of stealing from the joint, and when he was unhappy, it made the front desk clerks very uncomfortable when he came around. He always suspected that desk clerks took bribes to accommodate people who had no room reservations, and then would walk one of his customers. He may have been correct about the bribes, but we never walked one of his customers. We did not have the balls.

- Howie Engel was another owner who primarily worked as a host. He lived part time in Florida and did not have a permanent residence at the Dunes as the other owners did. However, when he was on site, he was around the casino working 24 hours a day. Because the Dunes Hotel was home to most of the owners, they all treated the facility like it was their personal house. The Dunes grounds and physical facilities were immaculately groomed, maintained and cleaned. Carpets were frequently replaced and rooms were renovated constantly. The thing I remember best about Howie Engle was his rapid response to a patron who had stamped out a cigarette on the new carpet in the lobby of the Dunes one afternoon. Howie had witnessed the person throwing the burning cigarette on to the floor and then putting out the burning ash by rubbing his shoe over the butt. Mr. Engle raced across the casino floor and confronted the man, yelling at him as he ran toward him. He screamed at the man, "Do you do that to the carpet at your own home, pal? This is my home and I don't like what you did. Now get the hell off our property." I was impressed. Howie Engel didn't even look to see if the culprit was a good casino customer. It was his opinion that the Dunes did not need a person like that, regardless of what kind of customer he might have been.

High-Level Characters:

- There were two more characters that come to mind that were role models. While not owners, they were high level executives or representatives for the owners and they carried immense weight around the property. The first of these guys was Sherlock Feldman. He was a little gruff Jewish guy about five and half feet tall, who I swear could run the hundred yard dash across the casino floor in less than 10 seconds flat. Sherlock was also from St. Louis and he catered to the hundreds of premium customers that Wyman, Rich and he himself had persuaded to visit the Dunes from all over the country, but especially from St. Louis and Kansas City.

Sherlock could not say "NO" to anybody, and whenever any desk clerk needed a room reservation or a special rate for friends or relatives, we would always go to Sherlock, who never turned us down. Sherlock loved to play the slots and you could see him late at night going to one of the change booths and grabbing rolls of coins to play right out of the booth. Likewise, it was not unusual to see Sherlock grab a few chips out of a table dealer's bank to give a cocktail waitress a tip if one of his good customers stiffed the server. These are things that would get you in a lot of trouble in today's world of casino regulations, but not then.

And speaking of cocktail waitresses, now that the Dunes had been open for over ten years, it was a common joke that most of the cocktail waitresses were now on the older side. Heck, some of them were almost 50 years old. Anyway, I remember the story of a customer who was complaining about the age and appearance of one of the cocktail waitresses, when Sherlock explained to the customer, "Do you want a drink or do you want to get laid? If you want to get laid, we have a separate department for that."

The most comical comment ever spoken by Sherlock Feldman was caught in an interview he had on television in response to the book written in 1962 by Professor Edward Thorpe, titled "Beat the Dealer." The book explained how the odds on the game of Blackjack could be manipulated into the player's favor through card counting techniques. When asked about the success a player could achieve from reading Professor Thorpe's book, Sherlock challenged the TV viewers, when he proclaimed, "If you come into the Dunes and implement Professor Thorpe's methods, you will leave dressed just like Professor Thorpe…In a ten dollar suit with a two dollar neck tie and a five dollar pair of shoes!"

- The other character that deserves a mention is "Big Julie" Weintraub. At about 6 feet, four inches and 275 pounds, he was a giant-sized jeweler from New York City with more gambling associates than one can imagine. Mr. Weintraub became the most successful junket operator in the history of Las Vegas gambling casinos. No less than twice monthly, Big

Julie would bring in a Boeing 707 jet full of players taking up at least 125 rooms of the Dunes 816 room inventory. There would even be times in which Julie would have his associates bring in back-to-back junkets so he could use the same plane to take the first group home. Consequently, the demand on rooms was always critical when Julie was in town. Unlike most of the other junket operators who usually left a small cash gratuity around for the front desk clerks to split up after their junket was settled in, Big Julie seldom parted with a nickel for the desk clerks. Some of the customers on his junket would ask us if we received any of the tip money that was collected by Julie from them on the plane for the hotel's service employees. We just played dumb and said it probably went to the bellman or Maitre d'. Nonetheless, Julie was good for business and he made the Dunes Hotel, (and himself) very wealthy by his ability to attract thousands of players into the Dunes. In those days, you could get a free jet ride across the country and stay for free in a Dunes hotel room for four nights and all you had to do was put up a $2500 deposit and bet $25 wagers for four hours a day.

Late in Big Julie's career, he was found inside an elevator with both of his legs broken. I trust it was from someone other than one of my fellow desk clerks, especially the not-to-be-named desk clerk who once checked Mr. Weintraub in and typed his name in the register as "Jewlie Weintraub."

My Fellow Employees:

The employees working at the Dunes came from all over the globe as well, but some of the more memorable ones from my standpoint were those that worked directly with me at the front desk and who eventually had a major impact on my life in some way. It is only fair to give a few of these folks a mention as well.

■ I spoke of my first boss, Jimmie Francis, earlier. While quite a self-serving guy, he did provide his front desk crew with the latitude to take good care of customers and let us earn an occasional gratuity ourselves. Jimmie was the ultimate hustler of customers and because he had an expensive drinking and sports gambling habit, he constantly was hustling in-coming hotel guests over for bribes and gratuities. He had an uncanny knack for identifying those people looking for rooms during sold out periods that had no reservations, but who he was confident would bribe him for an accommodation. His constant quest for more booze and gambling capital would cause him to sell a room to one of these non-reservation guests, often unfortunately at the expense of a customer who had advance reservations.

I would show up at midnight to take over the graveyard shift at the front desk, and often there I was, facing a group of incoming guests with reservations but no rooms to put them in. Jimmie would brief me on what was going on and then bid me farewell, leaving me to find alternative accommodations for these disgruntled customers. Whenever Las Vegas was totally sold out without a room in sight for a hundred miles, I often would have to make these customers wait all night for the first available early morning check out. As one can imagine, this was an uncomfortable position to be in with unhappy customers standing at the front desk all night complaining while waiting to check into a room accommodation that had been sold away to the highest bidder by my boss the night before.

Since these were the days before online front desk computers, the controls and registration processes were all manual. With my accounting knowledge and having access to the guest ledger, I devised a scheme to protect myself from these uncomfortable encounters with mad patrons. With necessity being the mother of invention, whenever I knew we would be at capacity for the next day, I would pre-register five or six ghost-reservations on my own every morning before I left my shift. I knew that these ghost-registrations would survive the physical housekeeper occupancy inventory reports for the day. Then, I would arrive for my work the next evening several minutes early and make certain that I pulled the guest accounting folios of the phony registrations from the ledger buckets before the night auditor began his nightly room revenue postings. I would wait for Jimmie to leave for the evening, and then I would have five or six empty rooms for my own disposal. Usually, I needed these empty rooms to accommodate the customers who had reservations which Jimmie had sold to others. I would save a couple of the empty rooms in case the casino bosses needed one or two for late night gamblers, and sometimes even I would get a "bribe" to give a room up to someone who had not made a reservation either. At any rate, Jimmie was a role model of sorts because he showed me how employees can manipulate the system.

- As I mentioned earlier, my good friend and original mentor was Madison "Spike" Cook. As I also said before, this fellow had the ability to sell ice to Eskimos and he was constantly hustling show reservations, Grand Canyon tours, or whatever he could convince a guest to do that might augment his base salary. I have enjoyed many good times with this guy and have more stories than I could ever recount. As you will see throughout every section of this book, Spike was part of my career and personal life and there is always a good story to tell about him, whether he was 25 or 55. Sometimes he steered me the wrong way in my personal life, but my determination to make hotel and gaming management my career objective was largely based on Spike's mentoring at the Dunes front desk.

Spike taught me how to hustle. My first encounter with a "Spike Cook" soft hustle happened one evening when the two of us were registering two very long lines of customers. At the time, the Dunes Hotel had 816 Rooms and suites. For a reason that I never understood, almost three-quarters of the accommodations had two twin beds with the remaining one-quarter furnished with a single King-sized bed. Yet, the demand from customers was just the opposite. It was a constant daily battle to find an adequate supply of King-bedded rooms to meet the request of the customers. We would frequently leave notes in the employee suggestion box for ownership to provide a better mix of King bedded accommodations, but our suggestions always fell on deaf ears. In fact it was not until I became the Dunes hotel resident manager several years later, that we were able to materially improve the mix.

While the lack of adequate King-bedded accommodations made for some serious confrontations between desk clerks and customers at the time of registration, it also provided a good potential source of "bribe" income. Just like a showroom maître d' who could move you to a better seat by slipping a worthy gratuity into his bent backward palm, a desk clerk could manipulate bed type and location in a similar manner. The only difference is our hand was always open facing frontward. On this first encounter of the soft hustle, as I was checking a customer into a twin bedded room in a back section of the hotel, Spike walks up to my window and throws a five dollar chip into the window in front of me and the new arriving guest. I turned around with a surprised look and asked Spike what the five dollar chip was for. Spike replied, "Mr. Jones in room 1804 stopped by and left it for you. He appreciated you finding him a nice King-bedded room in the tower." Before I could slip the chip into my pants pocket, the customer I was registering reached into his own pocket and pulled out a crisp five dollar bill. Without blinking, he asked me, "What about a King in the tower for me, too?" This trick didn't always work on everybody, but it was effective enough that we usually tried it several times a shift with pretty consistent results.

Another source of side income in those days consisted of commissions from different motels that solicited our referrals. Since the Dunes Hotel and its Royal Palms Motel subsidiary were frequently filled to capacity, the desk clerks had the opportunity to refer "walk ins", and often even overbooked reservations as well, to nearby motels that would pay us for each referral. While these referral commissions never made us rich, they did provide a steady stream of income to finance our beer purchases at the end of most shifts. It was customary for us to visit the motel where we sent the referrals immediately after our shift was up and we would sign paid outs at the motel and leave with cash.

This process revealed its shortcomings one evening in an event that I will always remember. What could have been a disaster turned out to be a positive public relations event, thanks to the quick thinking of Spike Cook. We had started that particular day almost 200 rooms oversold. Because of a serious clerical counting error by the room reservation manager, it turned out to be one of the largest relocation of confirmed reservations ever conducted by the Dunes. Our only good fortune that day turned out to be at the Bonanza Hotel located directly across from the Dunes (now the location of Bally's Casino at Flamingo and the Strip). For some reason, the Bonanza had over 100 vacant hotel rooms that day, so we were able to secure all of them for most of our referral requirements. Best of all, the Bonanza was going to pay us a $2.00 referral commission for each room we sent them. We could hardly wait for beer time at the end of the shift.

With the Bonanza Hotel located so close to the Dunes, we had a relatively easy time convincing most of the incoming guests with reservations at the Dunes to relocate to the Bonanza for one evening with the condition that we would bring them back to the Dunes the following morning with an upgraded status. Nonetheless, when you have to send over 100 rooms away, someone is going to scream. Wouldn't you know it? Spike encountered the "Screamer" at his window in the form of a New York man by the name of Mr. Goldfarb. Even with Spike's golden tongue, it took him over twenty minutes to get Mr. Goldfarb to finally consent to take a room for the night at the Bonanza Hotel. At the end of the day, we were all exhausted. We had farmed out over 120 reservations to the Bonanza Hotel and several other smaller motels and we were ready for our cocktail hour. But first we had to stop at the Bonanza and pick up our referral money. We had $180 dollars coming due. As Spike signed the paid out receipt and the Bonanza cashier handed Spike the referral money, up walks Mr. Goldfarb who is demanding to know what we are doing there. Without missing a beat, Spike turns toward the Bonanza Cashier and counts the money tendering it back to the cashier while loudly announcing, "One hundred, twenty, forty, sixty, One eighty. Thank you so much for taking care of our valued Dunes customers." Then Spike turned to Mr. Goldfarb and proclaimed, "Hi, Mr. Goldfarb. We are over here taking care of the Bonanza staff. You don't think we got these rooms for all those people like you that we sent here today for free, do you?" Mr. Goldfarb seemed satisfied and moved on to his room. Spike turned around and retrieved our beer money so we could leave, but not before leaving a twenty dollar bill for the Bonanza cashier for playing along so well.

One of Spike's greatest skills was his ability to motivate employees to work hard for him. Prior to working at the front desk, he had been the convention coordinator for the Dunes. In that role, he was responsible for all convention and catering hall set ups and he had a staff of porters, mostly African Americans that performed all the heavy work of moving tables, chairs and equipment. Leading the staff of porters was a huge black fellow named Clyde with a slight speech impediment. He was a gentle and very likeable guy, but looking at him you knew well you did not want to get in any physical altercation with him. He was just too damn big and he was strong as an ox. Anyway, Clyde and his band of convention porters loved working for Spike because they were always complimented for their good work and Spike also made certain that Clyde and his team shared in the gratuities often left behind by convention and meeting managers at departure time.

Anyway, as the story goes, one day Spike was checking in on a catering set up in the "Diamond Room," where a special luncheon was about to take place an hour later. He wanted to make certain everything was in order and no details were left unattended. As he entered the Diamond Room, Spike spotted a telephone repairman of giant stature from the Central Telephone Company tearing the wires out of the junction box on the wall of the meeting room. Spike confronted the technician and demanded that he pack up and come back later after the meeting was over. The telephone repairman responded to Spike's demand telling him that he refused to leave. He had a work-order for the repair and he was going to finish it up that day. He told Spike, "I have no intentions of leaving to accommodate your meeting. Get your crew of jungle bunnies and move the meeting to another room, period!"

Spike left the room and found Clyde. In his gentle manner, Spike told Clyde that the Diamond Room looked marvelous all set up the way Clyde and his team had done. Then he told

Clyde, "Too bad you guys have to tear it down now and move the meeting into the Ruby Room." When Clyde asked why, Spike told him what the telephone man had said. Without blinking, Clyde instructed Spike to go get a cup of coffee in the Savoy Restaurant and he would personally take care of the "telephone man."

Rather than get coffee, Spike took up a spot located behind a post in the lobby at the base of the escalator to the convention facilities in order to observe what he knew would soon be happening. About ten minutes later he sees two large convention porters carrying the telephone technician between the two of them down the escalator and Clyde was right behind them carrying the repairman's tool box.

Spike raced into the coffee shop and sat nonchalantly at the counter sipping his coffee and smoking his cigarette as Clyde came in with a big smile proclaiming with his slight speech impediment, " Misher Cook, the meeting will go on in the Diamond Room as shhhhkeduled." Over the years as I observed how Spike Cook managed people, it was clear through this colorful and humorous example, why Clyde and his team performed for him as they did.

- Another fellow employee that remains forever in my memory bank of life was often the butt of many pranks, but was also somebody we all would have killed for. Soon after I became a desk clerk on the graveyard shift, we hired on an information key clerk by the name of Georgia Luna. A diminutive lady of rich Italian decent, we early on coined her as the "Mini Wop." Georgia was a compulsive person who spent as much time cleaning and tidying her work station as she did performing her normal job functions. She was immaculate in her dress and fastidious in her work ethic. These key attributes she possessed also caused her much pain for we used her compulsiveness and her naiveté to dog her continually.

Speaking of dogs, remember back in an earlier part of this chapter when I mentioned the yapping dog that was the pet of the primary owner's wife. Anyway, we told Georgia to be aware that Mrs. Gottlieb's dog would often call the information desk and ask for messages. We told her the dog had been trained to almost talk in a barking-voice sort of manner, and that she should not be surprised when she heard the dog on the phone. A day or two later, Spike called the information telephone line from the back office. When Georgia answered the phone, Spike barked into the phone asking for messages in room 2201. Georgia looked at me and I asked her if it was a dog calling. When she replied in the affirmative, I said to pull all the messages out of the key box 2201 and read them to the dog on the other end of the line. She did and hung up. We did this again over and over until finally we had to tell her. If she was still alive today, she still would not forgive us.

The "Mini Wop" was only 4 foot ten inches tall, so she required the use of a foot stool to retrieve messages and mail from the key boxes that were high up on the rack. Because she was so compulsive, she could not stand to have any loose keys accumulate without putting them in their respective key boxes. One slow day on the job, we pulled all the keys out of key box 100, which happened to be the box highest off the ground and farthest away from her telephone station. For hours we would constantly throw these keys out on the desk where she would systematically pick them up, climb the foot stool and place them back in box 100. We repeated the process over and over for a full shift. Near the end of the shift, we scribbled a note and placed it in Box 100. The note read, "What kind of stupid fool would spend their entire shift putting the same five keys back in this box, except the Mini Wop?" Then we called her phone and asked her if we had any messages in room 100. As she grabbed her foot stool and headed to the box to grab the message, we headed out the back door to punch out. It is a good thing we did. Her Italian temper could be heard a block away when she realized we had made a fool of her that entire day.

- Bob Banse was another character who happened to be the fastest clerk I ever witnessed around a front desk. As fast and efficient as he was when he was on duty, he was also a person who could quickly and efficiently consume large quantities of alcohol after work and he smoked four packs of cigarettes a day. He also had no fear. Bob was a frail looking person with a lily white completion. His chest cavity was slightly indented and he had sloping shoulders. Nonetheless, as I said he had no fear. One day Spike and I were having beer with him in a neighborhood bar. For some reason after drinking a six pack of beer, Bob got into a disagreement with a pretty big guy who was just aching to take Bob apart at the seams. Just like that, Bob turned around and left the bar. The big guy asked Spike who the hell Bob was, and that is when Spike told the story of his life. Spike advised the big guy that Bob had just got out of prison for killing a guy in a bar. "That's why he looks so frail and is so lily white in his complexion," Spike said. "He probably left to get his gun." The big guy grabbed his bankroll, tipped the bartender, chugged his drink and left by the side door. When Bob returned from the restroom and saw that the big guy had departed, he immediately proclaimed with his great ego, "See, I ran that son of a bitch off, didn't I?"

- The first female desk clerk ever hired at the Dunes Hotel was a cute young lady with some Latina genes. She and Spike became an item and we soon were all calling her "Bon Bon".

That name was apparently the pillow talk moniker given to her by Spike. Anyway, the pranks we used to pull on Bon Bon in those days would put us in the penitentiary today, or at least get us fired for harassment. These were the days of the mini-skirt and the Bon Bon wore them exceptionally well. Unfortunately, a desk clerk is always facing the desk and the customer and does not have the ability to observe the antics going on behind them. Bon Bon was no exception. I won't go into detail about what we all did to her to amuse ourselves, but if she reads this book, she will be grateful that I left it out. She turned out to be a great hotelier and a good friend.

- When I moved to the graveyard shift, I shared the big desk with the night auditor by the name of Harold Veo. Harold had been on the desk for years and could play the old NCR 2000 accounting register as though it were a concert piano. Initially Harold was very standoffish, but as I slowly took on some of the mundane aspects of the night audit, he became a mentor and began showing me the ropes. As I got to know Harold better, he would ask me to have a beer after work at one of the neighboring casinos. "After work" for Harold and me was 8:00 a.m. every morning where we would take off for downtown "Glitter Gulch" and the long bar at the "Mint Casino".

On Harold's salary, I was always amazed at how much money he could wager on KENO whenever we went out after work. When I asked Harold how he could afford to gamble so much, like most degenerate people he merely proclaimed that he was just another lucky gambler. As a result, he became a role model of sorts (in a negative way), in that he showed me how easy it was to steal from an employer, even if the employer might be owned by the mob. Harold was eventually caught manipulating comps for cash in connection with his audit activities, and was discharged from his employment.

Everybody said he got away with it, but come to think of it, I never heard where he moved to or saw his name in the obituary column either. Who knows?

Interesting Customers & Celebrities:

Of course, the excitement of casinos in those days centered around the celebrities that frequently visited the casinos and the Dunes in particular. Except for Cary Grant, none of these celebrities were role models for me, but they did provide me with fodder to brag about when I was back In Boulder City visiting my parents or up in Montana visiting my relatives

- Cary Grant was the premier celebrity who not only visited the Dunes quite often, but also had a permanent suite. He was a special friend of Mr. Gottlieb and his suite was at the opposite end of the hallway on the 22nd floor of the Dunes Tower. Mr. Grant was a gentleman and very nice to the employees and I admired him.

- Telly Savalis was a frequent customer who loved to play 21. He visited the Dunes once or twice a month back then. He would call me after midnight at the front desk advising that he was on the way up to Vegas and would need a room. Sherlock had given me standing order to give him a room anytime he called, which was fortuitous for me because Mr. Savalas always had a nice five dollar bill wadded up for me when he checked in.

- Wolfman Jack was another guy who always found his way to my window with a nice five dollar bill.

- Jan Murray was a fine entertainer that visited often. He was known as being a little cheap when it came to the tipping department, but I had always admired him on the game show "Dollar a Second." One time he was waiting for his car at Valet and he apologized to the valet attendant that he had no tip money; only a hundred dollar bill. The valet attendant startled Murray when he pulled out a roll of currency and said he would gladly make change for Mr. Murray's $100 bill. It was one of the only times Jan Murray tipped big.

- Barry Gordy became a frequent customer of the Dunes and after creating Motown Records, was one of the Dunes best customers. Mr. Gordy was also an occupant of the elite 22nd floor when he came to town. Because of his position, he was constantly accompanied by the many Motown Recording Stars who loved to vacation in Las Vegas, and, of course, provided so much fun and excitement for customers and employees alike with their presence in the public areas of the Dunes.

- Another infamous character, Nate Jacobsen, spent months living at the Dunes Hotel and was occupying a suite when I first started working there. Mr. Jacobsen was one of the founding owners of Caesars Palace, which was being constructed next door to the Dunes. Jacobsen worked all day on the Caesars development, but was known to party hard and gamble big almost every night while staying at the Dunes.

Interesting "Signs of the Times" and a Little "Potpourri":

Las Vegas casinos in 1966 were built on the value proposition for customers. Rooms, food & beverage and show tickets were cheap or often free. It was easy to get a room discount even if you were not a casino player.

Room rates at the Dunes started at $4 single and $7 double for rooms in the back of the old Olympic Section facing the laundry and went as high as $15 single or $18 double in the new tower.

You could go to the stage show, "Casino de' Paris" for a five dollar minimum admission which also included two cocktails in the price. Created and produced by Frederick Apcar, famous French dancers Line Renaud and Jacqueline Duquet headlined the famous French show that was adorned by sixty topless dancers and showgirls. The lounge show, "Vive les Girls," also an Apcar production had a one drink minimum and drinks cost $1.00.

Art and Dottie Todd and the famous Russ Morgan Orchestra played nightly in the club on the top floor of the Dunes, appropriately named the "Top O' the Strip." I remember that the room specialized in roasted duck. I enjoyed my first roasted duck in this restaurant and still love it today.

"Antonio Morelli and his Magic Violins" provided the ambience in the famous Sultan's Table, no doubt one of the premier gourmet rooms of its time.

On graveyard, the casino put out a free buffet "Chuck wagon" in the lounge.

The casino games were run with minimal regulations and it was not uncommon to see chips transferred between tables instead of going through the accountability steps of the casino cage banks as is required today. Free drinks and cigarettes were always generously flowing with frequency and the kind of service seldom seen today in the corporate gaming world managed by accountants and Harvard MBA's.

I saw my first hooker at the Dunes. As closely as I lived to the strip (just 22 miles away in Boulder City), I had led a sheltered life. During the first month working at the Dunes, I noticed a certain number of very attractive girls (and some not so attractive but well endowed) would constantly parade from the front door to the hotel elevators, returning about thirty minutes later. I was amazed that most of them seemed to know the bell captain. They almost always stopped to visit with him and I thought they were dropping off mail. When I asked the bell captain who these girls were, he told me they were all "working girls." I wondered what department they worked in. I was embarrassed when I finally found out where they worked. Wow! How naïve of me when I think back.

Anyway, three of these gals remain in my memory bank. The first one was known as "Slow Boat." We didn't even know her real name. When she came through the front door, she ambled along as if time was no object to her. She was not extremely attractive, but the bell captain told me she had special talents and the guys would ask for her.

The second girl was a diminutive cutie named Joanie. Old Lou, the graveyard bellman told her I was infatuated with her, so she went out of her way to tease me every time she exited the building. Joanie was probably 36 years old at the time and she got a special kick out of picking on a shy naïve guy almost half her age. On one very slow night in January, 1967, I was working away on the audit not really paying any attention to the traffic in the lobby. Suddenly, Old Lou, the bell captain comes behind the front desk and says he has something to show me. He leads me back into the deserted office hallway behind the front desk where I run smack dab into Joanie. She lifts her mini skirt and says, "What do you think about this?" Red faced, I stammered back, "Very nice! Very nice indeed, but I have to get back to work." As I scampered back to the front desk I could hear Old Lou and Joanie laughing their butts off at my expense. But it was a learning experience. I never knew before that some women do not wear underwear.

The third hooker was a large Chinese girl that we all nicknamed "Hong Kong Suzie." Suzie liked Spike and one night after work we were sitting at the Dunes bar having a beer when Suzie pulled up alongside of Spike. Apparently when Spike made some obscene comment about her size, Suzie took it out by grabbing Spike's thigh and squeezing so hard, she left a black and blue welt that lasted for weeks on his legs. We continued to tell tales about Hong Kong Suzie but we never got within arm's distance of her again after that night.

Section 2

MY FRESHMAN YEAR IN MANAGEMENT — THE SANDS AND THE RAT PACK

IT WAS MARCH 17, 1970. My first day at the Sands was almost as frightening as my first day at the Dunes. The systems were far different and much more cumbersome than I was used to at the Dunes. The front desk was cramped and access to the room rack (the room inventory library) was far less convenient.

After I completed the employment enrollment at the personnel department, I met with Mr. Zike and he introduced me to the assistant resident manager and my new supervisor, a young guy by the name of Ted Ward. Ted was not particularly happy to see me on the scene. He obviously considered himself the king of the Sands front desk, and now he had to contend with a new upstart protégé of Mr. Zike, who was his boss, too.

Just prior to my employment, the Sands had been recently purchased from one of the old syndicate organizations by Howard Hughes. As part of the sales agreement, the key players of the old syndicate stayed on as consultants and executives for the Hughes organization. Robert Maheu, the initial kingpin for the Hughes Nevada Operations (HNO as it was known) was frequently seen on site meeting with Alvin Benedict, the new general manager. They were the new official bosses, but it was evident from observing the actions of all the employees that they still followed the direction set by the former owners. Key among them was Carl Cohen, a rotund guy with a calm but imposing demeanor. Next to Mr. Zike, who was my initial role model and mentor at the Sands, I found Mr. Cohen to be the guy I would like to emulate if I was ever the big boss. Carl Cohen was extremely respectful of his employees and customers, but also demanded honesty and loyalty from those who worked for him. That included Frank Sinatra. I wish I could have been there the day when Sinatra was put in his place by Mr. Cohen during an angry tirade where Sinatra turned over the dining table in the Garden Room Coffee shop while Mr. Cohen was eating a pastrami sandwich. In his anger, Sinatra had just driven a golf cart through the side entry glass door of the lobby and then made his way to the telephone operators' office where he pulled every cord from the old manual switchboard. Sinatra could have gotten away with doing all that damage without any recrimination from the bosses, until he turned over Mr. Cohen's dining table in front of guests and employees. That did it. Mr. Cohen popped Sinatra with one quick jab that nearly knocked him out. The incident caused Sinatra to sever his ties with the Sands and move his show as the senior member of the rat pack on to Caesars Palace.

I met another key person that first day on the job who became a lifetime special individual. The superintendent of service, a guy named Jerry Garvey, became a mentor on day one and our relationship evolved into a close friendship. I eventually became his next door neighbor for a time while living in Las Vegas in the early eighties. Jerry was a feisty, gruff and talented manager, who ran the bell desk, valet parking, front door and provided concierge services for customers and executives. He was the first to correct you when you were wrong, but he was highly protective of his friends and he was one guy at the Sands who always had my back.

As was the case at the Dunes, I was the youngest person at the front desk and somewhat resented by the older desk clerks, all of whom had no ambitions other than coming to work each day to methodically register people into the hotel, and hopefully maybe make a gratuity here or there along the way. The Sands was a hotel comprised of a small 200-room tower with another 550 rooms spread out in a series of ten bungalow buildings around immaculately manicured grounds. Unlike the Dunes where room types and suites were in similar numbering series, the Sands had many different room types and an unusual numbering system that took most people quite some time to learn. So the first week I was employed, I took it upon myself to create easy-to-understand maps of the rooms' layout in every building and framed the maps for installation on the Front Office wall. Drawing the maps gave me an instant understanding of the rooms' layouts, suite locations, bedding types and which rooms connected to each other. I quickly became the fastest desk clerk on the Sands staff and the resentment among the old timers made me keep my further ideas to myself until I won the promotion I hoped to garner at the end of my 120-day probationary period.

On July 1, 1970, I was summoned to Mr. Zike's office where he announced that I was being promoted to assistant resident manager, and on the next day I assumed my first management role. The day started off with some anxiety, but except for the old desk clerks out front and some apprehension on the part of my now-new counterpart, front desk manager, Ted Ward, I felt welcome in my new role by all the girls back in the room reservations office and all the cashiers, also all female, who worked on the front desk.

My first day on the job in my new role was also one of my most embarrassing. The day I was promoted, I headed off to a local haberdashery to buy a couple of new suits and ties, because now I could discard the front desk clerk uniform I was accustomed to wearing and be dressed like the executive I wanted to be. Showing up in my new suit complemented by cuff links and a pinky ring, I was ready to perform my new duties. I wasn't on duty more than ten minutes, when I squatted down to pick something off the floor and split my new trousers down the middle of the seam with a hole over fifteen inches wide. With my ass exposed to all the girls in the room reservation office, I ran out of the office red-faced and off to see the tailor in the uniform shop. Back in my old uniform pants, I completed my first day as a manager while my new expensive suit was being repaired.

While the tear in my pants was my first personal crisis as a manager, just three days later on July 4, I was placed through my first true management crisis and it was a key test of my ability to handle a critical problem. A fire broke out in the Hollywood Turf Club, one of the bungalow buildings. The building was safely evacuated, but my next ten hours following the fire tested my ability to handle an adverse situation. With the assistance of everybody at the front desk, we relocated the evacuated guests, helped the victims secure new clothing and creature comfort supplies and worked with security and insurance agents to file the customary claims. At the end of the experience, I had earned some respect from the old desk clerks who had earlier questioned the wisdom of hiring a young clerk from the Dunes but, best of all, I had impressed the executives of the casino, who made their pleasure known to Mr. Zike, my immediate boss. While the fire was a grueling experience for a young 22-year-old supervisor, it enabled me to accelerate my agenda at the Sands.

In my new role, I was able to suggest and implement operational changes for the front desk and hotel operations at the Sands which became a hybrid of the best practices at the Dunes and Sands. As a result, we were able to improve registration efficiency by 25% within just my first month on the job.

THE SANDS WAS probably the most famous and well known casino in Las Vegas at that time. While Caesars Palace and the International Hotel (now Las Vegas Hilton) had recently opened, the Sands still had that air of elegance and class, and the customer base was very loyal. Of course the Sand's lineup of stars helped it maintain its image. Even after Sinatra defected to Caesars Palace, the main characters of the "Rat Pack" remained as frequent stars in the famous Copa Show Room. Complimenting Dean Martin, Joey Bishop and Sammy Davis were Steve Lawrence and Edie Gorme, Al Martino, Rowan and Martin and Alan King, just to name a few. Most of the stars were cordial to the employees but I remember one encounter with Don Adams that got me in trouble. If you recall he was the star of "Get Smart." Anyway, as he was checking in one day when I was on the front desk window, he heard his name paged and asked me for a phone. I handed him my shoe instead. He was not amused.

In addition to my favorite old boss, Carl Cohen, I have fond memories of the other "Old Guys" on the new Howard Hughes payroll when I got there. These previous owners looked their parts. They included Sandy Waterman, Moe Lewis, General Charles Baron, Bucky Harris and impresario Jack Entratter. Almost every one of these old owners lived in a big suite in the various bungalow buildings, most equipped with outdoor swimming pools, guest cottages and carports.

As each of these owners eventually terminated their employment, the suites became part of the room inventory and the Sands became known as the first casino in Las Vegas to offer its very best high rollers the opportunity to occupy a Cabana Suite with private swimming pool. Of course today, the Mega Casinos in Las Vegas have multi-million dollar cabana suites that dwarf what the Sands initially offered, but in those days we thought they were something and they were.

In the early sixties before my arrival, President John Kennedy had been an occasional visitor of the Sands occupying the Presidential pool suite in the Churchill Downs Turf Club when he was in Las Vegas. Following my departure from the Sands, President Reagan occupied the largest cabana suite in the Aqueduct Turf Club on several trips to Las Vegas, and the famous arms dealer, Adnan Kashoggi was often on the property for months with his entourage, occupying three or four of these mega cabana suites along with upwards of 100 additional rooms for his party and entourage.

In my first few months at the Sands, I observed corporate politics in action for the first time in my life. When I was previously working for the Dunes, the operation was not political and it had more of a "family" atmosphere, albeit a Soprano-type family atmosphere. Problems were ironed out behind closed doors and never in public view. Nobody at the Dunes appeared to be jockeying for power or willing to cut somebody's throat to move up the food chain. The Sands was obviously different, at least now under the new Howard Hughes ownership. To exacerbate the political atmosphere was the fact that the owner was reclusive and relied on only several key trusted confidants to manage his vast holdings. As such, there were always the brown nosers and hangers-on surrounding the new Hughes executives, who reported to Robert Maheu. The newly appointed president and executive vice president of the Sands, Alvin Benedict and Bernie Rothkopf, had been around the mob operated Stardust Casino for years and were bringing a touch of the good old days of Vegas to the Sands where the Hughes executives tended to be out of touch and certainly not experienced in gaming. However, from our perspective as the lower level employees watching from the sidelines, Benedict and Rothkopf seemed to be using their superior knowledge of the everyday workings of a gambling joint and the Las Vegas "good old boys" political network to further their own personal agenda right under the nose of the novice new managers of the Hughes Nevada Operations.

Well, it did not take long for Hughes to shift gears from his penthouse at the Desert Inn. In the middle of November of 1970, Hughes turned the management of his Nevada operation over to what was commonly called "The Mormon Mafia," comprised of Chester Davis, William Gay and Randy Clark. On the first weekend of December that same year, they stormed the Hughes owned casinos including the Sands, taking over the Casino cages and front offices of each property. At the Sands, they commandeered the 18th Floor Penthouse level of the tower and stationed guards with semi-automatic weapons at the elevator entries. Randy Clark Sr. demanded that we not take any additional room reservations or walk-ins to avoid any covert press coverage getting inside the property. Then they went from office to office inside the executive suites cooridor with a locksmith from the Howard Hughes Security Group, *Intertel*, changing out locks thus blocking any existing management from access to their offices.

As someone who had his office in the middle of the Sands lobby, as I did on that fateful day, the events that unfolded before my eyes certainly made for the trailer of a good movie to come. The coup d' grace came about the very evening of the Mormon Mafia takeover, when Bill Gay brought in his new general manager and casino manager to take control over the Sand's management operations. The newly appointed general manager was Richard Danner, who had previously been in charge of the Frontier Hotel and joining him as the new Casino Manager was a diminutive-sized ball of energy in the form of Harry Goodheart.

Prior to working for Howard Hughes, Danner had been city manager of Miami Beach and had served as a lawyer in the FBI during the J. Edgar Hoover years. Danner had numerous influential connections in Washington D.C. and was a close friend of Governor John Connelly of Texas and Bebe Rebozzo of Key Biscayne, Florida. It was widely rumored that Danner had recently provided President Richard Nixon with a sizeable campaign contribution from Hughes that was delivered by Danner in cash obtained from the casino cage at Hughes's Silver Slipper Casino directly to Bebe Rebozzo in his suite at the Frontier Casino, where Danner presided as general manager at the time.

Harry Goodheart had learned the ropes of a gambling casino starting as a dealer in the Beverly Hills Club of Southgate, Kentucky. When the illegal gambling in Kentucky got too hot for Harry, he headed off with his wife and family to work in Las Vegas, where he started as a crap dealer at the Desert Inn. Goodheart had a keen sense of relationship marketing principles long before they were being taught in universities or practiced by marketing executives. He used his knowledge of gambling operations and combined his sense of promotional intuition to establish himself as an expert in strategic casino resort management.

Danner and Goodheart's walk into the Sands that fateful night in November, 1970, to take over the control of the Sands from Benedict and Rothkopf had all the ingredients of a gunfight at high noon. The four gentlemen met in the lobby adjoining the coffee shop and the tower corridor, tempers roared and fists were raised and a near scuffle ensued between Danner and Benedict. Ten minutes later, the palace coup d'etat had ended and the new management kings were installed by their own personal edict. Benedict and Rothkopf went on to join Kirk Kerkorian and built the MGM Grand Casino (now Bally's Casino in Las Vegas), which they opened as a major competitor of the Sands Hotel just three years later.

CHAPTER **3**

I GOT MY start in management at the Sands and this casino also provided me with some of the best experience and fun of all the places I have worked in this business. In fact, I was employed on three separate occasions at the Sands, being rehired by Richard Danner and Harry Goodheart twice after I left them and the Sands Company for a different career opportunity at other gaming companies.

The Sands also provided me with more role models and mentors than any other company in which I have been fortunate to work during my career. The two foremost role models and mentors were no doubt Richard Danner and Harry Goodheart themselves. Danner was about 60 years old and Goodheart was clocking in at 53 when they joined the Sands. I, on the other hand, was only 23 years old so I had little in common with them and my lowly position at the front desk was certainly off their radar, or so I thought.

But both Danner and Goodheart were well aware that the hub of a hotel operation anywhere is the front desk, and they made it their priority to know everybody working in the Sands Hotel front office. Goodheart also was building his reputation as a Las Vegas casino manager who had a tremendous junket network across the United States, Canada and Mexico. Second only to the operation at the Dunes Hotel, Goodheart's junket operation had been expanding rapidly at the Frontier Casino prior to his moving over to the Sands to take over the casino operations in our casino. What was retarding Goodheart's ability to increase the size of his charter groups was the inability of the Frontier Hotel and its front desk operation to expedite the rapid handling of big junket groups the way the Dunes had been able to do. When Harry moved his first junket from the Frontier to the Sands, I had the opportunity to handle the logistics of the arrival and departure of this first junket to our property. By coordinating it with the Sand's front services team the same way we had done it at the Dunes Hotel for years before, the processing of the junket was smooth and far more efficient than what the junket operator or Goodheart had ever seen before. When Harry Goodheart saw how efficient the junket registration process could be accomplished, I became his best friend at the front desk and from that day on, whenever possible he would only call upon me to handle his most important assignments or premium customers.

Danner and his administrative assistant grew accustomed to working directly with me for their needs as well; and, even at my young age, I became part of the executive round table with daily invitations to join the senior executives for lunch. It was also expected that we would all join Mr. Danner at his nightly roundtable in the Regency Lounge for cocktails. Cocktail hour was an event where ideas were exchanged in an informal way and much business was transacted that benefited the Sands. I will never forget my first interview or friendly encounter with Dick Danner. It happened to be soon after he took over the Sands and it was my first time to join him at his round table in the lounge. As it would happen, when I got to the lounge he was the only other person at his table. It was quite an intimidating event for me at my young age, and because I barely knew him, I was reluctant to sit down and join him. As I slowly cruised around the perimeter of the lounge, Danner spotted me and waved me over, motioning for me to sit down and join him. He broke the ice for me by comparing me to his own son, who was a lawyer in Dallas and then he hit me with a direct blunt questions. He asked, "Roger, do you drink booze at all?"

How do you respond to a question like that? Is it a set up? Is that why I am the only one sitting with Mr. Danner and now I am being tested? But then I looked up at the bottle of *White Label Scotch* on the table next to his rocks glass and stared into Mr. Danner's Irish nose that had obvious capillaries bursting through it for who knows how many years, and I quickly responded with my answer to this very blunt unexpected question. I said, "Mr. Danner, I love to have a beer or two every night after work and maybe three on my day off." ….To which Mr. Danner replied, "Good, because I don't trust no one who doesn't drink!"

And this guy could drink. "Mister. D", as we all called him could polish off a quart of White Label Scotch each evening, but I learned early that he always had his wits about him. How did I learn early on? Remember what my first boss told me? He said, "The boss ain't always right but the boss is always the boss." Anyway, one night as we were all listening to his stories during the cocktail hour, I had to slip away early. About fifteen minutes after I left, my beeper went off so I headed to a house phone to retrieve the call. We did not have cell phones in those days. It was Mr. Danner and in a slurred voice he told me about an idea he had for something he wanted done that evening that was going to take up a lot of valuable time on my part and also did not sound like a great idea to me. I figured it was one of those "brain farts" you get when you are out drinking with friends, so I elected not to pursue his request, figuring he would forget about it after he went home to bed. Since I was scheduled off the next day, I was anxious to get a head start on my free time. Early the next morning, my phone rang and it was Mr. Danner's assistant hunting me down. Mr. D had never called my home before so I was certain this must be an emergency. The emergency proved to be about his "brain fart" from the evening before and he was livid that I had not executed his instructions. That is when I remembered that the boss is not always right, but the boss is always the boss, so I quickly told him that I must have had one too many drinks myself and just forgot to get the job done. I offered to come in on my day off and finish what had not been done the night before, but he let me finish my day off without any disruptions. I came in the next day and implemented what I still thought was a bad idea, but it made Mr. Danner happy. Ironically, a few weeks later, he called the engineering manager directly and instructed him to remove the new installation because the idea was not working as he envisioned. Mr. Danner never told me he reversed the idea and while I knew he did, I was smart enough to never bring it up again.

AS I SAID in a previous chapter, the "Sands" was the most important incubator for my future career as a casino executive. At the Sands, I was exposed to more role models and had the benefit of numerous mentors who worked with me to teach me the many intricacies of the casino resort business. While working hard and learning, I was able to do it with a myriad of partners and friends who made me successful along the way. Forty years later, many of us still alive get together for frequent Sands Hotel employee reunions and talk about the "good old days."

If this were a textbook, I would have to delve into the strategies and tactics of how to run a casino or hotel business. But since this is written in the style of a novel, it is far more interesting to talk about some of the more exciting or humorous events that are worth re-calling. As I started describing earlier, my indoctrination as a newly appointed assistant hotel manager started with a fire in the hotel that occurred just four days after my appointment. Handling customers in diplomatic fashion is a trait all hospitality service people must learn to do well to succeed. For the most part, I was good at guest relations and I could generally console guests who might have grievances with the company. We actually prided ourselves in being able to take a bad situation for a guest and turn it around so that the guest actually became a loyal patron, with the genesis of the new loyal relationship coming about through solving the initial grievance.

One of the toughest aspects of the job at the front desk in those days was the task of "walking" customers with confirmed reservations. I touched on this a little bit in the last section where Spike Cook taught me some of the arts of soft hustling. "Walking customers" became an art at the front desk because it occurred so frequently and it was so unpleasant for both the hotel employee and the incoming customer. Unlike today where everybody provides advance deposits with credit cards, we preferred not to have deposits and instead relied on expected arrival times to plan our assignments of room accommodations and we further used the ETA information to purge the no-show customers for the day. It was the goal of the owners in those days to have people occupy all of the rooms, all of the time if possible. An empty room meant ZERO contribution to casino revenue, and in those days Casino revenues were the only real revenues that counted. Back in 1970, gaming revenues made up 95% of all the company's cash revenues, so collecting a deposit on a room reservation that amounted to a no-show was immaterial to profits.

As one can imagine just putting yourself in the shoes of an incoming customer with a confirmed room reservation, having a desk clerk tell you that you don't have a room after traveling for hours to get to your vacation destination was a very discerning event. Yet, with a ten to twenty percent no-show factor from people who made reservations but took no initiative to call and cancel when they decided not to redeem their reservation, made it incumbent upon the hotel management to anticipate no-shows and oversell enough reservations to ensure a full house of gamblers, potential gamblers and at the least warm bodies occupying every accommodation.

Even without taking deposits or asking for credit cards in advance, management was successful in offsetting the no-shows by accurately forecasting the number of reservations to oversell to reach capacity occupancy… At least most of the time! But occasionally the rudimentary actuarial projections made at the front desk in those days (and now today by computerized algorithms that control yield management hotel systems) were wrong for a variety of reasons. Sometimes fewer customers no-showed than projected. Other times, customers refused to vacate on their assigned date of departure and they would hide or refuse to answer phone calls or pages as the front desk clerks frantically tried to notify them of the necessity to vacate on schedule. Most prevalently, the casino owners, casino hosts and the casino marketing executives would make reservations for casino players or for political or personal contacts that had shown up without reservations, often on days in which special events or super star entertainment were taking place in the city.

As I said, most front desk management teams were very adept at forecasting the number of rooms to oversell by factoring in the average number of rooms generally called for by the casino owners and hosts for customers who had not made advance reservations, but whom were deemed important enough for whatever reason to bump somebody who had made an advance reservation. Front Desk management had a vested interest in managing room inventories perfectly, because the three goals of front desk managers in order of priority was to (1) Run 100% occupancy; (2) Never turn away the casino guest (3) Never turn away a confirmed reservation. In order to achieve priority number 1, sometimes priority number 2 and often priority number 3 are breached.

As I related earlier, management at the front desk had an additional vested interest in managing room inventories perfectly as often as possible because perfect management of room inventories also meant meaningful gratuities for desk clerks and front desk management. Just as the Maître d and his seating captains did in the showrooms of the early Vegas days, so did the front desk manager and his desk clerks work over the incoming guests as they registered into the hotel. Front desk management often had to forego gratuities when it was impossible to achieve the three priorities listed above.

Because business cycles and seasonal demand affect patronage in Las Vegas, achieving 100% occupancy is almost impossible 365 days of the year. Nonetheless, hotels in Las Vegas have long been successful in doing it for several hundred nights each year with annual occupancies in the high nineties. As such, there have been only a few occasions that I can recall in which we had to relocate or "walk" any premium casino customers to competing hotels or motels due to an oversell, and whenever it did occur, the customers were either the very low tier of gambler, or they were known gamblers who showed up so late that we no longer had expected them to arrive.

But breaching priority goal number (3) happened fairly frequently. Fortunately on most days we only had to "walk" one or two reservations, but I have witnessed long days In which, through some mathematical error in manual counting of advance reservations, (usually found through a group block error), upwards of two hundred advance reservations were required to be walked.

Going back to the art of walking customers with confirmed reservations, we all became adept at the task at hand. Generally, we knew several days beforehand that we were going to be in trouble. Rather than call people in advance and admit we were oversold, we usually took our chances that perhaps some guests would depart earlier than expected and that the no-show factor might be larger than anticipated. Then we embarked on the task of finding alternative rooms in nearby hotels and motels to relocate the reservations that would be denied on their arrival.

The usual "excuse" used by desk clerks was the reciting of the small print located on the bottom of the written confirmation that had been mailed to the customer. This small print is still contained on most confirmation documents all over the world..... *"Your room accommodations are confirmed subject to the failure of previous occupants departing on schedule or for maintenance or any other reasons beyond our control."*

Actually, we were often truthful when we said the previous guests had not departed on schedule, because that was a common occurrence. What we didn't tell the guest is that we also usually received the same number of early departures as we did unexpected stay-overs. Of course, sometimes we used a sewer stoppage, or a flooded floor as an excuse, and the one I used the most actually made me afraid of flying in an airplane. When we had a mass "relocation" of many reservations and the lobby was crowded with all kinds of people hanging around the front desk waiting to check in, we used the excuse that a charter airplane with a group of people on a gambling junket had canceled due to a mechanical problem and it was impossible to ask them to depart until their plane was repaired. This excuse was so effective that we used it almost to the point that I believed it myself... thus my fear of airplanes with all those mechanical breakdowns.

When we walked customers, it was never pleasant for anybody. The customers often cried, hollered, screamed, cussed and sometimes made threatening remarks to employees. Everyone in the front services area was a target for an irate customer and often they would take their wrath out on the bellman, the doorman, the parking attendant or the security officer. And, looking back, I could hardly blame them.

Anyway, in my life around a front desk I must have walked 5000 customers myself. Many of them I walked to motels that as I said in the previous section, often paid referral commissions and sometimes sent me gifts for the extra business. At the Sands, whenever it was necessary to walk customers, I attempted to relocate them to a hotel where I had friends, and more often than not it was back to the Dunes where I had previously worked. Fortunately for both the Dunes and the Sands, the friendships I had with their front desk manager, Spike Cook, enabled us to maximize room occupancies at both of our respective hotels. Both hotels were of comparative size and quality. We both operated junket programs that caused extra large group movements, but the Sands big arrival day was Thursday while the Dunes big arrival day was Wednesday. This enabled us to jockey rooms around to benefit both casinos in maximizing occupancies while also assisting each other with taking good care of relocated guests.

Generally we did not pick up hotel tabs for people we relocated in those days although we did arrange for transportation or cab fares at our expense. We also attempted to bring the relocated people back the next day and upgrade their accommodations. However, if we did

our walking artfully and with enough compassion, usually the customers stayed where we put them, and sometimes they found a new
home for their next trip to Las Vegas, certainly to our chagrin. But that
was part of the cost of achieving the three priorities.

The best example of a humorous walk was with a patron who arrived on one terrible day when we were almost 100 rooms oversold. A
couple comes to the desk with confirmation in hand ready for a great
time at the Sands. I had the pleasure of telling them the room we had
blocked for them failed to depart on schedule and it was going to be
necessary to relocate them across the street to the Castaways Hotel.
The Castaways was a nice, but small, Howard Hughes Resort with
limited food service and no show room. I offered to make show reservations and assist the guests with other needs they might have and
they graciously relocated across the street. Well, wouldn't you know
it, about a year later I look up from my manager's desk and see the
same couple trying to check in again at the Sands and wouldn't you
also know it? Yep! We were oversold and walking again. When they
arrived at the front desk window, they had already overheard the desk
clerk telling the previous customer that they were being relocated
across the street to the Castaways. I just knew there was going to be
trouble so I headed out to the front desk to assist the clerk with con-
soling the couple who were preparing for a Déjà vu letdown. Well,
the strangest thing happened. The husband said that they had really
enjoyed the Castaways Hotel the year before and wanted to go back.
However, when they tried to make a reservation at the Castaways
they were told that the dates were sold out but that the Sands had
availability. They figured they might get lucky and be relocated by
the Sands back to the Castaways if they booked again, and their wish
came true. This time I did give them complimentary show tickets and
this couple eventually became good frequent casino customers at the
Sands for years to come, but they stayed at the Castaways for their
room accommodations.

However, not all customers are that cordial when you screw
around with their fun. Some customers refuse to relocate and insist

on waiting, sometimes for hours and sometimes even for a day to check into their original room. Perseverance often paid off for them because the old adage, "the squeaky wheel gets the grease" works when you are annoying. These patrons would stand around the front desk like crows on a fence post and sometimes they would even conduct "sit ins" on the lobby floor. Some of you remember when sit ins were popular during the Vietnam War, and when you walk somebody, some grow a bit militant. Room clerks and front desk managers learned to wear tear away neck ties on days we were going to walk, because it was not unusual to have somebody grab you by the tie across the desk when you gave them the bad news about their room reservation. All in all, considering the number of people we were required to relocate over the ten years I worked on or around a front desk, while the initial disappointment for people coming to Las Vegas, the "art of walking" helped ease the discomfort and most of these people went on to enjoy a great time in the city, and the fistfights, tie pulling and sit ins were really the exception.

The good news is that most people with confirmed room reservations actually received their rooms as promised. Unfortunately, some of these guests think the world revolves around them and I guess, if you think about it, each of us is the center of our own universe so maybe that is a natural thing. Courtesy and being kind to your fellow guest is often lacking. In Las Vegas there were no clocks in the casino to remind patrons how long they had been there. Check out times were late; up to 3:00 p.m. in some of the strip hotels, so many guests did not bother to check out till very late, often cheating on check out time by several hours. Yet many guests who were told that check-in time was not before 3:00 p.m., showed up at 10:00 a.m. and hung around the desk, pestering the desk clerks for an early check in, over and over and over again.

CHAPTER **5**

AS HARD AS we try and as good as we get at it, we cannot make everyone happy and some days I was not even on top of my game. Sometimes an irate guest or an inconsiderate patron will get on your nerves to the point that you lose your temper. Losing your temper with the wrong guest could get you fired so you had to be very careful if you ever did get in an argument. Generally speaking, in our business even if you win an argument with a customer, you lose in the end because the customer stops coming.

In all my years of handling guests, I can only recall two instances in which I lost my temper in public. The first one occurred about two weeks after the fire at the Sands. I had been in my new management role for only two weeks and we were very busy on a Sunday afternoon registering a convention of Buick Motors Executives in town for the NADA Convention. There was a commotion at one of the check out windows where a guest was screaming and cursing at one of our older female cashiers. In all my years in the casino hotel business, while I had heard such profane words before, I had never heard them used in such a nasty manner in front of so many people in the lobby of a classy hotel casino. I raced over to the cashier's window and interceded. The female cashier was in tears and obviously incapacitated from the embarrassing experience. Then he started in on me using the same kind of language and swinging his arms in the air. Now keep in mind that I was only 23 years old and did not look like a manager to him. He was looking for the old gray haired guy to come out that he could scare into succumbing to his demands.

Anyway, I started in yelling back at him and threatened to have our security guards play basketball with him out in the middle of Las Vegas Boulevard, using him as the basketball. Then I told him, "Thankfully, pal, for every customer like you we fortunately have ten thousand good ones. Now get your ass out of here and never come back." The hundreds of people in the lobby started to clap and the cashiers behind the desk were forever my friends. It was all good until about two weeks later when I was called into Mr. Zike's office and he closed the door. Mr. Zike handed me a letter and asked that I read it. It was about ten pages long--- almost like a book. It had been addressed to Howard Hughes and it berated me and criticized my handling of the event at the front desk that particular Sunday. It went into every detail, magnifying the scope of the patron's embarrassment. The letter had been passed down from Bob Maheu, the head of Hughes Nevada Operations, then passed down to Al Benedict, managing director of the Sands and then on down to Ed Zike for appropriate disciplinary action.

I took time to read the letter and was swallowing hard. Finally as I finished, Mr. Zike asked me, "Well, is it true?"

I replied, "Actually most of it is, but let me tell you my side of the story first. I took this job because I thought I was moving from the classy Dunes to the classy Sands. I can tell you that no one at the Dunes would have put up with the conduct of the customer in this case and that the obscene conditions he was placing the cashier in were unbearable. It is my contention that if the Sands desires to put up with this kind of conduct, then they do not want me for a manager because I will not put up with it."

Mr. Zike took the letter from me and tore it into shreds in front of me and said, "No further explanation is required and no reply to the patron is justified other than this." And with that he dropped the shredded letter in his waste basket. Nonetheless, it was a lesson to be learned. You just cannot lose your temper in this business, because the guest always wins the war, even if he loses the battle. This experience was an exception to that rule. Also fortunately for me, the customer was not a good casino player and the letter had never really been read by Howard Hughes.

On another occasion I got into a heated argument on the telephone with a guest named Mr. Karp, who was way out of line, but I also knew that he was a good casino customer. I started to remember my old lesson and as I backed off with my hot-headed rhetoric, he yelled at me saying, "Do you know who I am? To which I replied, "Yes sir, but do you know who I am?"

When he said he did not know who I was, I said, "Good!" and I hung up the phone. Then I took off to the employee cafeteria to hide while Mr. Karp scouted the front desk looking for someone that sounded like me on the phone. He never did find me.

One of the most humorous customer interventions I ever saw, let alone participated in actually occurred at the Sands about a year after I became a manager. It was a classic event and one we still laugh and talk about. The chances of what happened that night are greater than winning any lottery ticket, but as luck would have it that evening we were all in for a laugh, and unfortunately for one desk clerk, a big black eye.

It was a relatively quiet day with very few reservations left to arrive, and the front desk was manned by just two clerks that evening. One of the clerks was a great guy named Frendy; he had been employed at the Sands in different capacities for several years and knew all the customers. He had been an athlete in college and was still in great shape. I was sitting in my manager's desk just adjoining the main front desk going over the next week's schedule, when all of a sudden a scuffle broke out in the lobby. It so happened that a young couple was checking in at one window of the desk when a second couple walked up to check in with Frendy, the clerk at the other open window. The two couples looked up at each other with a startled look in the two women's eyes and then all hell broke out as the two men started rolling around and punching each other in the lobby. I yelled for the bell captain to call for security guards to assist us and I, along with Frendy, raced out into the lobby and attempted to separate the two men fighting. As I pulled one of the men away, and Frendy was able to lock the other fellow in a full- nelson arm hold, we saw three security officers approaching the scene to assist us and take over the problem. However, the man I was trying to contain slipped from my grip and proceeded to take a full "round house" swing at the other guy who was still being tightly constrained by Frendy. Yet as the powerful swing of the one man's fist came flying toward the other fellow's face, the guy Frendy was holding managed to duck at the last instant and the powerful fist hit poor Frendy square in the eye.

As the security officer separated all of us and escorted the two "rowdies" down to the detention facility, we learned from the female companions of these two guys what caused the ruckus. Apparently each guy was stepping out with the other guy's wife for the weekend heading to Las Vegas unbeknownst to each other. When they saw each other's spouses at the check in windows, they became enraged and the donnybrook ensued.

We laugh about it today, but still are amazed by the odds of it happening. Even if two couples would sneak off for a Las Vegas tryst, in a city of twenty or more hotels at that time, what was the chance of them picking the same one? But even more astounding, what were the odds of the two couples checking in at the same time?

CHAPTER **6**

THREE YEARS WENT by quickly at the Sands and I was given more and more responsibilities, but they were all added to my current job title. As young people do, we are all impatient. I had expressed frequent interest to my bosses at every level that I had a desire to move into a higher level role and that I was willing to relocate to another hotel within the Howard Hughes chain of properties to achieve my goals. From time to time, an opening would occur at a sister property and I would voice my desire to apply for the position. Usually I was told the job had already been awarded, but then my bosses would give me a little raise in wages, I guess hoping I would stay put and just do my job every day. Things were running smoothly in my department and they liked it that way. A change in management always screws things up for a little while as it takes time for everybody to get used to each other, and as far as Mr. Danner and Mr. Goodheart were concerned, the status quo was the safest bet for the organization. They did not like people having to get used to each other.

Then one day I was informed that the hotel manager's position was open at the Frontier Hotel and the job description for that job was right up my alley and could lead to the natural progression toward a senior position several years later. I applied for a transfer only to be told that the position was being awarded to a fellow at the Sands who had no hotel experience at all. While this candidate for the position was a wonderful human being and a very cordial customer host for the Sands, I felt jilted. This guy was no more qualified to run the hotel operations at the Frontier Hotel than I was qualified to pilot a 747 airliner. Nonetheless, the transfer was completed and I was given another little raise in an effort to make me happy at losing out on this opportunity.

I left work that evening dejected and headed to my favorite watering hole at that time, The Guys & Dolls Lounge, located directly behind the Flamingo Hotel (Today it is known as the Stage Door Lounge). When I arrived at the bar, I was joined by my good friend and mentor, Spike Cook, who was now the front desk manager at the Dunes Hotel. I commiserated over my rejection for the hotel manager position at the Frontier, but we polished off enough Coors beer to take some of the sting out of my dismay.

With a slight hangover, I went to work at the Sands the next morning and about 11:00 a.m. I received a call from the general manager of the Dunes, my old boss and first mentor, Charlie Gustin. Mr. Gustin said he had been talking to Spike about my desire to take on additional responsibilities and he had a solution for me. Mr. Gustin invited me to return to the Dunes Hotel where I had received my start in the business just eight years before, and take over the position of resident manager. The incumbent had just resigned that previous weekend. It was not a great jump in pay, but I knew I had to move away from the Howard Hughes Company if I was going to give myself any chance at upward mobility. I slept on the offer and the following day I resigned my first management position at the famous Sands to take my first promotion in title back at the Dunes Hotel. As I expected, when I tendered my resignation with a polite written letter, I was offered a salary increase that would match my new position at the Dunes. I had learned early on that sometimes you have to take a step backwards in salary to move a step forward toward a career goal....and what the heck, I wasn't in it for the money anyway... Only for the Fun!

CHAPTER 7

THE SANDS HOTEL may have been the most famous of the casino resorts in the sixties and seventies. The home of the Rat Pack until the early seventies, it has a history unlike most of the other strip casinos. Some of the people who made history during the time I worked there deserve mention in this chapter before I move on to the next section of my book. The most famous of these was Howard Hughes.

During this period of time, Howard Hughes was in the news every day. He was reputed as wanting to buy up all the casinos in Nevada and he wanted to have enough economic clout to eliminate the underground nuclear tests that were taking place regularly at the Nevada test site just ninety miles northwest of his casinos on the strip. He had already purchased much of the land northwest of Las Vegas and controlled thousands of acres in Clark County. By 1970, in addition to the Sands and Desert Inn, Hughes now owned the Frontier Hotel, Landmark Hotel, Castaways Hotel and Silver Slipper Casino in Las Vegas along with Harold's Club in Reno. Nevada regulators were concerned that he would have too much economic concentration if he purchased any additional casinos and refused to let him go after the Stardust and Dunes. Nonetheless, he pursued and eventually owned every vacant piece of land on the strip between Sahara Avenue and what is now Sunset Road. He purchased every piece of land on the south side of the new McCarran Airport to bank for future industrial development, but he let the former owners live in their homes virtually for free until he needed the land for development. After his death, the Summa Corporation liquidated his casinos and strip land holdings, selling raw land to companies that have since built the Mirage, Treasure Island, Caesars expansions, the Forum mall, the Fashion Show Mall, Excalibur Hotel and Luxor Hotel. His land holdings in northwest Las Vegas were turned into the nation's largest master planned community, the famous upscale Summerlin Section of Las Vegas. The many myths and sagas of the reclusive Hughes live on today. From his alleged mysterious trips alone in the desert to his alleged slow death at the hands of the Mormon Mafia, where he apparently died with a long beard and five inch finger and toe nails. Truth or fiction, it was a great time to be at the Sands.

When Hughes purchased the Sands, he retained the original owners as consultants for a five year period. I spoke earlier about Carl Cohen. He was by far the best known and best regarded of the old Sands owners. Except for his outburst against Sinatra, he was seldom known to lose his temper and he was the most pragmatic of the bosses. While Cohen really ran the casino, the face of the Sands was its president, Jack Entratter. Entratter was best known for his impresario acumen and as such, the Sands enjoyed the reputation as the resort with the finest live entertainment and celebrity presence. Entratter started as a night club doorman in New York and eventually became a co-owner of the famed Copacabana in New York City. Entratter died shortly after I went to work at the Sands and we commandeered his luxury apartment to create one of the city's first casino cabana suites. Ronald Reagan was the most famous person to occupy the Luxury Cabana after Entratter's death

While I worked at the Sands, several others of the original colorful owners still lived on property in their respective luxury suites. They included Charles Turner, Sandy Waterman, General Charles Baron, Charlie Kandel and Bucky Harris.

Turner was reputed to have connections to Meyer Lansky, but he didn't look like a mobster to me. Next to Carl Cohen, it appeared to me that Turner had the second largest following of high rollers just based on the number of hotel reservations Turner submitted for players. While Turner was generally a very reserved and polite guy around the employees, his wife was the opposite. In fact, she was often perceived as ruthless--- the Leona Helmsley of the Sands.

Sandy Waterman served as the daily casino manager for the Sands. When I met him, it was evident that he was the nuts and bolts of the day-to-day operation on the gaming floor. He also had a nice following of good players, but nothing of the likes of Cohen or Turner. Like Turner, Waterman occupied a suite on the third floor of the Aqueduct Turf Club. Like Turner's wife, Waterman's wife was tough on employees, too. When Waterman's consulting agreement expired after the sale of the Sands to Hughes, Waterman moved on to manage the Caesars Palace casino. He is best remembered for pulling a pistol on Frank Sinatra in 1971 when Sinatra charged at him in the Baccarat pit at Caesars Palace over a wagering dispute. Waterman was arrested for pulling the pistol but all charges were dropped. Waterman was eventually arrested in 1973 on racketeering charges. Waterman was shot by an assailant in 1974 while driving his car to work, but he survived.

General Charles Baron was the Sands' Chicago connection. Known as the official Sands Greeter, the General was also reputed to be a Lansky operative. He earned his title as a Brigadier General in the Illinois National Guard while owning a successful car dealership in Chicago. The General lived in his modest suite in the Bay Meadows Turf Club at the Sands and was proud of his storied pistol collection, many of which he kept on hand in his suite to display for his friends and visitors. The General was a quiet but well organized man whom you would not suspect of having killed two people during his lifetime.

The kindest and gentlest of the old Sands owners was Charlie Kandel. Kandel was a very minor owner, but he was a magnificent host with a nice following of customers. He lived in a single hotel room back in the Aqueduct Turf Club several doors from the Turner apartment. He was well liked by the employees and he often sat and talked with all of us in the front office. Kandel was best known for his display of the American flag and for passing out those famous stickers you saw embossed with the American Flag and a slogan that read "Love it or Leave it." Kandel was single all his life, but apparently enjoyed an occasional liaison with a different female every now and then. He also apparently had a fetish. Except genitally, he apparently did not want to touch his lover. That explained the small hole he frequently cut in his top bed sheet. When the housekeeper told me about the frequently damaged linen, I told her I would put the story in my book after Charlie Kandel passed away.

Bucky Harris owned only a percentage of a point in the Sands, but everyone regarded him as Mr. Sands. Bucky and his wife, Mary, lived in their luxury apartment on the second floor of the Aqueduct Turf Club directly below the Turner Suite. As each of the old owners moved on after their consulting contracts expired, Bucky elected to stay on with the Hughes organization until he passed away. Unlike Turner or Waterman's wives, Mary Harris was loved by all the Sands employees. Mary Harris could be found wandering around in the employee cafeteria or the housekeeping office visiting with maids and porters. Bucky had been a bouncer at the Copa Cabana years before and he knew every customer worth any money that walked in the doors of the Sands Hotel. He had even a larger following than Carl Cohen and Carl respected him for it. I loved working with Bucky and always went out of my way to pay special attention to his customers' room reservations.

I will close this section with my favorite story about Bucky Harris. Bucky loved to bet the horses. Every single morning, rain or shine in summer or winter Bucky could be seen dressed in his sports coat and tie complete with white sneakers walking from the Sands north on the strip to the Rose Bowl Sports Book. The Rose Bowl Book was located where the entry road leads into the Wynn Resort today. Armed with his racing form, Bucky always studied the various ponies' racing statistics as he walked toward the book to make his bets. On this one occasion, an African American hooker approached him as he was walking and studying the racing form. She stopped him and inquired, "Hey mister, what do you think about a little black pussy today?" Bucky quickly replied with a question, "What track and what race is she running in?"

Section 3

MY SOPHOMORE YEARS IN GAMING — BACK TO THE DUNES AND THEN BACK TO THE SANDS WITH A STOP IN BETWEEN AT THE FRONTIER CASINO

CHAPTER **1**

MY FIRST DAY on the job at the Dunes the second time around was far easier this time. I knew all the players and I was no longer a total novice. However, now I would have to get used to being the supervisor of friends, mentors and in some cases previous supervisors, and at the age of 26, I was going to have to navigate a little gingerly.

When I left the Dunes employment the first time in March of 1970, the original ownership I talked about in the first section of this book was still in place. Now three and a half years later, the ownership structure had shifted and it was evident that there was some political maneuvering going on among the key leaders of the Dunes organization. Sid Wyman, the king pin of the Dunes Casino operations from its inception, had for many years been represented by the notorious St. Louis attorney, Morris Schenker. I recalled that Schenker had been a frequent guest of the Dunes during my initial days as a desk clerk. I had frequently checked him into one of the luxury suites on the 22nd floor of the Dunes Tower, and he and his wife Lillian were always gracious. While we knew he represented Sid Wyman and maybe even a couple of the other Dunes owners, his real celebrity involved his legal representation of Teamsters Union Boss, Jimmy Hoffa. By 1970, the Teamsters Union was beginning to invest some of its pension money into legitimate gambling businesses and Schenker steered some of that money into the Dunes coffers as he began his quest to take over eventual ownership of the now-aging facility.

At the time of my return to the Dunes, Morris Schenker had just moved into a suite on a permanent basis and was beginning to exert his power over different aspects of the operation. However, several of the old bosses were pushing back. The most severe "push back" was coming from George Duckworth, the son-in-law of Charlie "Kewpie" Rich. He was the new casino manager, taking over the day-to-day management of gaming operations. Apparently in Mr. Duckworth's quest to maintain control over general operations, he had placed certain restrictions on Mr. Schenker's ability to give directions or make demands on the Dunes staff, and he sent written instructions around to the various departments that prohibited Mr. Schenker from reserving hotel rooms or granting special rates and complimentary arrangements for rooms, food, beverage and entertainment. The "Power to comp" and give out free rooms and show tickets were generally recognized automatic rights of power that every owner and almost every high level casino executive in each Las Vegas Casino shared without any requirement on their part to seek approval from a third party. Yet, here at the Dunes were written instructions that Mr. Schenker was not permitted to make suite reservations or comp anybody without approval from Mr. Duckworth.

Well, with written instructions like this posted on bulletin boards around the company, one can only imagine how low level employees would interpret them. What was worse is that Mr. Schenker did not know these written instructions existed. The first night in my new position, I heard some panicked voices in the room reservation office just outside my office door. Apparently Mr. Schenker was calling in from San Diego, instructing the reservation agent to book a suite in the Seahorse Wing of the hotel for friends of his, and the agent was to mark the reservation as fully complimentary. The guest was also to be told upon his arrival that he was the guest of Mr. Schenker. The reservation agent, not being extremely bright, blurted out to Mr. Schenker that Mr. Duckworth had distributed a memorandum advising all personnel that Mr. Schenker was not permitted to make suite reservation or comp customers without Duckworth's written approval. One can only imagine the predicament my staff was in when Schenker retorted, "Do you know who I am? What do you mean 'dat' I can't comp. I am 'da' owner of the 'f—kin' hotel. Get Duckworth on the line right now!"

There I was my first day on the job in my new role and one of my reservation staff people had me in the middle of an executive donnybrook before I'd even had a chance to place my personal effects in my new office. Fortunately, Duckworth took the heat after getting a nasty phone call from Schenker and he rescinded the written instructions, although he came back and privately advised me (off the record) that he wanted to be made aware of any reservation Schenker might put in. In a quick backroom session with my closest front desk managers, Spike Cook and Bob Vannucci, we established an informal methodology to ensure we were always in the loop when Schenker called and we were able to quietly inform Duckworth when such arrangements for Schenker's guests were made.

Other than that one stressful moment my first day back, my transition to my new manager's position at the Dunes went relatively smooth, even given my young age. Some of the techniques I had developed at the Sands were easily transferable to the Dunes operation and with the cooperation of my old fellow desk clerks and the people I knew in the housekeeping and engineering departments, we were able to create a new hybrid of hotel operational procedures that improved productivity and efficiency. The Dunes front desk operations was already streamlined much better than that of the Sands, but the room inventory management system was antiquated and often inaccurate, which caused oversell situations that were needless. In 1970, the advent of the computer was still foreign at hotel front desks so, for the most part, room inventory was conducted solely by hand. Needless to say, when working with an 800-room inventory, hand tallies were only about 90% accurate at best. In order to maximize room occupancy and minimize the inconvenience to customers and employees alike because of the erroneous room inventory system that existed, I was able to talk the general manager, Mr. Gustin, into leasing a new fangled mini-computer that calculated room inventories for us based on three simple variables: namely, number of rooms in the reservation, the arrival date, and the departure date. We established simple procedures that required all reservations taken by the agents to be posted through the new mini-computer and stamped certifying the entry had been posted before the reservation was inserted in the reservation rack. Likewise, all cancellations and date changes or modifications to the number of rooms in a reservation had to be entered into the system. Though antiquated by today's standards, this simple system was a pre-cursor to the room's management systems that everybody takes for granted today in the hotel industry. Within one month of my tenure, we had improved inventory forecasting and made over a ten percent improvement in average occupancy.

IN MY ROLE as resident manager, I was still able to jump on a check-in window during heavy arrival days and help out to move the incoming lines out of the lobby. The desk clerks at the Dunes were as fast as any I have ever seen or worked with, and with the manual systems the Dunes had in place, customers could be checked in at a pace of over 40 check-ins per hour by each expert desk clerk, if rooms were clean and available for occupancy. That kind of productivity is mathematically impossible in today's computer world where the desk clerk now has to navigate around a series of screens to find the customer and then match him or her up with the appropriate room. Since the Dune's front desk clerks were very competitive, they frequently would each throw five dollars into a pot, and the clerk who recorded the most check-ins during an eight hour shift would win the pot. Likewise, to take the sting out of the pain of walking customers during oversells, they would each throw ten dollars into the pot, with the clerk doing the most walks getting the pot, winner takes all.

After a tough day on the desk where we would handle a 600 room arrival with three or four clerks, and especially if walking patrons were numerous, we generally retired to the closest bar after work to compose ourselves. It was on one of these early spring Sundays in 1974 that I came in to work to help the front desk with a particularly tough check in. At the end of the shift we were exhausted and my buddy, Spike, and I decided that we needed to relax in some place classier than our normal hideaway at the Guys and Dolls Lounge. We decided to head over to the new Bootlegger Italian Restaurant that was located at Tropicana and Eastern and enjoy a quiet beer away from the noise of the casino or our regular gin mill. We had just sat down and ordered a beer, when two big inebriated golfers showed up. They had obviously been out in the sun too long that nice spring day and the booze they consumed on the links was providing some false courage. They ordered a drink and then proceeded to throw their glassware into the speed rack behind the bartender.

Spike suggested to the bartender that he call the police, but the bartender hesitated, thinking they just needed to settle down after too much sun. Two more times they threw their glassware and still the bartender did not confront the two lugs. Then a fellow shows up, escorting his blind mother to a seat at the bar next to mine. He orders his mother a drink and tells her he will be right back after doing some shopping next door. Not one minute went by after he left his mother there, before these two clowns began throwing their glassware again. Only this time one of the glasses landed on top of the bar next to the blind lady and shattered leaving the poor lady hysterical. It had been a tough day at the Dunes, but this was making my day even worse. I told the bartender to call the police, and I got up and went out the front door of the bar to my car. I took off my coat and tie and then came back in the Bootlegger front door. With one round house swing, I put one guy on the floor and cracked his head open, banging it on the rung of the bar stool. When I let him up, he and his buddy ran out into the parking lot and the police showed up (finally).

I figured I was in a heap of trouble now, so I called my wife and told her to get some bail money as I waited for the police officer to come into the restaurant and arrest me. By this time, the owner of the Bootlegger had gotten my name and sent Spike and me a beer on the house with his thanks. When the police officers came in, they said, "Are you Mr. Wagner? When I acknowledged that I was, I prepared to put my hands behind my back to accommodate the handcuffs. That's when the cop asked me if I wanted to press charges for assault and battery. It seems that Spike had adequately demonstrated to the many witnesses eating their spaghetti in the dining area of the Bootlegger that I was attacked and hit by flying glass and had thus defended myself along with the honor of the little old blind lady. I told the cops that I did not want to press charges…I said, "Just send these two clowns home and let me finish my beer in peace."

CHAPTER **3**

AS I HAVE said before, the front desk of a casino hotel back in those days was the hub of the operations and communications-central. If something was going on someplace in the building (good or bad), the front desk and certainly the telephone operators knew about it. The front desk at the Dunes was also the first and last place a customer saw upon entering or leaving the hotel or casino. Without a doubt, it was the best vantage point in the casino to observe the diversity of customers and, of course, witness some outrageous incidents.

Looking back, some of these incidents are pretty funny to talk about, but they were very serious when we encountered them. It is only fitting that I recall a couple of these stories that have survived the test of time for those of us that witnessed them or were even directly involved.

On one occasion, we heard a lot of hollering at one end of the casino floor and then we saw a fellow running out of the casino into the lobby and heading for the front entry way to escape the security officers pursuing him. It seems he had reached into the chip tray of one of the blackjack games and grabbed a handful of $100 gaming chips and then started running to make his escape. As he was dashing through the lobby with three security officers hot on his trail, one of the owners was on the house phone in a booth adjoining our front desk. The boss heard the commotion and saw the perpetrator running toward him, so at just the right moment he stepped out of the phone booth and stuck his leg out in front of the thief, tripping him up and sending him crashing to the lobby floor with his stack of gaming chips flying in every direction. By this time the security officers jumped on the guy and then all the action was taking place below the front desk level where none of could see what was really happening…but we could certainly hear the pounding this poor soul was getting. Then they dragged him off to the security office located back by the big vault and we never did see the thief again. It kind of made us wonder what other uses the old bosses had for their big sound-proof concrete vault.

One of the more memorable incidents took place one Saturday morning in April of 1974. I remember it like it happened yesterday. On the prior Wednesday, we discovered that there was a guest in one of the tower hotel rooms by the name of Harry Zeff, who had unwittingly attached himself to a high-roller's entourage and then conned a pit boss into giving him a room. Once Mr. Zeff had checked into the room, he started ordering expensive liquor and food from room service and began to run up a sizeable tab. When the front desk cashier flagged the account as suspicious, our front desk manager called the casino manager to inquire about how we should handle this account. When it was figured out that Mr. Zeff was a fraud, we called his room and asked him to come down to the front desk and pay on his account. However, Mr. Zeff decided that it was in his best interest to just duck us and avoid our further phone calls. So after a couple hours passed by and still no word from Harry, we sent a security officer to Mr. Zeff's room with instructions to "double-lock" the door. In those days, we were able to lock a patron out of his room manually with a special key (known as an "E" key), if we deemed it was in our best interest or it was necessary to get the patron's attention.

Well, Harry never came back that night or the next day either. So by Thursday evening, with room occupancy running at capacity, we sent security and housekeeping staff up to Harry's room and packed his belongings for safekeeping in the lockup.

Wouldn't you know it? Harry shows up on Friday morning looking for his belongings. We tell him that as soon as he arranges to pay his bill, we would release his suitcases, but until then we were keeping them as a lien against what he owed the hotel. I kiddingly told him that the brand new suit he had hanging in his closet, that we were now holding as collateral, was exactly my size. I then added that if he did not show up by Saturday with payment for the account, that I would then own his suit and would be wearing it on Monday to work. In the meantime, I told Harry that he was no longer welcome at the Dunes and that if he came back on property again without the funds to pay his bill, I would have him arrested and jailed for trespassing. Harry left the desk in a very foul mood but indicating that he would figure out how to come up with some money to pay the bill and get his clothes back.

Then on Saturday morning, I was in my office behind the front desk when I heard a commotion. Harry had returned. But Harry had not returned in a conventional manner. Instead he came into the back office through a restricted door and confronted the desk clerks in their work area. Evidently Harry was also looking for me, the guy who was going to abscond with his new suit. So I obliged him by coming out from my office. In the meantime, I gave Spike the nod to call Security and we made small talk with Harry while we waited for the security officers to arrive. Harry was fidgety and most evidently high on something and we did not know if he was armed so we were taking no chances. Finally two security officers showed up, one being an older fellow named Jim. Once they arrived, I told Harry we were going to file charges against him for defrauding an innkeeper and also for trespassing. I then instructed the officers to take Harry off to the security offices to hold for the Las Vegas sheriff. As the officers attempted to handcuff Harry, all hell broke loose. Harry kicked old Jim in the groin and made a dash for the exit.

Out through the lobby he ran. As he exited the front entry way and through the Porte cochere he began heading north up the strip. He knew old Jim was not capable of catching him but he had no idea that the hotel manager, an old UNLV track star, would chase him down. There I was in my suit and tie racing after Harry. I finally caught hold of him on the center median of the Las Vegas Strip directly in front of the MGM Grand Hotel (now known as Bally's). As I grabbed Harry by the back of his neck, I glanced across the highway and there was Jim, still reeling from the kick in his groin, and now pointing his 357 magnum at both Harry and me. Worse yet, his gun was also pointed at several dozen people directly behind us, standing in the valet entryway of the MGM Casino. Fortunately, another security officer, a huge black guy named Clyde, showed up and talked Jim into putting the gun down. In a previous section, I identified Clyde as a special employee who once worked for Spike Cook in the convention services department. Clyde had moved up the ladder into a role of sergeant in the department and I was sure glad to see him that Saturday morning. Clyde came out into the middle of the highway median, handcuffed Harry, and took him away.

As Clyde was escorting Harry through the Dunes parking lot back to the security detention room, apparently Harry tried to kick Clyde like he had done to Jim. Nobody saw it happen, but Clyde being about 290 pounds slammed Harry's head into the hood of a Volkswagen Beetle that just happened to be parked nearby in the Dunes parking lot. Harry was eventually booked into the Clark County jail where he spent several weeks before some relative finally bailed him out. To my knowledge, he never did pay his bill and we eventually donated all his belongings to charity, yes even his suit.

I called Clyde after Harry finally was carted away and thanked him for stopping Jim from shooting at us. And then I asked him about how the big dent occurred in the hood of the Volkswagen Bug out in the parking lot, to which Clyde responded with his slight speech impediment, "It muuushed have been a pasherby!"

Another crazy guest I had to stifle was a nut case out on the Dunes Golf Course driving range. In those days, the Dunes had one of the nicest golf courses in Las Vegas, the famous "Emerald Greens." Located next to the golf course and actually bordering on the strip wedged in between the Dunes casino and the Jockey Club Towers, was the Dunes driving range. One afternoon, a mentally challenged patron purchased a bucket of golf balls and started driving balls, but not in a west to east direction in line with the natural footprint of the range. Instead, this guy was driving golf balls perpendicular to the natural footprint of the range. Occupants of the Jockey Club started calling our telephone operators in panic as their glass sliding doors and windows were being knocked out one at a time by this nut on the driving range. By the time we got out to the range and had him arrested, he had knocked out over 50 windows and sliding doors. He may have been mentally challenged, but he had a wonderfully accurate golf swing.

I HAD ONLY been working at the Dunes in my new role for three months when I began getting telephone calls from the Summa Corporation offices (the new company name for the old Howard Hughes Nevada Operations). The head of the gaming operations, a guy named Steve Salvodelli, had always been happy with my work at the Sands and was dismayed that I left, but he admitted that the company had passed me by for promotions because they liked keeping me where I was in the Sands. Anyway, he now wanted me to consider coming back to the Hughes organization and wondered if I would accept a position at the Xanadu in the Bahamas, which Howard Hughes had just acquired. I thanked him for his continued interest in my career but told him that I had an obligation to my new employer and furthermore had no desire to move my family to a foreign country. Two months later, he called again asking me to consider taking the hotel manager's position at the Landmark Hotel which had recently become available. Again, I told him that I was already in a hotel manager position, and my current position was in a hotel casino with much more prestige than the Landmark, but thanks again for his interest in my career.

Mr. Salvodelli and his team knew that I was still sore about missing the chance to be the hotel manager at the Frontier when the position had become available several months prior and was then awarded to someone without any hotel background. So in October, 1974, just ten months after going back to the Dunes, Mr. Salvodelli called me with an offer I could not refuse. They were going to make the hotel manager's position at the Frontier available for me, with a nice salary increase, a big office and some beefed up comping privileges that I did not enjoy in my current role at the Dunes. But most enticing of all, they indicated they wanted me to be placed on an upwardly mobile path to higher positions with greater responsibilities, and with six casino hotels in Las Vegas, I saw that as being a fair reason to leave the Dunes.

It was tough to go into Mr. Gustin's office to tender my written resignation. I had a great deal of respect for Charlie and he appreciated my work and always told me so, which so many bosses fail to do. I learned from him and always try to compliment my employees when they try hard and do well for the company and themselves. He begrudgingly accepted my resignation, understanding how I thought the move would improve the trajectory of my career path, but he insisted that I talk to the owner, Mr. Schenker, before I finalized my decision. With butterflies in my stomach, I reluctantly went upstairs to the executive office to visit with Mr. Schenker. When I was escorted into his office, he was there with his wife, Lillian, and they both tried to persuade me not to resign. Mr. Schenker being a skilled and successful trial lawyer said to me, "Everything should always be up for negotiation. What will it take to make you stay?" All I could say was to thank him for his support but that I had made my mind up and saw my move to the Frontier as being an important step in achieving my long term career goals. When I left his office, I never talked to Mr. Schenker again.

CHAPTER **5**

I STARTED TO work at the Frontier Hotel on October 18, 1973. It was comfortable to be getting back with the Howard Hughes affiliated casinos. The company was now called the Summa Corporation and the Frontier Hotel was a relatively new facility and the management team headed by Jack Pieper was in direct competition with the management team at the Sands headed by Dick Danner and Harry Goodheart.

I think Pieper was annoyed that the headquarters for Summa had engineered my employment at his hotel casino, but he treated me kindly on my first day on the job and laid out my job responsibilities as he saw them. After working at the Dunes and the Sands where the action was much faster, the Frontier almost seemed boring for me from the first day I arrived. The desk clerks were like robots and their efficiency was horrendous from my point of reference. Morale around the front office was dour and the effects of past bad blood in union relations were evident. This was an operation where the Teamsters Union had pitted their front desk members against the Frontier management, and the quality of service for the customers was suffering badly. It seems that an African American desk clerk had been terminated for unbecoming conduct with a guest, and then won an acrimonious arbitration award against the Frontier that required the company to pay out substantial back wages and reinstate the fellow back to his original position with full seniority rights. The reinstatement did not go over well with the manager who had directed the termination, and mutual resentment permeated the entire front office environment.

With my arriving on the scene as a newcomer, I took the opportunity to bring the problem desk clerk into my office and lock the door. I informed him that with my predecessor and his former nemesis now departed from the Frontier management team, it was time for the two parties to clear the board and start over. We had a very frank discussion in private about how the company and he were going to press the "re-set button" on our business relationship and he was going to become a productive member of my front office team. I also told him in the privacy of my office that while I had no chip on my shoulder over the fact that he had won his arbitration against the company, his return to employment did not grant him any special privileges or the right to treat fellow employees or our guests with anything but courtesy and respect.

I reminded him that I had never lost any arbitration and that I had special ways to ensure that I would have a verifiable paper trail of evidence that would be available to me and the company if I ever had to terminate him. I told him, "No threat, Leonard! Just fact!" We shook hands and he left my office and returned to his station at the front desk.

I tested him several times during the next month. I had casino guests of mine purposely check in with him. I had outside secret shoppers work him over when they checked in. To his credit, he remained calm and did his job. While this guy never became a star employee, he did become a team player and employee morale improved right along with much better guest service levels. The front office operations were now as good as any other casino hotel on the strip and upper management, especially the casino hosts and pit bosses, noticed the difference and began commenting on it.

Well, it happened that Mr. Pieper, the general manager had been thoroughly disappointed with the conditions at the front desk, but because my predecessor was a dear friend of his whom he had hired personally he was unable to demand the changes necessary to correct the impediment to service. When he discovered that I had solved the problem, essentially in the first month of my employment, he began to soften his stiff attitude toward me and I became one of his inner-circle group invited to lunch and after hours cocktails almost daily.

OF ALL THE casinos I have worked in during my 44 years in gaming, the shortest run was at the Frontier. Consequently, I made fewer close management acquaintances and was unable to get to know many of the employees by name, as I had been able to do at the Sands and Dunes. Nonetheless, I did come across the most professional room reservation manager of my career in a demure and thoughtful woman named Charlotte Ellsworth, and to this day I still regard her as one of the most guest-oriented managers with whom I have had the pleasure of working. The people in her department adored her and emulated everything for which she stood. She had been a fixture at the Flamingo Hotel for twenty years, starting there just shortly after Bugsy Siegel opened the doors to that first strip hotel. In 1967 she moved over to open the Frontier and she had seldom been out of Las Vegas. Little did I know when I met her that she would eventually agree to transfer to Reno and open the MGM with me several years later.

Working closely with Charlotte, my hotel team was able to re-engineer many of the business processes in the front office and housekeeping that enabled the Frontier to improve occupancy, while speeding up the cleaning and rooming process. The improvements were noticed at the Summa corporate headquarters and Jack Pieper was getting the credit. At the same time our success was putting the pressure back on the Flagship hotel, the Sands.

Seeing our success, Pieper handed me additional responsibilities with engineering, security operations and even had me negotiating purchasing agreements. Pieper volunteered the Frontier to be the beta site for testing an online computer application for the front desk, something that we take for granted today but which was foreign, untested and unreliable back in 1973. He also volunteered me to teach front office operations as an adjunct instructor for the new Community College that had just opened its doors the previous year.

As I took on more responsibilities, he let me have my first glimpse "behind the scenes" of the gaming operations. Pieper had me reading books by Scarne on the rules of the games and he had me work with the finance people to garner a good understanding of the numbers and metrics that enable casino operators to measure the successes of promotions and help ensure the integrity of operations.

Up until then, I thought there could be no more fun than hotel operations. After all, the hub of a casino operation centered around the front desk. At least, up until then I thought this way. But getting a taste of the casino operation from the general manager's viewpoint was not only exciting; it was priceless, especially at my age.

IN NOVEMBER OF 1975, my previous co-worker Ted Ward, now the hotel manager of the Sands shot a cannon ball across the Frontier bow. It seems he was coaching a flag football team comprised of Sands employees and he was challenging other hotels to a weekly contest. The Sands was undefeated against other opponents and the rivalry between Danner, the general manager of the Sands and Pieper, his counterpart at the Frontier, fueled the challenge. Since Pieper was aware that I knew most of the Sands employees, he thought I should lead the Frontier Team in defending the challenge put forth by Ted Ward and the Sands. Ted, known for his boastful demeanor, predicted that the Sands would win by two touchdowns and he was constantly encouraging people to wager on the outcome.

The big game became quite a morale builder at both companies, and the big night took place at the football field of a local junior high school. The weather that evening was a crispy 35 degrees, but that did not deter the crowd of spectators, mostly family and friends of the employees of the Sands and Frontier. The hotdogs were cooking on portable hibachis while brandy and coffee were flowing from the many thermos jugs on both sides of the field. But best of all, Danner and Goodheart were making giant wagers with Pieper and Sam Hogan (the Frontier casino manager), over which team would take the trophy. While the game was called to promote morale and a good time for employees and their families, we all felt the pressure when we heard that several thousand dollars was wagered on the outcome of the game that night. Today that doesn't sound like a lot of money, but to somebody taking home a little over a thousand dollars a month as the hotel manager in 1975, it was a lot of money to lose for our bosses.

The Sands football squad started out with a bang by scoring a touchdown on the first play and it appeared they would run away with the game, as they had been doing for several previous weeks against other opponents. But we kept the play close and with seconds left in the game, the Frontier quarterback threw a *hail mary* to the fastest black guy we had on our team and the rest was history. Danner and Goodheart glared at me, but they headed back to the Sands several thousand dollars lighter. Come to think about it, that was the last game they let Ted Ward coordinate, and football at the Sands came to an end that night.

The next day, Pieper called me to his office and I just knew he wanted to talk about the success of the game. Instead, he gave me the news that he was resigning as the Frontier's general manager to take on a position as the new president of the MGM Grand Hotel Casino development in Reno, Nevada. I was stunned by the announcement because it was so unexpected and, of course, in our business, a change at the top often brings about changes in management at every level when a new general manager takes over.

Pieper told me that he had discussed my future with the officials at Summa Corporation and assured me that I would still play a major role in the company's management development program and I should not be concerned about my job security. Pieper indicated that the company was planning to transfer and promote the assistant general manager at the Sands, a man named Merle Coombs into the general manager position at the Frontier as Pieper's replacement. This was good news for me because I knew Merle personally and thought he was a fair and genuine guy who deserved the promotion and it would be an honor to work for him. I told Pieper that I appreciated his willingness to bring me into his inner-circle and teach me an expanded version of the business and that I was looking forward to using what I had learned to add value to my position with Summa Corporation, at whatever property they might want me to work in.

Pieper then confessed that he had been giving me extra responsibilities and teaching me casino operations from a selfish standpoint. He told me that during the next eighteen months I should continue to learn as much as I could about all gaming and resort operations, because he intended to offer me a senior position on his team at the MGM in Reno, when the time was appropriate to start bringing his management team together. Jack Pieper worked out his notice and closed out the year at the Frontier, departing the property on New Year's Eve, 1975.

MERLE COOMBS STARTED as the Frontier's general manager on January 3, 1976. It was a pleasure and a lot of fun assisting him with his transition. One of the great benefits of being a general manager for Summa Corporation in those days was the chance to live in a luxury suite on property if you ran the Frontier, or in a company furnished home on the Desert Inn Golf Course if you managed the Desert Inn or Sands Hotel. Merle Coombs and his wife moved into the hotel and from day one they both were a hit with employees and customers.

Two weeks after Coombs came on board and his transition was almost completed, I received a call from Steve Salvodelli at the Summa office asking for a lunch meeting that particular day. With Merle Coomb's transition to the Frontier successfully completed, Salvodelli informed me that the company now wanted to transfer me back to the Sands and into the position just vacated by Merle Coombs, as assistant general manager."

It just couldn't get any better than that. A new executive office on the mezzanine level, a nice increase in compensation and benefits and a chance to again work with Danner and Goodheart who I still felt were two of the greatest bosses in Las Vegas at the time.

Salvodelli arranged a meeting for me to meet with Danner later that afternoon and one week later I started work at the Sands for the second time. Danner told me he forgave me for the lost wagers at the football game and expected me to make up for it by working hard and being loyal to him and Goodheart.

CHAPTER **9**

IN MY NEW role as assistant general manager, I found that what I had learned about the casino operations and the new responsibilities I had taken on in the administrative and security areas would really benefit me in my role as Danner's assistant. In fact, he was pleasantly surprised that I was able to add value almost from day one. In addition, since I was keenly familiar with the Sands physical plant as well as many of its employees from my first tour there just two years prior, my learning curve was greatly reduced this time around.

Unfortunately for my old co-front desk manager, Ted Ward, Danner decided to eliminate his position as hotel manager and combined those hotel responsibilities into my new job description. Ted was knocked totally off guard with his dismissal, much as he had been when I knocked him out of the day-shift spot when I was promoted into my first management job at the Sands several years prior. Unfortunately, this was not to be the last time I displaced poor Ted, and I will delve into that later in the next section of this story.

These were exciting times for hotel operations in Las Vegas. The role of large conventions was playing a more important part in establishing the city as more than just a gambling destination. With the opening of the MGM, the expansion of the International Hotel (now the Hilton) and the growth of the Las Vegas Convention Center, the largest conventions in the United States were beginning to flock to the southern Nevada City for their annual meetings and retreats. This new element of consistent business opened up opportunities for new revenue sources within the resorts and the importance of the hotel and catering aspect of the casino hotels made for nice increases in salaries and other benefits that previously had been reserved for the casino executives only.

Also exciting was our opportunity and ability to participate in the development of the first real-time hotel computer systems that instantly could manage guest accounting and room inventories, advance reservations, housekeeping activity and guest phone services. Previously this was all handled manually with the technology of the day being telephones, walkie talkies, telautograph machines and pneumatic tubes. Hotel accounting was accomplished on large cash register machines, mostly the Series NCR 2000 or its updated, more modern version, the NCR 4200.

The most difficult part of designing the new computer applications was finding an electronic methodology for replacing the famous "Room Rack." The Rack, as we called it, was a huge inventory control system using basic inventory cards to keep track of guest room availability. All relevant guest registration information for every guest in the hotel was readily visible and could be accessed by multiple desk clerks simultaneously. Even to this day I believe the rack was the best tool for managing room inventories. Even the best computer rooms-management systems today are unable to provide the kind of visible "look" at the hotel occupancy and availability that was afforded by the old room rack. But that is where the old manual system superiority ended. The computer applications instantly created on-line information for the telephone operators, restaurants and bars and all the retail outlets. Room charges were now posted instantly on guest accounts instead of on a batch basis hours after the charges were incurred, as was the case in a manual system. Room charge postings previously accomplished over several hours on the old NCR register were now able to be posted instantly, and most elements of the night audit were accomplished by the computer.

However, the new computer applications were not very reliable in the early days of their existence. For several years, we maintained simultaneous manual backup systems because the computers would constantly crash. Like most companies in those days, we blamed many of our customers' complaints and grievances on a computer error. Obviously, then as is still the case today, effecting change is difficult, especially in the minds of the older workers. Many of the employees in the front office were terrified of the new computers, mostly because so many initially believed they could not learn or adapt to them. In their minds the end result would be their job termination if they couldn't catch on. As such, our training efforts were fraught with resistance and, no doubt, we experienced sabotage when it came to handling the hardware, and data integrity was always in question.

Like all technologies today, great advancements in hotel management and accounting systems came quickly. The early systems became obsolete and their successor systems became faster, more reliable and much easier to use. Initial programs that required the desk clerk to move around a series of menus to find the proper applications slowed the registration process and caused lines in hotel lobbies. To overcome the slower registrations required larger front desk staffs and more computer terminals. However, the efficiency of online accounting and room's inventory control made the slower registration process worth it. Today, the current systems use Window technology and kiosk self-registration programs to speed the check-in process, but the one dynamic still left unsolved by computers remains: When will the guest depart the room?

Unlike airline reservation and theater or concert seats, managing the room inventory in a hotel (and worse in a casino hotel) becomes a function of guests checking in and out on schedule. In 1966, check out time at most of the Strip Hotels was 3:00 p.m. Also in those days it was common for the casino pit bosses to extend late check outs to almost anybody that requested one. Common, too, was the audacity of many guests to just stay for a couple of extra hours knowing they could get away without an extra charge just by talking their way out of one. Consequently, many customers stayed in their rooms until 6:00 p.m. or sometimes even later. One can imagine the problem this posed for the front desk staff when advance room reservations projected a full house.

Time zones make the situation even worse in Las Vegas. Most of the visitors to Las Vegas that arrive by airplane come from the east coast or the mid-west. Consequently many flights arrive before noon or just thereafter. The incoming reservations arrive at the front desk to learn that rooms are not yet cleaned or ready to occupy. In the old days, incoming reservations that arrived early were told that check in time was after 3:00 p.m., but often due to the late check outs, they could not be housed until the dinner hour.

As occupancy levels increased city wide, the policies governing check out times at most of the hotels evolved from the 3:00 p.m. in the 1960s, to 1:00 p.m. in the 1970s and finally to 11:00 a.m., which today seems to be the standard across the nation. Yet even with the early departure policies, the problem with late check outs and guests staying beyond their contracted departure dates are problems that make simple inventory control complicated in a hotel. They were a problem then and still remain a problem today.

CHAPTER **10**

ON APRIL 6, 1976, Howard Hughes died. The date is clearly etched in my mind because my first son was born two days later and we almost changed his name to Howard. Anyway, I remember the confusion in the company that resulted from the death of America's only billionaire. Like many eccentric people, he apparently left behind no will, so alleged heirs and kinfolk began to show up staking a claim. Eventually, a most gracious person emerged to become the executor of the Howard Hughes estate in the person of William Lummis. Mr. Lummis was a cousin of Hughes, and he actually looked very much like the photos of Hughes taken when he was a public celebrity in the days before he edged into reclusiveness.

Lummis was an attorney from Houston, where most of Howard Hughes's kinfolk apparently reigned. Lummis took charge and became a much respected leader of the Summa Corporation. He was able to convince the Hughes's relatives to stay united in their court battles to settle the estate for the rightful owners. This effort alone took over eight years, but Lummis was able to keep the casinos and other Hughes enterprises operating in a manner that preserved their value for the heirs. It became clear that he was going to develop a strategy to systematically liquidate all of the Hughes Nevada holdings, beginning with the casinos first, and then the vast sections of raw land that Hughes had banked in and around Las Vegas. Some fifteen years later, his job was totally completed and he retired from his position as CEO of Summa Corporation. Summa Corporation eventually changed its name to the Howard Hughes Corporation in the early 1990s and merged with the Rouse Company in 1995, which gave the heirs the liquidity they were seeking in the form of Rouse Company Common stock.

CHAPTER **11**

THE YEAR 1976 was a great time for some other innovations on the Las Vegas Strip and I am proud to have been a part of two precedent-setting events. Even though the civil rights laws had been legislated in 1964, it was rare to see any minorities or people of color in management positions. I was determined to be one of the first managers to change that at the Sands.

Lubi Draskovic, our Director of Food and Beverage, made me aware of a very bright and articulate young African American fellow who was finishing up his degree in hotel administration at the University of Nevada, Las Vegas. Lubi had sneaked out of Yugoslavia during the communist regime of Tito, and he managed to immigrate into the USA. As a foreigner with limited command of the English language, he got a break in his search for a career in the hospitality business when he landed a job as a dishwasher at the Sands at its opening in 1952. His boss mentored Lubi, and he quickly moved up in the organization to a position as the most respected food and beverage executive throughout Las Vegas.

As a result of Lubi's experiences, he constantly championed the cause for employees he saw who looked like they had promise for upward mobility, and many successful individuals working in the casino industry today were the product of Lubi's mentoring and lobbying.

Dan Napier was no exception. Here was this good looking, well educated and smooth-talking "executive-in-waiting" working for Lubi as a dishwasher in the main kitchen, a job he had been doing for almost two years. He was reliable, never missed work and was a de-facto leader of the dishwashing and stewarding crew whenever he was on duty.

We transferred Dan to the front desk and put him through intense training. Obviously the environment at the front desk was a night and day change from the inside of a dish room in the main kitchen. Dan was a quick learner and in less than four months, we promoted Dan to the role of assistant hotel manager, making him the first African American to hold that position in any major Las Vegas hotel at the time.

Dan was a hit with customers and his fellow department managers and we were all proud of his achievements. He eventually landed a senior executive position at a big casino in Atlantic City in the late seventies when casino became legal in New Jersey, and I recently saw him and his twin brother on the cover of a magazine in which Dan and his twin brother, Dana, were spotlighted as two successful executives for one of Detroit's new mega-sized casino hotels.

THE SECOND PRECEDENT-SETTING event took place that same year at the Sands. While in those days it was assumed that all management positions should only be held by white people, it was also assumed that certain jobs could only be handled by men, while other positions could only be handled by women (such as making beds or serving cocktails).

The position of bellman was one of those roles it was thought women should not take. Why? Because! That is why the position is named "Bell Man."

In those days at the Sands and in the other premium Strip hotels, Bellmen made a very good living. Customers' tips were bountiful and the union contract under which they performed had a very generous guaranteed gratuity provision built in for package plans and group movements. The position was coveted throughout the industry and one needed *juice* to get management and union bosses to agree to send an applicant out for a rare open position.

At the time, women were also rattling their sabers for the right to be considered for well paying positions that had heretofore been a private domain for males only. Women had recently won a lawsuit permitting them to deal in strip casinos where, until the lawsuit, by county ordinance women were only permitted to deal in casinos off the strip and in downtown Las Vegas. With that victory behind them, some women were applying for typical male jobs in engineering, gardening and truck driving and now others wanted a piece of the action with big tips like gourmet room waiters, valet parking lot attendants or best of all, the position of "Bell Person." With this pressure on, the recruiters at the human resources center were careful to ensure that all qualified applicants were referred to department heads for open positions, regardless of color, sex religion and all the other protected classes according to the law.

It seems we had one of those rare openings for a bellman (or should I now say bell person?) and when I told the bell captain that we were going to have to consider a female for this position, I thought all hell was going to break loose. The bell captain was my mentor and good friend, Jerry Garvey, whom I described for you back in the second section of this book. Jerry was an old timer who believed the woman's role is in the kitchen, and this new mandated personnel directive was considered an affront to his ability to manage. Because of his stubbornness, I told him that I planned to sit in on any interview he conducted with any female candidates.

Wouldn't you know it? The first candidate was a hot looking lady named Cathy who drove in for her interview in a nice Corvette. She got two points right off the start in my book because, (1) she was hot and (2) the Corvette was my favorite car at the time. The interview went along quite well and it was evident that Cathy could handle the job. She was in wonderful shape and strong enough to lift any reasonably sized piece of luggage. She had a good gift of gab and her humor would be an asset with our guests. As the interview was winding down, up to this point Jerry was handling himself quite well considering his aversion to having a female bell person on his staff. Suddenly he blurted out, "You know you can't call in sick every twenty-eight days." Cathy looked at him with a straight face and replied, "Don't worry, Jerry, I show up every twenty-eightdays just like the full moon, Period! Did you get that Jerry? Period!" For the first time, I saw Jerry speechless.

Cathy proved to be a good bell person and she worked out well for a couple of years before she finally decided to get married and retire. Before I leave this story of Cathy, the bell person, it is appropriate to relate the most humorous bellman tales of my recollection. The Sands Hotel had a policy that bellmen would not transport luggage unless the guest's suitcases were packed and ready to go. Jerry Garvey also had a strict policy that bellmen were not permitted to assist a customer in packing his or her luggage. The rule was, "If the guest is not packed, politely excuse yourself and ask the guest to call the bell desk when he or she is completely packed and ready to go."

Well, it happens that Cathy, the first Sands female bellperson, is dispatched to a departing guest's room on her very first Sunday, when the hotel is experiencing an unusually large room turnover. When she reaches the guest's room, she finds that the patron has not yet packed his luggage. The patron requests that Cathy pack his luggage for him, but, knowing the rules, she tells the guest that she is not permitted. The guest insists that she call down to Jerry and get his permission to make an exception to the rule. When she calls the bell desk and explains the request to her boss, Jerry yells out to her, "Screw him! You know the rules. We don't have time to pack him. Get back down here now!"

Cathy responded to Jerry, "What do you mean screw him? Hell, if I have time to screw him, I have time to pack him up." Nonetheless, she scampered back to the bell desk to receive her next dispatch so as not annoy Jerry any longer. Later she told me she received a black chip from the guest, just for talking to Jerry the way she did. The guest was still chuckling as he departed the Sands.

By the way, a black chip was big money in 1976---- $100.00.

WITH ALL THE good things happening in Las Vegas, 1976 had a couple of *down times* due to two major instances of civil unrest. This chapter will describe how management of the Sands reacted to each of these events.

The first was an effort to bring attention to alleged discrimination against black people by the strip hotels. It started out with groups of black people dining in strip hotel restaurants and demanding individual checks. When these groups finished dining, they would get up and walk out without paying their bills.

When the hotels started detaining the people involved and filing charges for defrauding an innkeeper, the arrests set forth actions throughout the minority community that culminated one Saturday with a march down the middle of the Las Vegas Strip and through several major casinos by several thousand people organized by the local chapter of the NAACP. The march was to start at the Las Vegas Convention Center and proceed up to the strip where the marchers would traverse through the Stardust Casino and then get back on the strip where they would head south to Caesars Palace. After making their tour through the Caesars Casino floor, their next destination was to be the Sands.

When Richard Danner heard about the planned demonstration, he said, "No way are these people coming through my casino to terrorize my customers and my employees." Mr. Danner held a quick staff meeting and we collectively made the decision to lock down the entry ways to the Sands during the hours of the demonstration. We were going to do everything within our legal power to stop these demonstrators from entering the Sands. With cooperation from the sheriff, we commissioned twenty or more armed policemen with helmets and shields to stand inside the lobby next to the window glass that separated the hotel interior from the outside valet parking area. Our own security officers were armed and took positions at every entry way into the hotel. Guests who needed to come in or go out of the building were escorted by security officers in and out of the hotel through the side entryways while the lockdown was in effect.

The march took off as planned, and although the demonstrators had toured the Stardust and Caesars Palace Casinos with no apparent violence or damage being done, Danner still insisted that they would not be permitted to "tour" the Sands.

As the throng of demonstrators flooded the valet parking area, totally sealing off the front driveways, they encountered doors that were fully locked and revolving doors that had wedges driven under their wings. While they appeared to be peaceful, they were loud and angry over finding the doors locked. Tempers began to flare and the crowd became more unruly. At that point, Danner instructed the chief of security, a scrappy young man named Kurt Wilcox to open one door, go outside and address the crowd. Kurt removed his coat, tie, and weapon and left them in my care behind the front desk. Then he opened the door carefully and slowly made his way out into the screaming crowd. He finally got their attention when he fired up his air-horn to advise the crowd to dispense or face arrest. He looked helpless out there all by himself, but for some reason the crowd sensed that he was just doing his job and they began to move back out onto the strip. The leaders of the movement were losing control and with members of the press and television crews present, they started chanting for a *sit-down*. Within minutes, half of the crowd dispersed leaving the other half sitting in the middle of Las Vegas Boulevard, impeding traffic in both directions. With the customary efficiency of the Las Vegas sheriff, adequate paddy wagons and police personnel were dispatched to the scene and the more militant of the dissidents were carted off to the city jail. Just the presence of people being rounded up and dragged into the paddy wagons was enough to break up the remaining demonstrators. The event ended and Danner got his way.

The second major event of the year was a labor strike sanctioned by the Culinary Union. It turned out to be the longest strike affecting the entire industry, lasting 15 days. Leading the efforts to get to an impasse with the union was Richard Danner. During the previous strike in 1972 the hotels stayed open and operated the restaurants and hotel with minimal replacement staffing and with minimum services. However, Danner was determined to lock up the joint this time and just close down. With the deadline for the strike looming, guests were informed to vacate and our security forces were beefed up. For safety purposes to guard against fire or vandalism to our outside cabana buildings during the strike, the entry ways were boarded up. At this time in Sands history, only one executive, a distinguished older gentleman named Walter Kane still lived in the hotel. This person was a close confidant to Howard Hughes and he now was serving as the Summa Corporation impresario. Prior to his working with the Hughes casinos as its vice president of entertainment, Mr. Kane had been the president of RKO studios in Hollywood. For security purposes, Kane was relocated from his ground floor cabana to the penthouse in the tower. When the strike began, the first few days were like a party inside.

The fun started when I received a call from Walter Kane's bodyguard, Jim. He asked me to come up to Mr. Kane's penthouse suite. I did not hear or see Walter Kane in the suite when I arrived. His bodyguard had a terrified look on his face and I thought maybe Walter had died or something else bad had happened to him. Then Jim told me that Walter had gone to Los Angeles for the day, and while he was gone, Jim had been practicing "quick draw" with his pistol against the image in the mirror on the wall in the penthouse suite living room. Accidently, Jim discharged the gun shooting a hole through the mirror and into the concrete wall behind it.

Jim was in panic, worrying about his job if Walter ever found out. Furthermore it was embarrassing.

"Not to worry," I told him and quickly called housekeeping and instructed the housekeeper, Bessie Thompson, to send me up a replacement mirror. Since all the union employees were on strike, I told her I would install it myself. Jim and I cleared the broken mirror and threw the remains in the dumpster. A temporary worker delivered the replacement mirror to me in the 18th floor utility room, and I carried it into the Kane Suite and installed it right over the bullet hole in the wall. I know I probably should have called security to report the incident, but because all the officers were busy with the strike and Jim, the bodyguard, was such a good person, I decided to handle the incident the way Sinatra would have. … my way. To my knowledge, the mirror was still in place with the hole in the wall behind it many years later when the Sands tower was imploded to make way for the new Venetian Hotel.

But the fun did not stop there. One of the craziest characters at the Sands was "Vegas Vic" Friedman, a junket representative from Virginia Beach, Virginia. As we were trying to clear all the outside buildings of occupants, we overlooked the suite Vic was occupying, because we assumed he departed with his junket that had already evacuated the day before. As we were conducting the final inspections before applying the plywood to the entry doors of the bungalow buildings, we open the door to the Arlington Royal Suite (room numbers 208-9-10) and there sitting Indian style in the middle of the living room floor in his underwear, was Vegas Vic. Surrounding Vic in a huge circle were fifty or sixty empty green Heineken beer bottles. He had been on a full scale bender and had passed out, missing his junket plane which had departed the day before. Upon waking from his stupor, he just sat mummified, drinking the remaining Heinekens.

As we were trying to get Vic to stand up, out of the guest bedroom emerged a young working girl, maybe 22 years old, all dressed up in corset and garter belt. She introduced herself as Judy Levine, and claimed she was befriended a day earlier by Vic (yeah sure!) when she was tossed out of Caesars Palace due to the strike. Vic told her she could use his extra bedroom, and it was evident she had turned it into a brothel. She bragged that yesterday she had laid a preacher in the men's restroom at Caesars Palace and bagged a priest the evening before in the Aladdin Hotel. She was gunning for the trifecta when she learned that Vic had a rabbi on his junket. Little did she know that the rabbi had left on the junket plane, the one that Vic had missed when he passed out.

Anyway, later that evening I retired to my suite where I was living during the strike. With me was my friend, Jerry Garvey, the famous superintendent of guest services I have spoken about in several chapters of this book. Wouldn't you know it, but Judy Levine shows up banging on my bedroom door. I guess maybe I looked like a rabbi or something. I let her in just for the heck of it. Then for fun, I sent her into Jerry's bedroom. She must have thought Jerry was Elvis Presley when he started yelling, "*Return to Sender* and get your ass out of my bedroom, you whore!"

CHAPTER **14**

ONE OF THE classiest of all special events started at the Sands in 1976. In an effort to keep the biggest high rollers loyal to the Sands, the first of what became a coveted annual event by the biggest gamblers in Vegas was initiated in early June. The Sands rented the entire Mauna Kea Beach hotel and all its facilities for five days, and flew the best customers on its players' roster on a chartered 747 loaded with liquor, treats and many other wonderful amenities. The guests were greeted upon landing in Hilo by pretty hostesses in Hawaiian themed Super Buses to take the guests in luxury to the five star hotel on the big Island of Hawaii. Guests were treated to a three day golf and tennis tournament, ocean fishing and shopping sprees in Kona.

To qualify for invitation to this special event, a player at that time was required to have a minimum line of credit exceeding $25,000, with gaming play that matched a theoretical loss of $25,000 during the previous year and all markers had to be paid current. That was big money in those days.

Furthermore, to be eligible for boarding the charter 747, customers were required to arrive at the Sands and register for the trip at a special luau party on the Saturday prior to the scheduled departure, which was initially scheduled for early the following Monday morning. With over 150 players of this caliber, along with their wives, arriving two days before their charter airplane departed Las Vegas, one can imagine the play on the casino floor for two evenings before the Hawaiian venture even started. We usually paid for the event before the plane left the ground for Hawaii.

After five hard days of play and dining in Hawaii, we timed the charter aircraft to arrive back in Las Vegas on Saturday evening late enough that few customers could head homeward until the following morning, thus giving the Sands one more opportunity to have these good players gamble. In 1976, the first event cost the Sands over $1,000,000, which covered the price of the charter aircraft, 200 rooms for five nights at the Mauna Kea Beach Hotel, golf, tennis, food, beverage, shopping sprees, ground transportation and, of course, three nights room accommodations and parties in Las Vegas at the Sands before and after the trip. The first trip generated over $3,000,000 in gross gaming revenues, which in those days was considered quite large. The success of this event became well known throughout Las Vegas among all our competitors. Even if we hadn't won so much money, the event proved to have so many side benefits. For instance, many of these customers who attended could afford to vacation anywhere in the world, but this became a social event that many of them wanted to be part of every year thereafter. Consequently, almost all of these customers started gambling at higher levels each year to ensure they would maintain their invited status, and many of them were afraid to stray to a competitor's property for fear that Harry Goodheart would find out and strike their names off the invitation list. Best yet, it ensured that markers were paid in a timely manner.

This special event continued on for five additional years surviving one additional year after new owners purchased the Sands in 1981. However, the concept was copied by competitors both in Las Vegas and Atlantic City, expanded and eventually taken to a level in which the high expectations of the invited guests could no longer be achieved and still enable the casinos to make a profit, so such excursions finally came to an end.

CHAPTER **15**

SPEAKING OF COMING to an end, in late December of 1976, I received a telephone call from my old boss, Jack Pieper, who had moved away to Reno the previous January to take over the helm of the soon-to-be-built MGM Grand-Reno. He wanted me to come up and visit with him regarding an opportunity he thought would accelerate my career growth. I was loving it back at the Sands and knew I could probably work there for years with a great deal of job security. Yet at age 29, the thought of being part of the team that was going to open the largest casino under one roof in the world certainly merited a trip to Reno.

My wife and I drove our small RV the 450 miles to Reno in the snow and cold to meet Jack Pieper and his wife at their luxury home on the posh new Lake Ridge Golf Course. Jack had no office and was working out of his home, but his sales pitch included all the blueprints and renderings necessary to sell me on joining his team. He described the position he would give me and advised that it would come with a title of executive vice president. Taking this job would be risky because everyone I knew that opened a new casino hotel generally did not last long in their position after the hotel opened for business. Yet I believed the chance to improve my compensation by 50%, coupled with the experience I would garner opening a new casino, (especially of this size and magnitude) was worth the risk.

Furthermore, I thought I was smart enough to survive the purge that always seemed to take place once we opened the place. Based upon our positive relationship at the Frontier just a year or so before I admired Pieper as a role model, so it seemed like a good shot to move my career along at an accelerated pace.

I returned to Las Vegas to handle my responsibilities related to the New Year's events at the Sands, and during the first week in January, I phoned Pieper to advise him that I would agree to take the position he was offering as long as I could bring along several of my trusted friends in the business to work for me, assuming they might have an interest in moving to Reno. When Pieper assured me I could, I asked him to set a date for my employment, which he indicated would ideally be February 1. However, since Danner and his wife were going on vacation during the last two weeks of January and I was to be acting general manager at the Sands, I told Pieper that I could not give my notice of resignation until after Danner returned from vacation on or about February 1. Three days after Danner returned I fearfully made an appointment with him to tender my resignation at the Sands, now for the second time in my career. To my surprise, Danner was actually quite happy for me and threw a big party in my honor, even though I had only worked for him this second time around for less than 14 months.

Luck continued to be on my side. I placed my house up for sale and had it in contract within ten days. The closing took place three days before I moved to Reno, with my moving van leaving for Reno as the new owners were moving in. We rolled out of town behind the moving van in our little motor home and a Chevy Malibu. With two kids and a dog we headed to the Kietzke Avenue apartments, where we'd reside until we could find a home to purchase. We arrived in Reno on Saturday, February 26 and on Tuesday, March 1, 1977 reported to work in the Mill Street construction offices of the MGM Grand.

DURING THIS SHORT second tour of duty at the Sands, many additional interesting characters and events had crossed my path. Several of these became role models. First and foremost was a wonderful Italian lady named Rosie Merranto. Rose hired on to run the telephone call center as our chief operator. Like Charlotte Ellsworth at the Frontier, whom I described earlier, Rosie was another gentlewoman. When you were around Rose, regardless of how crude you might otherwise be, you just knew you had to keep it clean. She had that air about her from the first time you met her. We all loved to listen to her when she got a little riled up, because she knew no cuss words. Instead, she'd yell out, "Great Gussie's Ghost" or "Mother Goose," as a substitute. Heck, I even found myself yelling "Mother Goose" instead of "Oh S__t" when I got angry.

The second set of characters was George and Wick MacCall. George MacCall was initially forced down my throat by Steve Salvoldelli to become the Director of sports activities at the Sands. MacCall had apparently befriended somebody at the corporate offices by providing them with some complimentary tennis lessons, and now I felt my department operation was going to have to pay for that so-called freebie. Remembering that the boss is not always right, I reluctantly hired George on and turned him loose with his array of screwy ideas. One after another, his special events failed. They failed not because George was not smart or creative, but because he ap-proached our team as an arrogant know-it-all. To his credit, George had enjoyed a life of celebrity of sorts. He was the Davis Cup captain and the creator of World Team Tennis. His wife adorned the front page of Life Magazine in the late fifties. Finally as I was in the process of leaving the Sands to join the MGM in Reno, George came into my office and pleaded for some advice. With nothing to lose now that I was headed out the door, I gave him a piece of my mind and set him straight. I left for Reno betting him $100 that I was right and he was wrong on a matter we disagreed on. Two months after I had relocated to Reno, I received a telephone call from MacCall conceding that I had won the bet. He wanted to know where he should send the $100. I asked him to send it in my name to his favorite charity. He then added that he had taken my advice and approached his latest special event as I had recommended and the event turned out to be highly successful. I congratulated him and wished him well, never expecting to talk to him again. Little did I know that several years later we would become lifelong friends.

My favorite celebrities to play the famed Copa Showroom on my second tour were Wayne Newton, Robert Goulet and Al Martino. My least favorite entertainer was Don Adams and I told you why in a previous section of my book. Wayne Newton played the Sands Copa show room for up to thirty weeks a year while I worked there. Without a doubt, he was the hardest working celebrity to play any stage in Las Vegas, back then or today. Robert Goulet was a favorite of mine, too---not so much because of his singing, but more for the pranks he played on Wayne Newton, including sending a naked streaker across the stage on one late night Wayne Newton performance.

I met Al Martino at the Sands and later rekindled a lifelong rela-tionship with him when I managed the Claridge Casino in Atlantic City several years later. Al Martino had one of the strongest and most beautiful voices of his time and he retained his great sound right up to his passing at age 82.

The most memorable customers that stood out during this stint at the Sands included Japanese millionaire, Kenji Osano, Adnan Khashoggi and CBG Murphy.

Osano came to the Sands with one goal: break the bank. In those days, Baccarat was played with cash and Osano brought bags of it. I had never seen that kind of money before, and it is eye-opening even for someone who has. Put $3,000,000 in hundred dollar bills in the center of a big baccarat table and there is not much room left for the cards. Anyway, Osano played for three straight days, winning upwards of three million dollars before losing it all, plus another three million he had in the bags. With Osano begging for credit, Goodheart eventually gave in and extended another million dollars. Twenty four hours later, Osano was busted and heading back to Japan. A few months later, Nevada regulators required that gaming chips be incorporated for baccarat play and accounted for like other table games.

The biggest gambler in the history of the Sands Hotel was Adnan Khashoggi. While he lost his greatest amount of money in 1979, he was still the biggest customer even in 1976. The notorious Saudi arms trader played all table games but was primarily attracted to roulette. He was a smart businessman but a very poor gambler or money manager. He loved to show off and when he had a pretty woman on his arm, he would bet in ways that made her think he was winning, even when he was not. On some occasions, he was known to bet every single number on a roulette table, just so he could guarantee he would hit the winning number. He would bet $1000 on all thirty-six numbers along with the zero and double-zero for a total of $38,000 on just one spin of the wheel. When the number came up, he would be paid out at odds of 35 to 1 for a $35,000 payout on the winning number. He would lose $3,000 just to show the gal he could always hit a winning number.

The most mysterious player we hosted was an eccentric philanthropist named CBG Murphy. Murphy was once found wrapped in a bed sheet at the craps table. When a pit boss told him he couldn't wear a sheet, he removed it and stood there in his birthday suit. After that little surprise, the pit boss allowed him to wear the sheet. Murphy had a big Cadillac convertible with Texas Longhorns adorning the hood. One time in the heat of July, he left the Sands in his Caddy to make a lay down at Binion' Horseshoe in downtown Las Vegas. He parked his car on the curb at the front door of the Horseshoe with the motor running and went in to make a few bets. Several hours later he returned to find his car engine all burned up. The radiator hoses had burst and his car engine just kept running until it died. The Horseshoe paid for the repairs, though, after CBG lost several hundred thousand dollars. Murphy was an odd ball out of the casino, as well. One morning at dawn, he was discovered by security officers fly casting his fishing line into the Sands pool while standing totally nude. Charles B.G. Murphy died at a Lake Tahoe casino two years later.

The most memorable event that year occurred in early 1976, shortly before Howard Hughes died. It made me believe that Hughes was more involved and cognizant of his surroundings than history gives him credit. Richard Danner had decided he wanted to build a warehouse facility for the Sands Hotel and thought the best place to construct the facility would be on land just north of the Sands employee parking lot. Danner had us mobilize a contractor and commence laying out the foundation. Then suddenly Danner received a telephone call from the Summa Corporation offices demanding he cease construction. It seems that Hughes had looked out his Penthouse suite windows at the Desert Inn and witnessed the warehouse construction taking place. Hughes made it known through Salvoldelli that the construction was taking place on land that did not belong to the Sands. Hughes owned the land through another subsidiary and he obviously was well aware of where the boundary lines existed. Needless to say, the construction stopped and the construction site was restored to natural desert.

The most humorous event to be witnessed by many occurred one night in the Garden Room lobby lounge that comprised about twenty five plush seats around a circular bar. Our assistant chief of security, Richard Ruble, happened to be touring the property when he observed over twelve prostitutes sitting at the lobby bar. Richard Ruble quietly announced to the twelve working girls, "Would you ladies of the evening please depart?" As Ruble walked away from the bar, about six of the girls got out of their seats and headed toward the exit. However, the rest of the girls decided to remain. Ruble circled the casino and returned to the lobby bar about ten minutes later. When he saw the remaining prostitutes still seated at the bar, he raised his voice and yelled, "Now, all you whores get your asses out of here now or you're going to jail."

And it was here at the Sands that I learned a new accounting term. It was well known that the casinos picked up airline transportation tabs and outside restaurant expenses for their best customers and such reimbursements were made by use of a "paid out" at the casino cage. The Sands was no different. However, one night as I was standing next to the Sands cage with Harry Goodheart, I witnessed a casino shift boss authorize a paid out to an obvious "working girl" who had apparently just serviced a big player. I saw that the paid-out document was marked as "CODB." I asked Harry what that stood for. He simply replied, "Cost of doing business."

Yes, the Sands was a great place to work in those days and moving on to my next career adventure was a tough decision. I would be remiss if I did not redundantly reiterate how honored I was to have the privilege of working for Richard Danner and Harry Goodheart. Hands down, they were the best combination of casino resort managers in Las Vegas during the decade of the 1970s. I credit these two men with helping me build the strategic foundations of my career in casino resort management. In my career, I have been fortunate to be tutored by six key mentors along the way. My first two mentors were Spike Cook and Ed Zike. My final two career mentors were Bill Dougall and Jack Binion. In between, both Danner and Goodheart provided the tools for me to progress to the next level.

Section 4

As a junior, I was a junior executive — a chance to open the MGM in Reno, back to the Sands, and finally exiled to Laughlin in my first general manager role at the Edgewater Casino

LIFE AT MGM proved to be a bit trying at first. In other job starts, someone had shown me around and explained what I was expected to do. In this new role it was evident that I was on my own. There was absolutely no administrative infrastructure in place. The temporary offices had been recently leased and, fortunately, some office furniture had been purchased and was in place on the day I arrived for work. If I recall, I was the fifth or sixth person to be hired for the new hotel casino company who was not directly involved with the construction.

While Jack Pieper had been on the MGM payroll for over a year, it was also evident that he had not engaged in any measure of detailed planning from an administrative standpoint. It appeared that he assumed the management team from the MGM property in Las Vegas would just send up a team of people, a box of standard forms and procedures; and, magically, we would be in business. To some extent, his assumptions were correct because we were eventually inundated with "know-it-all" management people from the Southern Nevada Casino who intended to show us the best way to run one of these joints.

On my first day I took a tour of the construction site. It was massive. The steel was out of the ground and the general footprint of the building was visible. Based on the newly poured slabs and wooden concrete forms ready for more concrete, the foundation demonstrated the immensity of the future building. It was March 1, 1977 and the announced date for the grand opening was to be May 3, 1978. It was hard for me to imagine that we could meet that date.

MGM had successfully opened their $100,000,000 mega-casino resort at Flamingo Road and the Strip in December, 1973. It was the last major construction on the Strip until Steve Wynn opened the Mirage Casino in 1989. In 1976, they decided to forego entering the Atlantic City gaming market in favor of putting a sister operation in Reno. The new MGM Grand-Reno was estimated to cost $125,000,000 and be the largest casino resort under one roof in the world--- almost 18 acres of enclosed space.

The competitors in Reno laughed at the MGM executives when they purchased the 110 acre parcel on which to build their new Reno Casino. The parcel was actually part of Sparks, Nevada (not Reno) and while MGM only paid $2.5 million for the land, the parcel had been a former gravel pit, and the interior elevations of the land were many feet below the surface elevation of the adjoining roadways and neighboring real estate. It was estimated by our competitors that the cost of acquiring fill dirt to bring the level of the property up to grade would be a multi-million dollar expense and the time to transport the fill dirt would take several years to accomplish.

However, nobody in Reno had ever seen the likes of Fred Benninger, the chairman of the MGM Grand in Las Vegas, who was spearheading the construction project. Fred was an out-of-the-box thinker and a shrewd businessman and relentless negotiator. Taylor Construction Company of Las Vegas had done a wonderful job completing the MGM Las Vegas project on time and on budget, so they were commissioned to build the Reno facility. The Taylor engineers had figured out that if they excavated approximately 20 acres of the 110 acre parcel by digging a hole 300 feet deep, they could transfer enough fill dirt from the new hole to bring the remaining elevations of the parcel up to the desired grade. Since the MGM parcel adjoined the Truckee River, the engineers knew that digging the new hole would be like digging a well. The engineers constructed two de-silting ponds and continually pumped water from the excavated hole into the ponds as the Euclids transported the fill dirt to its new location on our building site. The clean de-silted water in the ponds was then discharged into the Truckee River. When the excavation was completed, the pumping of the seepage water was discontinued and the 20 acre hole in the ground began filling with water, creating an attractive but very deep lake with an especially steep shoreline. For safety reasons, the lake was fully enclosed with security grade fencing.

CHAPTER **2**

WITH A LITTLE direction from Jack Pieper, I began to prepare the plans for the best administrative infrastructure I felt would foster a smooth and efficient hotel operation. Pieper had turned over casino operations to his long time friend and gaming veteran, Glenn Neely. Pieper had delegated convention sales to a very able guy named Joe Esposito. He left the rest of the operation to me to figure out. However, he did not tell me that I was going to get more assistance from my counterparts at the MGM Grand in Las Vegas, than I ever counted on or even wanted. About the only activity I performed without some interference was getting the U.S. Postal Service to provide the MGM-Reno with its own personal zip code. The Reno postmaster told me that it was impossible for a single company to obtain a personal zip code, but one month later he called to tell me that "89595" now belonged solely to the MGM, and we were the first in the nation to be awarded a private zip code.

To cover my flank, I immediately reached out for my old friend, Spike Cook, and was successful in getting him to leave his position at the Dunes Hotel and join me in Reno in the position of hotel general manager. I knew there was no one more suited to cover my back in the important hotel arena while I was dealing with and coordinating the other aspects of my responsibilities in food & beverage, security, and property maintenance. With Spike in place, I knew the hotel would be staffed with professionals and operated better than the MGM casinos executives were used to in their Las Vegas property.

Within one month of Spike's arrival in Reno, he had recruited five key hotel employees from different Las Vegas properties that set the foundation for the best front office operation I had ever witnessed. Most importantly, he was able to recruit my favorite room reservation manager, Charlotte Ellsworth, from the Frontier Hotel in Las Vegas to manage all the room reservations and group sales aspects for the new MGM-Reno. Since Charlotte was well regarded by Pieper from his days at the Frontier, as well as the senior executives from the MGM Vegas from their days working with Charlotte at the Old Flamingo Hotel, the affairs of the hotel department ran perfectly from day one.

CHAPTER **3**

THE CLOCK TICKED on faster and faster, making the planned opening date with Pieper at the helm, quite worrisome. Jack was a wonderful host and a skilled public relations figure for the company, but his organizational skills were his shortfall. It was evident that he had never opened a facility from scratch, and therefore he abdicated much of the pre-opening chores to the people he had hired, with little oversight on his part. Worst of all, he let the Las Vegas management people come to Reno and "piss" all over the efforts of our newly recruited executives and managers in virtually every department.

While I personally understood that the senior executives of MGM-Las Vegas had financial incentives to make certain the new Reno casino resort opened on time and as ready as possible to be efficient and provide good customer service, I was unhappy that neither Pieper nor his senior counterpart in Las Vegas, Al Benedict, recognized the morale problem they were creating. Many of the problems that ensued could have been mitigated with a brief series of meetings between the managers of the two MGM casinos, where departmental responsibilities and accountabilities could have been outlined and sorted out among the two management teams, as directed and communicated by the presidents of the two MGM entities. I pledged to myself that if I was ever in the position to be the "head honcho" of a new start-up casino operation, I would do it differently. Unfortunately for me, I never did open another casino hotel from scratch, but I did use what I learned from this project to better manage whatever projects or expansions came before me during the next thirty years of my career.

On the other hand, without the involvement of the Las Vegas executives in the construction aspects of the project, especially those of Fred Benninger, the Reno project would not have opened on the aggressive schedule the company had set forth in the beginning. Fred was meticulously detailed and was the most profound negotiator with vendors and contractors that I had ever seen. It was evident to me from the start why Kirk Kerkorian, the major shareholder of MGM, had Benninger on his executive staff. Benninger played with millions of dollars in his budget, but fought for pennies and nickels with every vendor and supplier. He was relentless and knew how to use psychology to wring out the best deal for the company. I remember one day when we were all sitting around the big conference table in the construction trailer with a contractor, haggling with him and his manager over the specifications and pricing for some aspect of the job. We had started the negotiations immediately after this vendor had arrived after a four hour drive from San Francisco that morning. Deliberations began at 7:00 a.m. and at about noon, we could all hear each other's stomachs growling for lunch. Yet Benninger just kept deliberating and negotiating over minutia. Then as he had it planned, several chefs Benninger had brought along with him on the company jet from the Las Vegas hotel showed up with an array of mouth watering deli food and began setting up a nice buffet in the back of the construction trailer. The aroma of the deli meats and spices was overwhelming and as hunger set in even more profoundly, Benninger stepped up the tempo of the negotiations. Finally, the contractor caved in and agreed to Fred's last offer, just so he could get at one of those giant corned beef sandwiches. I used some of Benninger's tactics when I became a purchasing executive several years later and found them even good when negotiating with union bosses for labor contracts.

CHAPTER **4**

MY 30ᵀᴴ BIRTHDAY coincided with the topping off party we held in a big tent under the steel works of the giant Porte Cochere. It was July 13, 1977 and we were less than ten months from opening day, and looking at the structure in its current state that day made it still difficult for me to imagine that we would get the place open on time. Red carpet and limousines decorated the construction site that evening and every dignitary and invited guest received a monogrammed hard hat and a small bronze Lion as a keepsake, the lion representing the face of the MGM logo. To this day, I still have my Lion on its pedestal in my office.

The party was the talk of the town and for the first time during my short residency in Reno, I detected panic in the eyes of some of our competitors who were present that mild night in July. While the building was far from completed, the immensity of the soon to be opening facility was mind boggling. It was evident that this facility was going to add huge capacity and supply to the current market and that every casino operator within 100 miles of the new MGM was going to be in a costly war for customers and employees alike. If the MGM was to be successful, it had to attract a higher caliber customer to Reno than currently existed. Except for Harrah's downtown Reno hotel casino, the nearest premium caliber casino resort was sixty miles south at Lake Tahoe. To exacerbate the overload of new casino space and hotel rooms was the fact that six additional new Reno casino hotels were scheduled to open within three months of the MGM. The key in our minds to accomplish our goal of expanding the regional Reno market to a nationwide market would depend primarily on expanded airport capacity.

To their credit, Reno officials had been planning for the onslaught of new business they expected this supply glut would create. They were in the process of expanding both the convention center and the Reno International Airport. A new freeway had recently been constructed with convenient access to both major entryways to the new MGM Casino, and access to the newly expanded Reno airport was especially conducive to patron convenience.

As we ramped up the construction and began to hire on staff that would operate the MGM, our sales people and local officials worked diligently with several airline companies to both enter and expand service to the Reno marketplace. With several months to go before our opening, the airlines began their aggressive advertising promotions. One airline in particular, Braniff Air, began selling advance tickets between Las Vegas and Reno for $1.00 each way. Even though the promotional tickets were only valid for the exact date of travel purchased, my buddy, Spike, went down and bought several dozen tickets, just in case he decided to go back and forth between the two cities after we got the MGM open for business in May. By opening day, we had attracted three new airlines to serve Reno and we even had non-stop service from New York, something never heard of before in Reno.

Ramping up the staff was the other major hurdle we faced. With six additional casino resorts opening in the same window of time during the spring of 1978, the competition for employees was intense. At that time as we were approaching the new year in 1978, the Reno metropolitan area was experiencing an unemployment rate of fewer than 2%. Of the approximately 2000 people unemployed in the region back in early 1978, only about half were truly employable and then even some of them were in doubt.

This is a case in which the team that worked for us staved off a huge problem for both Spike and myself. We did not want to be the company that increased the wages and salaries of rank and file employees throughout the Reno area, so we embarked on advertising and solicitation programs that would hopefully attract new potential employees from outside the Reno area. Unfortunately, Reno had limited affordable housing at the time, so most of the interested recruits found no place to live when they came to apply for employment either with us or the other six casinos opening at the same time. Eventually, as we got closer to opening, the situation became more critical. We discovered that several hundred new employees we had just hired were living in tents along the Truckee River in violation of the law.

Necessity being the mother of invention, our most creative inventor went to work. This character was Charlie Pinto. He had been the assistant executive housekeeper for the MGM in Las Vegas and we were impressed with his ability to motivate the housekeeping team in Las Vegas. Charlie liked Spike's management style and asked his supervisor in Las Vegas for a transfer approval to take on the executive housekeeper position in Reno. Reluctantly, approval was granted and Charlie became as important a fixture for us in the back of the house as Charlotte Ellsworth was for us in the front of the house.

With unemployment so low, the pool of available workers, especially entry level workers such as housekeepers and bus boys was slim. With 1000 rooms to clean at the new MGM, Charlie required over 120 housekeepers and another 30 housemen to handle the expected room occupancy. Ten days before opening, Charlie only had 50 people committed to work for him. Since response to classified want ads was poor and employment agencies we engaged were unable to fill our needs, Charlie Pinto took matters into his own hands. He managed to sneak into the back of the house at Harrah's and several other smaller hotels and visit with maids and porters in their respective linen closets and in the hotel hallways. Charlie passed them each his business card and promised them a 20% increase in pay if they would come to work for him. On opening day, we started with a full staff and a city full of competitors that were mad as hell over our tactics to steal their scarce workforce.

Our executive chef was enamored over Charlie's success in the housekeeping department, so he decided to employ the same tactics to fill his shortfall of employees. He started his solicitation by sneaking into the kitchen at John Ascuaga's Nugget Casino in Sparks, Nevada, just across the river from the new MGM project. The Nugget had the largest culinary operation in northern Nevada and the employees were known for producing a quality dining experience. Unfortunately, the chef did not fare as well as Charlie did over at Harrah's. Ascuaga's security people grabbed the chef and his assistant at their first entry into the Nugget kitchen and they found themselves thrown in jail for trespassing. After we bailed them out, we found ourselves in the position of having to increase wages substantially to entice employees to leave their existing employers. This drove the cost of payroll up for everybody operating in Reno, but we had to get open and we couldn't do it without an adequate number of employees. We took our lumps in the media and from our competitors and made a mad effort to close the shortfall. On opening day, the food and beverage team was still over 100 persons short of required headcount, but with overtime we knew we could get the doors open.

The casino department was able to staff up relatively easily. The MGM had a great reputation in Las Vegas for hosting premium customers, something all the Reno Hotels, even Harrah's, lacked. The idea of working for a new and classy casino company appealed to many dealers and casino supervisors throughout the Reno area. The new MGM casino also elicited substantial interest from casino personnel in Las Vegas who were interested in moving from the desert to a more normal climate without losing the benefits of working for a big Vegas-style company.

The MGM bosses did a great job overall of meeting the goals of opening this new project on time and on budget. They were masters at managing the Gantt chart and navigating the critical path through the construction project. Where they misstepped in my estimation was the strategy and planning for the opening parties of the casino. First of all, the Las Vegas bosses decided that very few premium customers from the MGM Las Vegas would be invited to the grand opening parties because they did not want to dilute the player visits of their exiting patrons. This proved to be a fatal mistake because many of the loyal MGM players thought they should be included in the festivities of the grand opening of the new sister MGM Casino in Reno.

The second mistake involved the timing for the grand opening festivities, themselves. With the hotel and casino scheduled to open on May 3, 1978 we were given instruction to host our grand opening party starting with a three day menu of festivities that would begin on May 4, just one day after opening.

When Pieper learned he could not use the MGM Las Vegas VIP customer list as a foundation for his grand opening of invited guests, he became visibly upset. While Pieper and his casino manager, Glenn Neely, had a small list of good customers themselves, they did not have near the number to create a gala party. On top of that, they had hired two or three casino hosts that had previously worked in small clubs at Lake Tahoe, and it was learned early on that none of these guys had any serious players that would qualify to be invited to the grand opening party. Pieper had no idea of how he could fill the grand opening party with properly qualified casino patrons. He knew he could shill empty seats, but the profitability of his party would be a disaster, and he knew that as well.

It so happened that both Spike Cook, who reigned from the Dunes Casino, and myself had a substantial list of good casino customers who frequented the Dunes and the Sands prior to our moving to Reno. We volunteered to coordinate the effort to develop an invitational listing of prospective names for the grand opening party. After culling together every casino executive and casino hosts' personal list of good customers, we went about eliminating duplicate names and then sorted the customers by city of origin and gaming worth. At the end of our exhaustive effort, we had developed a listing of over 5000 high rollers worthy of an invitation to the party. When presented with this opportunity, it was decided to host three successive grand opening parties beginning with the first party to start one day after we opened.

We carefully sorted the invitations geographically and by player worth so that we could be relatively certain to have adequate air transportation and suite accommodations available for the best of the premium guests who accepted our invitation. The expensive gold foiled and embossed invitations were mailed and we waited with bated breath for a response from the recipients, most of whom never would have thought of coming to Reno for a gambling vacation before.

The response was unbelievable. Our goal to have 500 invited guests for each party was met just ten days after the mailer went out, and responses were still coming in. Now we were worrying about how many guests we would have to turn down due to reaching a full house. As we approached opening day, we were oversold for each party, but we hoped the cancellation and no-show factor would bail us out.

ON MAY 2, 1978 my team made its final inspection of every hotel room and every square foot of the public areas of this giant plant. We were proud of the fact that not one television set had been stolen during the installation of furniture, and that every room had its complete complement of amenities even including waste baskets, which had been forgotten in the MGM Vegas opening. The restaurants were all cleaned and ready to go and the new staff of culinary employees was scurrying around conducting training exercises. The casino dealers were finalizing several weeks of live training, with team members taking turns being customers. The slot machines were still being coin tested but we were assured everything was ready to go and few problems were anticipated.

On the morning of May 3, I drove my new Cadillac up in front of the Porte Cochere hoping to be among the first people to have his car parked by a valet attendant. I knew the day was not going to go well when the first thing I did was lock the doors of my Cadillac with the engine still running.... and the car sitting in the middle of the Porte Cochere in the way of soon-to-be-arriving day one customers. Fortunately, our new resort project included a Shell Service Station on site and a mechanic showed up to open the door and get my car parked and out of the way.

As I entered the front doors to the MGM that day, I sighed in relief, knowing that we had met the deadline and that in a few short hours we would be opening those same doors to the public in an epic event for Reno. I walked past the massive front desk and was quite proud of the professional staff all decked out in their new uniforms conducting last minute training drills and making certain all collateral materials were readily available to them for servicing our soon to be arriving guests. I stopped off in the new coffee shop where employees were also tending to last minute affairs prior to the noon opening. Fortunately, the coffee shop was open for trial business of our executives and managers who were testing the new outlet by ordering coffee or one of the breakfast items from the exciting menu. The cashier struggled a little with my check, and that made me wonder if this was going to be an extension of my car-locking incident. I finished my coffee and headed straight for my office where I wanted to make a few last minute phone calls, mostly to congratulate the various department heads on their achievement and wishing them good luck for the opening.

The scheduled opening was to be twelve noon, but by 10:00 a.m. the parking lots were half full of cars and approximately 2000 people were waiting outside the entry doors in their quest to be first to enter the new casino. It was a mild day in May and the crowd standing outside the facility was relatively calm, but obviously anxious and impatient to get inside. As the morning wore on, the crowd outside became larger and more impatient.

Finally Pieper gathered all of his executives together to determine if we were possibly ready to open early. Were the restaurants ready to serve? Were the rooms ready for occupancy? Were there enough bellmen to escort people to their rooms in this massive building? Were the dealers on the games? Were the cashiers in the cage prepared for thousands of people hitting the casino floor? Were the slot people ready to sell change and handle jackpots and fills?

All of us indicated to Pieper that in the interest of crowd control, it would be prudent to open the doors early. The public relations people had the press already lined up at the entry ways, so at 11:30 a.m., we let the flood gates open and the huge crowd poured in from the outside, with people running in every direction but with most of them heading to the slot machines and the table games. By noon, the casino floor was crowded and it looked like a New Years Eve party. The Coffee Shop and Deli were full and the lines were backed up for miles it seemed. Unfortunately, the lines were not moving very fast and bickering soon consumed the people standing in line.

Even though the first VIP Grand Opening party was not going to begin until the next day, some of these premium customers began arriving on opening day. The front desk and the hotel operation operated without flaw. Housekeeping was staffed to capacity and the rooms were all exquisitely appointed to specification. The valet parking people handled their jobs quite well and the casino table games employees operated as if they had been working at the MGM for months.

But that is where things stopped going well.

By 3:30 p.m. that first day, over half of our 2000 slot machines were out of order and the slot crew was overwhelmed. The coffee shop and deli could not keep up with the demand and it was evident to me that we would not be able to fix the problems by the time the big wave of invited guests hit us the next day.

The MGM RV Park adjoining the Truckee River was denied its certificate of occupancy that morning with the city demanding that we reduce our spaces by half from what had been approved in the original design. Apparently the fire marshal got a hair up his butt during the inspection and did not feel the spacing between camp sites was safe. While we frantically changed the signage to comply with the city inspector's wishes, we had to detain some 200 campers who lined our entry ways with their big rigs. Finally by 6:00 p.m., we received the approval to commence registration in the MGM "Camperland." It took over three hours to get the campers situated, only adding more frustration to the opening day's events. By midnight, we finally saw the light at the end of the tunnel with the slot floor clearing up and the coffee shop and deli serving the last patrons standing in line.

Pieper was livid over the problems in slots and also dismayed by the problem with handling the volume in the coffee shop. I had long wondered why the Vegas bosses designed the coffee shop so small, given that the MGM was going to be a conventions hotel, but I guess it was a given that these guys were so-called experts and knew how to right-size a facility. They had done it successfully at the International Hotel (now the Las Vegas Hilton) and at the original MGM in Vegas (now Bally's). I learned later that their wisdom in design was driven by their belief that the Reno customer was a buffet customer, and therefore a large buffet would negate the need for a large coffee shop. Even though this was an incorrect assumption on their part, no one ever did anything to correct the problem and the property struggled for years with an inadequately sized coffee shop and long slow-moving lines daily.

On May 4, we were geared up for an arrival of High Rollers, the likes of which Reno had never seen before. Every customer was pre-registered with room keys and welcoming materials all ready in nice sealed "gold foiled and embossed" envelopes. Extra limousines had been imported from Las Vegas to ensure seamless transportation service from the airport to the hotel. As the casino geared up for volume business in the morning, it appeared that many of the problems with the slot machines experienced on opening day were alleviated.

As the onslaught of VIP guests arrived and the volume turned up on the casino floor, once again many of the new slot products broke down. On this day the coffee shop was really a mess. VIP guests started using room service as an alternative to the coffee shop, and that actually solved some of our problems on the casino floor. However, we soon discovered that we had not developed an efficient method for retrieving room service carts, and soon our entire inventory of 500 carts was gone, locked away in some 500 room accommodations throughout the hotel. The room service department closed temporarily while a search for the carts ensued. It took several hours to retrieve enough carts to begin serving food again, but with a new plan for cart retrieval we never encountered that problem again.

The Friday night gala featured Shecky Green in the ballroom and the Saturday night premier in the new showroom presented Dean Martin. Both events were handled professionally and successfully, but the problem with the coffee shop tainted the opening parties for all.

Over the next two weekends, we hosted identical parties; and, as would be expected, each one became more efficient. The table drop in the casino exceeded one million dollars a day during the first month of our opening, which rivaled any casino in Las Vegas in those days. Likewise, even with the problems in the slot department, the slot machines won over $200,000 per day in the first month of operation, which in the end more than met expectations.

However, after the grand opening parties were over, business levels in the casino did not stay at these levels. By the first week in June, Pieper was getting heat from the south for missing his budgeted projections. While hotel occupancy was very high, the occupants of the rooms were not converting into gaming patrons in an adequate quantity to fill the 100,000 square foot casino floor. Pieper made several comments to me that made it seem like it was my fault. I reminded him that I was the hotel guy, and not the marketing or sales guy for the property. I guess my helping get the place open with the grand opening parties made him think we could keep that momentum up for him indefinitely.

Then the next morning after my unpleasant conversation with Pieper, as I was coming into work, I noticed that the shuttle bus was missing from the valet parking lot, and yet an unusually large number of people were waiting for a ride to the airport. I inquired of the doorman as to what time the bus had last left for the airport and when could we expect it back to take these folks to their flights. After much "hemming and hawing" I learned that six pit bosses and six cocktail waitresses from the late swing shift had commandeered the shuttle bus after imbibing cocktails for several hours in the lobby lounge. We later learned that they had driven the bus to the Mustang Ranch, a brothel owned by Joe and Sally Conforte. It seems that Joe Conforte had been in the MGM Casino the night before with a two of his working girls on each arm and a big cigar in his mouth. While playing a big hand at craps, he passed out comp tickets to the pit bosses and casino floor supervisors for a free trick at his Mustang Ranch.

Apparently, six of these swing shift bosses decided to collect on their comp, and with enough liquor and prodding from the cocktail waitresses they were hosting, all of them stole the bus and headed to the Mustang Ranch. While it was quite funny when we look back at it, it did not go over well with Pieper and Neeley; and, needless to say, all involved were relieved of their employment when they returned the bus later that morning.

Pieper was outraged and blamed my operation for letting the casino people commandeer the bus. He failed to understand that in Reno, the hotel employees felt subservient to casino pit bosses and were not about to deny any pit bosses' instructions. I suggested the blame should be with the casino manager, not the hotel manager. I understand today that maybe I was a little cocky when responding to Pieper back then and I should have reflected on the words of my first boss in the business who said, " Remember, son, the boss is not always right, but the boss is always the boss!"

CHAPTER **6**

EVERYBODY IN THE casino hotel business should be fired ONCE! It is a humbling experience and it reminds one that nobody is indispensable. In fact as Jack Binion, the most respected man I know in gaming, would later profess to me, "If you think you are indispensible, place your hand in a bucket of water. When you pull it out, see what kind of a hole you leave!"

On June 12, 1978 just six weeks after the grand opening of the MGM, Jack Pieper called me down to his office early that Monday morning. Expecting to be briefed on some new aspect of business, I was caught totally off guard when he told me that he was asking for my resignation. He never gave me a reason and to this day I resent that aspect of my termination the most. I suspect that he needed a scapegoat for the problems we encountered at opening and I could have lived with him giving me that excuse. I vowed from that point on that, however uncomfortable I might be when having to terminate somebody, I would tell them why. Knowing why is the only way one can take appropriate positive measures to correct whatever impediment caused the termination. For the next 32 years, whenever I had to let somebody go, I made it a point to always give them the real reason they were being fired.

MGM was good to me when I departed. They gave me a reasonable severance allowance and paid for my moving van back to Las Vegas. I sold my house in three weeks for a tidy profit and left for Las Vegas to look for a new job.

CHAPTER **7**

WHILE MY TENURE at MGM was relatively brief, I did learn much about how, and more importantly, how not to manage various aspects of the resort casino business. I tried hard to carry that knowledge on in my later management ventures. In the meantime, it is appropriate to mention a few humorous moments that surrounded the people I met and dealt with at MGM in this chapter.

Fred Benninger was the chairman of the board of MGM. He had been a confidant of Kirk Kerkorian and he was a master at organizing the elements of a huge construction project. Of all the people that reigned from the MGM Casino in Las Vegas, Mr. Benninger was the one that played the most positive role in supporting and working closely with the Reno Management team. I wish I could say that for the other top executives at MGM, most of whom are dead today.

I will never forget the one negative comment made by Benninger that involved the fire codes in Washoe County. During both the designing and building process, Benninger constantly was looking for elements of the design that could be eliminated in his quest to reduce the costs of construction. He had identified a very expensive fire safety element that had just been mandated by new building codes in Washoe County. He let everybody know that he strongly disagreed with the code, and he was looking to remove the expensive automatic door closers in the elevator lobbies of the tower which were activated by equally expensive smoke and heat detectors. When the Reno Fire Marshall refused to support his variance request, I remember Benninger yelling at our construction manager, "What in the hell is wrong with these fools? Don't they know that a steel and concrete building of this type will never burn down? Why are we wasting our money on safety items that will never ever be used?" I will bet money he never recalled making that statement three years later when a terrible fire at the MGM Grand Hotel in Reno claimed the lives of 85 guests and employees. The MGM in Las Vegas had no such fire doors to secure the elevator lobbies on each floor.

While Pieper disappointed me with his administrative talents, he did hire several great guys to help guide the company at the very senior level. The vice chairman of the Board was a classy fellow by the name of Barrie Brunet. Barry eventually became president when Pieper was fired and he was a damn good one, I hear. Brunet had been a trusted executive at the MGM Studios and Kerkorian sent him to Pieper to be the eyes and ears of the major stock holder. Coming on board as the chief financial officer was Merle Coombs. Coombs, you will remember, was the guy who had been transferred from the Sands over to the Frontier to take Pieper's place when Jack resigned to become president of MGM Reno. Merle was a likeable guy who got along with everybody. Having served as a high level officer in the military, he was a much disciplined leader. While he had little practical knowledge of hotel or casino operations, his tenure as an assistant general manager to Richard Danner at the Sands enabled him to move into the president's role at the Frontier quite readily. With his financial background and his fundamental knowledge of gaming and hotel operations, he communicated easily with my hotel operating group and the team in the casino.

The most colorful character on the Pieper team was Glenn Neely. Glenn was a good old boy who became the vice president of casino operations. He was an avid hunter and fisherman and he was the only senior executive to show up to work driving an old pickup truck with a camper shell on the bed. Of all the people that Pieper brought to the management team, Glenn was one that fit in with everybody and he was always upbeat, even on bad days. Along with Glenn Neely, Barry Brunet and Merle Coombs became the only role models for me at the MGM property. None of them were ever my mentors, but Glenn and Merle were good partners and friends, even after I left MGM.

I did have other role models on the MGM team, though. Topping this list was Bob Ostrovsky, who was transferred from the Las Vegas MGM operation to assume the senior role in human resources. Bob was quick to adapt to the team of managers that I had recruited to MGM, and he quickly developed employment policies and procedure that were a hybrid of the best ideas that he could pull together from the diverse group of people that came to us from almost every big hotel in Las Vegas. While we were building the MGM and planning for the operation of the business, Bob Ostrovsky, Spike Cook and Charlie Pinto would meet me out for cocktails almost every day after work. Our usual haunt was the Pioneer Casino downtown where we could talk over business in the far corner of the dark and intimate "Iron Sword Lounge." The three of these guys always brought their assistant with them and we would drink *separators* for several hours as we solved the problems of the world. In fact the team became known by the Iron Sword bartenders as the *dairy queen group*, because the *separators* we consumed were made with Kahlua, brandy and mostly cream.

One night while I was sitting with this group near the fireplace, I saw Ostrovsky passing a joint around under the table and everybody was taking a hit on it. Everyone, that is, except me. I almost crapped my pants. Didn't these clowns know that the company did not yet have a gaming license, and I in particular was under investigation for approval of my Key employee license? Worse yet, sitting at the bar across the room were two detectives from the Reno Police Department who soon would smell the waft of marijuana. I jumped up and left. The next morning I called all these guys (my so called role models, partners and friends) into my office and chewed their asses out. I think they got my strong message. If they ever repeated this stunt again, they never did while I was present. Somehow, the two police detectives never caught on. Maybe they were smoking their own.

On another occasion, the group was partying at the "Foggy Notion," a night club in the Old Town Mall down on Peckham and Virginia Street. That was the night Ostrovsky credits me with saving his life. It seems we all had consumed a little too much tequila and mescal, and as Ostrovsky swallowed the worm out of the bottom of the Mescal bottle, he found an emboldened level of courage. Ostrovsky was a tough wiry guy with a relatively lean build. As the courage juice sunk in, he decided to cut in on a couple dancing in the club. The girl was gorgeous and her partner was a jealous 250 pound fellow who declined to let Bob dance with his lady friend. An argument broke out and the big guy picked up a cocktail table and threw it at Ostrovsky who did not see it coming. Luckily, I jumped in and diverted the flying table. Spike and I grabbed Ostrovsky and ushered him out the side door. Fortunately, we never saw the big guy or his pretty lady friend in the *Foggy Notion* again.

One night, we took a female executive from the MGM in Las Vegas down to the Foggy Notion to show her our classy night club. We all sat at the bar that night. Wouldn't you know it? This inebriated guy walks up to her and zips his fly down on his pants right in front of us exposing his genitals. Before we could stop him, he was asking our guest what she thought of his physical equipment. Without gasping or cracking a smile, the young lady told the drunk, "Gee, it kinda looks like a penis, only smaller." Then the police arrived and took him away.

One other character on our MGM management team was the hotel sales director, George Lysak. George did not hang out with our daily cocktail group, but occasionally he and I would meet for drinks and dinner. One night after dinner in the Pioneer Steakhouse, George and I decided to play a little Blackjack in the Pioneer Casino. It was a lucky night for both of us and we each pocketed over $2000.00 in winnings. As we were preparing to leave, George says, "Have you ever been to the Mustang Ranch?" I had not. He says, "Come on, let's go out and see what kind of trouble we can get into there." Since he was driving, I had little choice in the matter. Anyway, I was always curious about what a brothel looked like inside, so I said to George, "What the hell, let's go!"

The Mustang Ranch was a notorious brothel located ten miles east of Reno, owned by Joe and Sally Conforte. The government had taken over the ranch because the Confortes had evaded paying their income taxes. But since the government cannot seem to run anything efficiently, the Whorehouse under government management failed miserably. Subsequently, the government had to hire back Joe and Sally to operate the ranch.

George and I entered the brothel and it looked like what you always see in the movies. There was a little five seat bar with an older black female bartender that reminded me of Aunt Jemima. We sauntered up to the bar and each of us ordered a beer. I threw the bartender a $25 chip from my winning that I had not yet cashed out. About that time, six or eight working girls paraded into the parlor adjoining the bar. George sized up three ladies that he liked and headed off with all three. I sat and drank my beer. Finally a diminutive little blond girl mozies up to me and said, "High, I'm Honey! Do you want to party?" Nervous, I told her that I really wanted to finish my beer, so she asked me to buy her one, too. We had three or four more drinks as I waited for George to return. I kept telling her she should come to work for MGM and be a cocktail waitress. We had plenty of openings and I was certain she would do well making tips with her appearance. Finally, with my inhibitions waning, she made her sales pitch. "Fifty dollars for this and seventy-five for that!"

What the hell? Why not? So I said to Honey, "Give me $300 dollars worth of everything," and handed over three black Pioneer gaming chips. She ushered me back to her room where I immediately proceeded to fall asleep. Two hours later, I woke up and rushed out to the parlor where I found George sleeping on the couch waiting for me. The sun was already rising in the east and I told him we had to get home quick and clean up. "We have a staff meeting with Pieper in two hours."

As George and I were headed for the door, Honey came around the corner and said to George, "Tell your buddy to come back soon. He has a lot of time coming!" I never did go back.

That was not the end of Joe Conforte. After MGM opened, during our first month Joe was a regular customer in the MGM Casino. He frequently came in late at night with two or three working girls on his arm, and he always had a ten inch cigar in his mouth and a wad of money in his hands. He may not have paid his taxes, but he was apparently good to his workers. He bought them dinners in the gourmet restaurants and even sponsored a Mustang Ranch bowling league for his working girls. The Conforte Bowling League started its bowling at 4:00 a.m., which I guess is the slow part of the business day for a brothel. Come to think of it, when George and I left during my one and only experience, there was nobody else around.

Since I departed the MGM payroll one month after the opening, I only had a chance to become involved with three or four celebrities and entertainers. The classiest of these was Cary Grant, who showed for the opening in his capacity as a board member for MGM. He still looked as dapper as I remembered him from my days at the Dunes a decade before. The opening act in our main showroom was Dean Martin, and I had the opportunity to see how eccentric he had become since leaving the Rat Pack and the Sands hotel nearly seven years prior. I personally picked up Dean Martin at the Reno airport where he had flown in from Los Angeles on the MGM De Havilland jet. Martin got off the plane swinging a golf club over his shoulder as he walked down the stairs. When I saw his condition, I wondered why he hadn't floated down, he was so high. A bellman and I drove him back to the hotel where we ushered him into a two bedroom suite on the lowest floor of the tower. Apparently Martin had become claustrophobic in his older age. He did not want to ride in an elevator, so we positioned him where he could walk down stairs. He did not want to be surrounded by customers and autograph seekers, so we provided him with a golf cart that he could ride to the showroom through the basement hallways located four floors directly beneath his suite. He was so paranoid about being locked into his suite, that he required the double doors on the hallway entry to remain open. We set up a desk in the hallway at his suite entry and posted a security officer there 24 hours a day, so his doors could remain open. Inside his suite, we set up a bank of six television sets so he could watch multiple programs simultaneously. He would pace back and forth in front of the televisions with his remote control, constantly changing the channel on each TV set about every thirty seconds. He was really much different from the star I first saw at the Sands in 1970.

BEFORE I LEAVE this section, I will relate a story of an incident that occurred at Harrah's Reno Casino while we were building MGM. You will read in later chapters that I have never been a fan of Harrah's operations. Likewise, after Charlie Pinto raided the Harrah's house-keeping staff, Harrah's has never cared for me, either. I guess that's why I enjoy telling this story.

Harrah's had a bar off the casino floor in their annex on Center Street that was troubling the accounting department and the beverage manager for quite some time. Based on the drink prices and the portion specifications, the bar was supposed to operate with a cost of goods to equal somewhere around 20% of gross sales. Yet for months, the bar percentage at this outlet was over 27%.

Harrah's management brought in outside shoppers and watched the bar with closed circuit television cameras. Yet, nobody could detect any defects in the operation. Not one bartender appeared to be stealing. Portion Controls were pretty accurate. Every sale was rung up in the registers and every customer always received a receipt. Finally after hiring their third or fourth secret shopper, the problem came to light. This final shopper had been a bar owner in his past. When he inquired why this particular bar with three bartenders was equipped with four cash registers, the accounting people said his observations were inaccurate. They claimed the bar only had three cash registers. It turned out that the bartenders had purchased their own cash register, which was the identical make and model of the three company registers. Working in collusion, the bartenders stored the cash register in a storage cabinet at the bar and placed it on the bar when they opened the outlet for business. They had their own bank to make change and they produced sales receipts identical to the ones that were printed on the three company registers. It was embarrassing for the beverage management and even more embarrassing for the audit team. The bartenders were all fired, but this is one of the more clever scams I had ever heard about and I have to give credit to the bartenders who pulled this off so overtly right in front of the smartest casino and resort operators in Reno.

CHAPTER **9**

ON THE FOURTH of July, 1978, I attended a party in Las Vegas at the home of an old Sands hotel executive, Lubi Draskovic. Harry Goodheart, the sr. vice president of Casino operations at the Sands attended and was surprised to hear that I left the MGM. Harry suggested that I call Richard Danner and tell him I was looking for a job, and Harry said he would call Danner and give him a heads up. Danner set me up for an appointment on my birthday, and he offered me a position as director of purchasing & project planning for the Sands Hotel and said I could start the following Monday. I told him that I knew very little about purchasing. Danner told me I would need to learn it, because that is where he wanted me to work. After admonishing me for leaving him and the Sands on two previous occasions, he said I had to serve my time in purgatory at the back dock for a while, but he had bigger plans for me down the road. What a birthday present! I loaded my office materials in the trunk of my car and headed off to my new place in back of the Sands. On July 17, 1978, I started my third stint at this famous hotel casino.

CHAPTER **10**

I TOOK OVER the reins of the Sands purchasing department following the retirement of Larry Spencer, who had been an old friend during my past two stints at the Sands. The Sands purchasing procedures were antiquated beyond belief. While I had never participated formally in the purchasing process for a casino hotel, I had studied the internal control procedure that had been instituted by Mike Mavros of the MGM –Las Vegas and I was impressed by the controls they provided and by the ease by which they could be implemented to create efficiency in the material handling processes for a casino hotel. I slightly plagiarized the Mavros purchasing manual and related forms to create a hybrid system for the Sands. The vice president of finance liked the new procedures and endorsed them for me. Barbara MacDonald, my buyer and two clerks bought into the new program which made implementation easy. Our back dock receiving clerks and warehouse manager were all anal by nature, so the new procedures fit them just fine. With my overall knowledge of hotel and casino operations in general, I discovered that I could use my intuition to set inventory pars at more appropriate levels than what had been on the books and I established a "just on time" delivery of products so we would not have to tie up money in unnecessary inventories.

The MGM had been successful at obtaining discounts from suppliers and vendors for early payment of invoices. I notified all the suppliers of the Sands that we would also like to obtain discounts for early payment of their invoices. Interest rates were very high in 1978, so getting paid early was very important to vendors. Yet after I notified the vendors, I saw that we received no takers. That is when I discovered that our accounts payable office paid all invoices every seven days, regardless of terms. That had been the policy for years and it had never changed.

I convinced the controller that we could earn over $100,000 in discounts if he would have the accounts payable department pay according to terms of the purchase order. By the end of the first month, we had suppliers coming in to the office inquiring if we had cash flow problems or might be going out of business, because they were not receiving their weekly check. When they learned the reason for the delay, they were not happy at first but eventually understood the business reason behind discounts. And sure enough, we earned over $100,000 in discounts in the first year alone.

After the first month in my new role, Danner expanded my role to serve as events buyer and project planning coordinator. In this role, I was able to work closely with Harry Goodheart and his casino marketing people to identify and develop promotional parties and events for the casino. Most of these events included valuable gifts that would be purchased and given away to the event participants. The opportunity to be involved with the casino proved invaluable to my future career roles down the road. Having to serve my time in purgatory at the Sands purchasing office proved to be another stroke of luck for me in my career.

The most humorous aspect of my role in purchasing at the Sands involved the chores we were forced to perform for the biggest gambler on the Sands player roster. When I took over purchasing, Adnan Khashoggi, the famed Saudi Arabian arms broker was frequenting the Sands for months at a time. He and his flunkies, Robert Shaheen and Eugene Warner, enjoyed making Sands employees and executives jump through hoops on their behalf. They got a kick out of sending high level employees on scavenger hunts and they had no regard for an employee's personal time off.

The first assignment I received for something unusual happened a week or so after I started my new job. It seemed that Mr. Khashoggi wanted to purchase an electric barber chair and he wanted it delivered that day. He did not want an hydraulic model; only an electric one. My buyer and I sourced a myriad of vendors. Makes me wish we had "Google " back then to make it simple. Nonetheless, we finally located a company in Kansas City that manufactured the type of chair "Mr. K" desired. We were informed by the manufacturer that there was a model in stock at a barber supply house in Thousand Oaks, California. But how was I going to get this chair for Mr. Khashoggi in time? It was 2:00 p.m. in the afternoon so I called the fellow that ran our Beverly Hills field office located inside the Beverly Wilshire Hotel and asked him if he had anybody in Los Angeles that could drive to Thousand Oaks and pick up the chair. Harry Goldenberg, the field executive, knew a maintenance man at the Beverly Wilshire with a pickup truck, and he told the guy he would give him $300 to run up to Thousand Oaks, get the chair and deliver it to the Air Research Terminal at the Los Angeles Airport where I'd have Khashoggi's Boeing 727 pick it up and fly it to Las Vegas. The maintenance man agreed and Harry Goldenberg tore three hundred dollar bills in half giving the guy the three halves. Harry told him he would get the other three halves to tape together when he returned with the chair. By 6:00 p.m. that evening, the chair was installed in Mr. Khashoggi's suite.

Later that week, Bob Shaheen called and said that the "Chief" (their nickname for Mr. Khashoggi) wanted us to procure the finest and largest *Snapper* riding lawn mower ever manufactured. I located a model and had it delivered to his plane and loaded into the hold. He asked us to mark the crate for Nairobi, Kenya where he had recently purchased the William Holden Safari estate. Khashoggi needed a lawn mower for his gardeners at the estate. I guess he wasn't in a hurry for it, though, because a year later, I sent four pallets of supplies he was carrying to Cannes, France out to the plane, only to find that we had to remove the Snapper lawn mower and store it in the warehouse at the Sands so we could accommodate the load of pallets in the hold of his plane. I think the Snapper was still at the Sands years later.

One of the strangest missions I performed for this guy was definitely a scavenger hunt. I woke up one Saturday morning from a slight hangover to answer a phone call from Eugene Warner. "The Chief is desirous of you buying him one thousand different magazines for his airplane library," Warner demanded. I inquired as to what type of magazines Mr. K preferred, to which Warner said, "It does not matter, as long as each of them is different…No duplicates, period." Warner told me to go to the front desk and draw a cash payout from the Khashoggi master account of $3000 and start shopping.

Did you ever start calling around to magazine and book stores asking how many magazines they have? They think you're nuts. As luck would have it, I located a magazine shop in the Commercial Center down at Maryland Parkway and Sahara Avenue, who said they had well over 1000 different types of magazines including the latest pornographic issues. I told them that would be fine and requested that they gather up one of each and put them in a box so that I could come by and pick them up. Naturally, they thought it was a prank and declined to do so. So I grabbed an idle bellman and took him with me in the hotel station wagon down to the magazine store. We took possession of 1000 magazines and went through the painful checkout one at a time with the store cashier. The tab was over $2000 and we headed off to the airport with a station wagon full of magazines, all destined for Mr. Khashoggi's Boeing 727.

In the spring of 1979, Khashoggi moved into the Aqueduct building of the Sands Hotel. This building was comprised of 87 rooms including two swimming pool cabana suites and eight additional luxury suites. The building had attached garage facilities for Khashoggi's motor pool and a helicopter pad was located just 300 feet behind his suite. We commissioned the telephone company to install a dedicated phone system for this building to be exclusively used for the Khashoggi party, complete with its own private telephone number and switchboard attendants. From that visit on, the telephone system, which was modular, was disassembled upon his departure and reassembled just before his return visits.

Shaheen and Warner were especially mean to the employees of the Sands and they used their leverage with Khashoggi to push many employees around. It is a miracle that nobody ever physically confronted either one of them, but I guess out of respect for the company and especially Mr. Goodheart, the employees put up with the abuse. I personally got along with both Warner and Shaheen, but I sometimes had to bite my tongue. The redemption was that Mr. Khashoggi single handedly covered our annual bonus several years in a row. After leaving the Sands, I later learned that the employees in the coffee shop frequently spit on Mr. Warner's eggs on mornings in retaliation for his abuse. But then, the Coffee shop employees were not participants in the bonus, so how could I blame them?

IN THE FALL of 1979, Danner called me to the office one morning and told me he was moving me into the position of executive vice president of the Sands non-gaming operations. I was now in the position I had long dreamed of and working with a bunch of colleagues who all shared similar values toward serving customers and making the work place environment a true place of fun. I vowed never again to leave the Sands.

Danner promoted a family environment for the employees. While he declined to host any more intra-casino football games, he championed the Sands employees' tennis league that was coordinated by the Sands Tennis and Sports Director, George MacCall. While George had been my nemesis during my last round at the Sands, during this stint at the Sands he and his wife, Wick, had become close personal friends.

The year 1979 was a banner year for profits. The Sands had beat Khashoggi for over $22,000,000 and we had almost collected everything. For the first time in my career, I was going to qualify for a nice bonus. In March of 1980, Danner and his wife Martha headed to Maui for a vacation. Two days after they left, I received a telephone call from Danner advising me that the Summa Corporate offices had approved a bonus pool to be divided up among the Sand's management. Since Danner was anxious to get the money distributed, he told me to grab the next airplane flight to Hawaii and bring him the management roster. For the first time ever, I rode first class in a Boeing 747. A limo picked me up planeside at Honolulu airport and drove me across the runway to an Aloha Airlines shuttle that flew me immediately to Maui. I called Danner on my arrival at his Wailea Beach Hotel and he told me to bring the paper work and meet him at the pool. It was a wonderful spring day in Maui and the food and booze were flowing at the pool when I arrived. As Danner and I finished allocating the bonus pool so I could head back to Las Vegas to cut the bonus checks, I commented to Danner, "I wonder where all the poor people are?"

To which Danner answered, "Who cares? What the hell did they ever do for me?" It was an off the wall comment for a guy who always seemed to value the little guy at work. But everybody is entitled to at least one off-the-wall comment in life.

In the late spring of 1980, Richard Danner was complaining of headaches and shortness of breath. Danner's good friend, Dr. Michael Debakey of the University of Houston diagnosed Danner with clogged caratid arties and recommended bypass surgery. Danner declined and the situation deteriorated. In the summer of 1980, Danner checked into Scripps Hospital in San Diego to undergo the surgery, but shortly thereafter checked himself out, deciding to forego the surgery. Just several days later, Danner experienced a massive stroke that paralyzed much of his motor system and seriously impeded his speech.

Phil Hannifin, then the chief gaming executive for Summa Corporations, named Goodheart and me as acting co-general managers for the Sands, positions we would retain until Danner's health improved. It was evident after our first meeting with Danner when he was discharged from the hospital in a wheel chair that he would never return to the work again.

Goodheart and I worked well together. Harry was the best casino manager I had ever been around. He was the first of the old breed to use computers as tools to gather as much information about good customers as he could, so he could forge very personal relationships with them. Goodheart, with just two or three people on his staff, could out produce many of the large marketing departments of the modern day casino. He was gifted with a near-photographic memory and hardly ever forgot the name of a customer, or the name of the customer's spouse and kids for that matter.

In Danner's behalf, Harry and I continued to manage the Sands operation according to the successful business plan we had been following. Adnan Khashoggi had lost over twenty two million dollars in 1979 and now he was on track to exceed that in 1980, so we were looking at another banner year.

Two of the most memorable events in my career occurred in 1980.

The first event was the tragic hotel fire at the MGM Grand that claimed the lives of 85 persons on that fateful day, November 21. As I woke up that morning to ready myself for work, I turned on the radio in my bathroom only to learn that the MGM Hotel was on fire. How could it be? As Fred Benninger had said in Reno, these types of buildings just cannot burn down. I finished shaving and dressed for work. As I drove from my home on the western outskirts of Las Vegas eastward toward the Strip, I could see black smoke billowing thousands of feet in the air. As I drove over the ridge at Decatur and Spring Mountain Road, the flames were now visible reaching several hundred feet into the air. I got into work and quickly checked our room inventory. It was a Friday and usually Fridays were sold out. However, the weekend before Thanksgiving is historically one of the slower weekends and this year was no different. I saw that we had about fifty rooms left to fill. I immediately instructed the room reservations department to stop sales and we would hold all our empty rooms for refugees from the MGM fire. I had no idea how many rooms they might need, but I figured our fifty or so rooms might help. As Goodheart and Danner showed up for work, we all headed for the Penthouse Suite on the eighteenth floor of the tower to view the fire. It was bad.

People were hanging over the balconies on the east side of the MGM Tower trying to get air. Other people had run up the fire escapes onto the roof, trying to escape the smoke and flames that had entered the fire stairways due to a construction breach in the fire wall. Helicopters were braving the heat of the upward drafts in their attempts to rescue the folks on the roof. When I watched the first guy jump from his balcony, I couldn't take it any longer. I had to leave the penthouse and go down to my office and watch the further events unfold on the local news channel. I just could not stand to stay and watch others jump to their death, which continued to occur for the next hour. The MGM fire changed the course of fire codes for hotels all over the world. Certainly hotels are safer today than ever before and the tragedy at the MGM in 1980 showed that the wisdom of the Reno fire Marshall was ahead of his time when we were building the second MGM in Reno back in 1977.

The second event began just two weeks later. On December 3, Harry Goodheart had scheduled a promotional trip to Detroit to celebrate the opening of the new office of our Detroit representatives, Ernie Anastas and Emery Volpe. Several executives from the Sands, including me, were going to attend along with Harry.

I woke up early the morning we were to depart for Detroit and as I was shaving and listening to the morning news on the radio, the broadcaster said that "Summa Corporations announced the sale of their crown jewel, the Sands, to *Inns of America*."

This caught us totally off guard. I called Harry Goodheart at home and he had not yet heard the announcement. Yet, just minutes later the word was all over Las Vegas and, of course, all over the Sands. To compound problems for the staff at the Sands that day, all of our executives had left town for Detroit. It made them feel we knew about the sale and just left. Summa Corporation had done a poor job of communicating the announcement.

The Detroit party went off without a hitch and then we all returned home to start the process of passing the baton to the new owners. "Inns of the Americas" was a company based in Dallas, Texas primarily owned by the prominent Pratt Family. Their hotel company owned numerous hotels in Mexico and other Latin American locations and they had a distinct affinity for Hispanic business.

It was well known that the Sands had a very effective marketing reach into Mexico itself, and this was intriguing in itself to the Pratts, coupled with the Sand's $17,000,000 bottom line profit the year before in 1979.

The Pratts were frequent customers of Caesars Palace and were very close to a Caesar's Executive named Neil Smyth. Smyth was a well regarded Las Vegas casino executive who spoke fluent Spanish and was very effective at marketing South America and Mexico for Caesars Palace. The Pratts were able to convince Smyth to resign from Caesars and take over the reins of the Sands when their purchase was completed.

Harry Goodheart and I closely coordinated the due diligence process between the two companies, trying to balance the interests of the current owners with our own self-interests of being retained on the payroll of the new company once the transaction was completed. During the escrow period which lasted over six months, Smyth and many members of the Pratt family along with executives from their Dallas office spent many hours meeting with Sands employees and participating in the myriad of promotional and employee events that we conducted in the normal course of business.

The closing of the purchase was slated for the third week in May, 1981. Several days before the company changed hands, Hannifin met with me to advise that Goodheart was going to be retained at Summa Corporation and Harry would be moving his offices to the Desert Inn Hotel. Unfortunately, no other Sands executives would be offered jobs with Summa Corporation and we were on our own with the new owners. Shortly after my meeting with Hannifin, I made an appointment with Smyth to determine where I stood with the Pratt organization.

Smyth seemed genuinely appreciative of the work we had done and the cooperation we had shown his transition team, and he assured me that I would be an important part of their new team. While he admitted that there would be some material changes in their methods of doing business, he was confident that I would adapt.

At first, the new company seemed electrifying. The Sands had not seen any serious renovations for years under the management of Summa Corporation, and the Pratts commenced with an immediate expansion of the casino floor and hotel lobby, starting construction the first week they took title. While I disagreed somewhat on their design approach, I remembered the axiom, "The boss is not always right but the boss is the boss!"

As summer approached, construction disruption was negatively affecting business volumes greater than expected by the Pratts. On top of the lower volumes of business, the new Latin American customers being brought in by Neil Smyth and his son, especially those from Brazil and Argentina were slow to pay their markers. Then Adnan Khashoggi showed up and began making greater demands for amenities and discounts on his markers. Competition for his business was increasing now that Harry Goodheart had gone to the Desert Inn and Morris Schenker was wooing him over to the Dunes. On top of that, several high rollers including Khashoggi had been on a hot winning streak, and the win percentage was unusually below par.

Cash began to get tight and the Pratts missed their first mortgage payment to Summa Corporation. As the situation became graver, the family members involved in management became more involved in dally affairs of the company. Jack Pratt called the shots but his brothers Bill and Ed Pratt, Jr. were also involved in the financial minutia. The heir apparent was Ed Pratt III, (who we referred to as (EP3-O). After he permanently moved into a suite on the grounds of the hotel he began to assume many of the responsibilities that belonged to me and I could see the handwriting on the wall. My position would soon be redundant and with cash flow waning, I would probably soon be a victim.

I scheduled a meeting with Neil Smyth and asked him to square with me. Did I or did I not have a future with the Sands? To his credit, Neil advised me that if I could find another opportunity somewhere else, it would be in my best interest. He did not give me any definitive dates, but indicated there would probably be some management personnel reductions in the near future.

In the Pratt organization, I had not identified any role models nor had any of the Pratt executives shown a desire to mentor me or even be friends. Unfortunately for me, they valued new relationships that they brought onto the Sands organization more than the old "tried," (and in their mind "tired") relationships they inherited when they purchased the property. Remembering again the old adage, "The boss is not always right, but the boss is always the boss," I knew it was my time to leave.

Well, luck was with me again! I left the meeting with Smyth and wandered down through the casino floor with my hat in my hand, a little miffed by what had just transpired in the president's office. By chance I ran into my old friend and now Sands casino host, Frendy Dejong. He was chatting with a good Sands customer from Seattle named Bradley Hill. Frendy told me that Brad was an investor in a new casino hotel in the upstart gambling destination of Laughlin, Nevada and that the new company was looking for a general manager. They were both wondering if I might know of somebody that would fit the bill.

CHAPTER **12**

I MET WITH Brad Hill the following morning at the Las Vegas Country Club for breakfast to discuss the potential of my taking on the position he needed in Laughlin. I learned from Mr. Hill that he had been solicited by a Detroit investment group to passively participate as a minority owner in the Edgewater Casino project along with a group of six or eight other wealthy individuals. Initially the new casino was to be managed by principals from the Detroit investment group. The new casino had just opened its doors when the Nevada Gaming Commission determined that the Detroit investor group was not suitable to own or operate a casino in Nevada. The commission required the Detroit investors to withdraw their equity and exit the operation, leaving the fledging operation in the hands of the minority owners, and with no meaningful capital to run day-to-day operations. The state intended to close the facility down unless the remaining ownership group could hire on a licensable general manager and controller, and also provide enough working capital to satisfy the minimum bankroll requirements.

I could not imagine that the state of affairs at the Edgewater Casino was as bad as Brad Hill described, but Brad assured me that he wanted me to know that the upside for success at the Edgewater was limited and the downside risk to my career was substantial. Brad did not want me to take the job unless I was prepared to accept the worst case scenario.

With the environment at the Sands deteriorating daily, I felt that the only negative thing about moving into the position at the Edgewater was the fact that I would have to live in Laughlin, Nevada. I had recently visited Laughlin and recall telling my wife, "Now this is a town that I am glad I don't have to live in."

Next to Death Valley, Laughlin records probably the highest temperatures in the Southwest desert. Located on the Colorado River bottom in a valley between two giant mountain ranges, the arid desert acts as a Dutch oven from May through October. In 1981, the Colorado River bottom was infested with gnats, and it was not unusual to stumble upon Tarantula spiders and Sidewinder rattlesnakes.

The city of Laughlin was named after Don Laughlin, the entrepreneur who in 1966 initially opened a bar and bait store with eight hotel rooms, several slot machines and a blackjack table. Laughlin's store became the post office for the community that was located just across the river from Bullhead City, Arizona and roughly five miles south of Davis Dam. By 1972 he had expanded his facilities to 48 rooms and was on the forefront of taking advantage of the big boom caused by the construction of the Mohave liquefied coal-fired power plant. The construction workers who built the plant, and then the local and out of town boilermakers who operated and routinely provided the maintenance and overhauls to the plant facilities provided a steady flow of customers.

Soon the Bobcat Casino (later named the Nevada Club and now the location of the Golden Nugget), Regency Casino and the original Colorado Belle Casino opened to cash in on the boom at the power plant. All of these casinos were extremely small sawdust "joints" with four or five table games and maybe a hundred slot machines. Simultaneously, the population of the retirement communities across the river in Arizona was expanding rapidly. The popularity of Lake Havasu as a vacation venue for boaters and fishermen, just sixty miles south of Laughlin, expanded north to Davis Dam and began to make Laughlin a favorite spot for summer water sports despite the temperatures. Compared with Las Vegas, Laughlin was closer to Phoenix and an equal distance to Los Angeles, so these casinos started to become popular, especially with customers who yearned for the good old days of downtown Las Vegas Glitter Gulch and the great values they had grown accustomed to in the past.

The Edgewater was the first casino in Laughlin to feature a high rise hotel, although by current day standards, this 150 room six-story building now seems quite small. Before accepting the assignment, I took a tour to Laughlin to see what I would be facing. As Brad Hill had warned, the situation did not look promising. The casino had very little business, the restaurant food was horrible and the hotel was operating at about 30 percent occupancy. The slot machines were mostly used models. The mix and variety of slot machines were not competitive with the other casinos and the attitudes of the employees were not in line with the down-home feeling that other casinos, especially the Riverside and the New Pioneer were emitting.

I looked around for housing only to find that the total extent of residential neighborhoods on the Laughlin side of the river was comprised of a 40 space trailer park and a 31-unit condominium complex on the hill directly underneath the Mohave Power Plant. Every casino had its own sewer processing plant, and the stench on my first inspection of the Edgewater almost made me vomit.

I headed back to Las Vegas with my wife, pondering over what decision we should make. The next day at the Sands, it became more evident than ever that my time would soon be coming to an end. I finally determined that it would be better for me to select my fate than have it selected for me by the Pratt family or Neil Smyth.

I telephoned Brad Hill in Seattle and told him I would accept his offer and I could start work on the first week in December, but he had to provide me with a suite in the hotel or rent me a condominium on the Nevada side of the Colorado River as part of my compensation. I would not take the job if I had to commute back and forth from Arizona. Brad said he would fly down to meet me the next day and finalize the terms of my employment.

On November 15, I resigned my position at the Sands. After three engagements at this great hotel, it was finally my last.

NOT EVERYONE AT the Edgewater was happy to see me join the team. My old co-worker, Ted Ward, (remember the football game between the Frontier and Sands), had been the acting general manager at the Edgewater on the day I arrived on the scene. Yes, you guessed it. He was terminated the day I showed up, and I don't think he ever forgave me.

Brad showed me to my new office, which turned out to be the corner room of a triple wide trailer facility located just fifty feet south of the hotel tower. Upon entering the "Executive Office" trailer complex, Brad introduced me to William Farmer, who had joined the company three days prior as the new director of finance and company controller. The directive from the Nevada Gaming Commission required that both a licensable general manager and controller be hired, totally independent from the ownership group. Bill Farmer and I fit that bill. Farmer was a straight-laced family guy who had been an outstanding auditor with one of the Big Five accounting firms. Bill had previously worked on the Edgewater account and was familiar with its genesis and its now very weak financial underpinnings. He was an excellent selection by Brad Hill and we became good friends.

The first order of business was to meet the executive team of department heads and then tour the facilities, both front and back of the house to understand the physical lay of the land. Then, Farmer and

I pored over the departmental books and financial analysis to determine where the strategic opportunities might be, given our limited resources and lack of capital.

After assessing the strengths and weaknesses of the competition, by working closely with the department heads, Bill and I embarked upon developing a workable business plan that was easily understandable and measurable. It has always been my practice when taking on a new job assignment to work with existing management, and not come in with a big broom and start all over. When I arrived at the Edgewater, I only hired one trusted person to assist me in the transition, a shrewd food and beverage professional named Stuart Sherman. Stuart covered my butt in the back of the house and scoured the procedures and practices in purchasing and warehousing to determine where we might have material leaks and weaknesses in the internal control systems put in place by the Detroit management team. Stuart was so intrusive and examined every aspect of the operation in such detail that the employees referred to him as "the Eye in the Carpet," a force to be reckoned with by the employees (similar to the venerable "eye in the sky" surveillance cameras).

By the end of my first month on the job, it was evident to me that I would have to make some management changes to effectively carry out the tactical implementation of the new business plan. This would not prove to be an easy task, since the three key people I needed to discharge were also minority stockholders, confidants of the Detroit investors, and they held political connections with the remaining board of directors. Did you ever try to fire an owner? Well, I did. In fact I fired all three of them during my first sixty days on the job. At first it seemed to be an impossible task, but I soon learned that I had an outside force on my side that would help me make the necessary terminations.

After I quickly came to the conclusion that I needed to fire some key people, I was not aware of the fact that the Nevada State Gaming Control Board also held the same feelings regarding the qualifications and integrity of the original management team, as well as a very large contingent of the employees who were hired on at the Edgewater from day one. The second week after I started work in Laughlin, I received a request from the Nevada Gaming Control board for copies of every employee's personnel files. This seemed like an odd request, but I obviously complied. Bill Farmer photocopied all the files of our 300 employees and we hand delivered them to the control board office in Las Vegas the following day.

A week later, we received the identical request from the control board. I thought perhaps they misplaced the first batch of documents we had sent up the past week, so we duplicated the personnel files again and hand delivered them to their offices in Las Vegas.

When they called the third week with the identical request once again, it finally dawned on me that the control board was sending Bill and me a message. As we finished copying the files for the third time, I had the accounting clerk make an additional copy for me as well. That same evening, I invited Bill Farmer and Stuart Sherman to my condo on the hill, and we began scrutinizing every personnel application in our file to see if we could identify something common among the applications or something weird that would stand out in an unusual way, causing the Control Board investigators to continue to ask for these redundant files each week.

Our analysis of the personnel applications initially focused on each employee's past work experience and admitted criminal records, if any. This did not flag any unusual findings on our part. After several hours of analysis and a couple of beers each, we decided to look at the previous residence of each employee. That is when the revelation hit us. Of the 300 employees in this little hick town of Laughlin, Nevada, we discovered that over fifty of our employees had previously all lived in Steubenville, Ohio. The chances of this happening on a random basis were nil.

The following day, we called in the department heads and gave them each a list of names and instructed them to terminate these specific fifty employees as part of our down-sizing program. We never told them why.

A few days following the mass layoff, the investigator from the Gaming Control Board called and said they no longer needed a weekly update of personnel.

Along with the fifty terminations of the Steubenville contingent, I let the casino manager, slot manager and culinary manager go, as well and replaced them with three trusted associates from Las Vegas. I also hired my old Sands buyer to head up the purchasing effort for us.

Skimming is a term often associated with casinos. It is usually assumed that skimming takes place only in the count room when some of the gambling winnings are stolen. At the Edgewater, we discovered that the skim could be accomplished more readily by taking money out through affiliated vendors. Again, we were provided with subtle hints from our friends at the Gaming Control Board. It started with our company airplane.

Yes, even though the Edgewater was almost bankrupt, it owned a two engine Cessna 421 aircraft. The control board investigators constantly wanted to look at the plane and there was innuendo that we were possibly using the plane to shuttle drugs up the Colorado River valley from Mexico. I never understood why a little company like ours had an airplane, but Brad Hill and the other minority owners did not want to part with it, even with all the heat on us from the state.

Then the *eye in the carpet* discovered a revelation. He discovered that we were paying huge lease payments for both our airplane and our coin counting equipment to a company in Las Vegas. Stuart Sherman pressed deeper and found that the Cessna aircraft we owned had an appraisal value of about twenty percent of what the company had paid for it through our leasing arrangement. On top of that, he learned that the alleged brand new coin counting equipment we leased through the same finance company was actually used equipment that had been salvaged from the MGM fire the year before, and its true value was less than ten percent of the capped cost of the lease in place. Further investigations found that the Edgewater had leased several other major pieces of food service equipment, shuttle busses and a tow tractor and trolley from the same financial entity under the same shady circumstances.

After sharing our findings with Brad Hill, he gave me the approval to begin defaulting on the leases. He further agreed that we would tender the plane back to the leasing company and replace the antiquated coin counting machines with brand new Cummins state of the art equipment in a deal that I was able to negotiate for less than one third the cost of what we were currently paying.

I summoned our airplane pilot and told him to fly the Cessna to McCarran Airport and park it at the fixed base operation on Tropicana Avenue. I told him to call me from a pay telephone when he tendered the keys to the dispatch office, and I would have a driver pick him up and bring him back to Laughlin. After the pilot called to confirm the plane was secure at the airport in Las Vegas, I called the leasing company and advised them to take possession of the plane and that we would not be making any further payments. Then I called the control board investigator and advised him that we no longer owned an airplane. The agent said to me, "You are making progress, kid."

A few days later, I called the leasing company and told them we were no longer going to make payments on the coin counting equipment either. When they threatened to come down to Laughlin and repossess their equipment, I told them to do so, because the equipment was outside on the back dock and we had already replaced it with new and efficient machines.

I had no idea who owned or was associated with the leasing company, but I learned years later from a friend at the Gaming Board that I was apparently a potential target for physical harm because of my actions.

CHAPTER **14**

IN JANUARY, 1982 we engaged the services of Lamar Owens Advertising Agency in Phoenix and embarked upon the first ever television advertising of a Laughlin casino. Television advertising in Phoenix was relatively inexpensive in those days and there was an added benefit in that Phoenix television was broadcast to most outlying towns in Arizona, including our primary local feeders of Kingman and Bullhead City, Arizona. Our advertisements were simple still shots created at very minimal cost, and our efforts paid off handsomely. Overnight, our room occupancy skyrocketed from 30% to capacity. In fact the demand for rooms spilled over to the other casinos and the motels on the Arizona side of the Colorado River. The full hotel helped ease the financial burden, but we knew we still had a huge hole from which to dig out. While we had an advantage with our hotel in an environment with a scarcity of good hotel rooms, we faced an over-capacity of casino space that occurred when the Edgewater and Pioneer Casinos opened almost at the same time, nearly doubling gaming positions in Laughlin. With our less popular slot machine product and our inability to finance any replacement equipment, we slogged along depending on our promotional programs to attract trial and repeat business.

A major source of business for all the casinos in Laughlin is the casino employees themselves. As such, we provided every employee with a free drink every day after his or her shift was over and in fact the free drink was referred to as a "shifter." When I first arrived at the Edgewater, I discovered that many of the employees were taking cash advances against their pay checks directly from the casino cage. It was a huge bookkeeping burden, but was even more devastating to the personal lives of the employees who were abusing the program. You would have thought I was the bogey man when I stopped payroll advances during my first week on the job.

A practice I could not discontinue, though, was the cashing of employee payroll checks. With no banks in Laughlin, and limited availability across the river, all the casinos cashed their own as well as competitor's employee paychecks both as a service to the employees, as well as a revenue source. Payday was always a good day for all of the casinos.

Because of cash flow being negative for so long at the Edgewater, cashing payroll checks became a burden and required significant cash planning and management by the cage manager and controller. I changed pay day from Friday to Monday so that the casino cage would have the benefit of cash being built up over the busy weekend, to exchange for payroll checks on Monday evenings when the employees all got off work.

In those days, it would often take five to seven days for a check to clear the bank when it was routed through different banking districts. Since Brad Hill, the company president, agreed to fund a $200,000 loan to the Edgewater, we established an account with his Seattle bank. We established our payroll account with a bank in Las Vegas, but did most of our general payables banking through a small bank in Riviera, Arizona. With three banks in three different banking districts, we could manipulate the peaks and valleys of our cash flow.

However, even with good cash management in place, we often found it necessary to take almost all of the coins out of the vault and include them with our Monday deposits to clear all our outstanding checks. Business improved enough to hold our own, but not enough to ever pay the outstanding balances due that had been generated from day one of opening, but had never been paid. The general contractor, a minority shareholder, was owed money and was threatening a lien. Likewise, the company attorney, also a minority shareholder, was owed considerable money for his past services. After five months of hard work we felt like we'd been running in a squirrel cage. Brad Hill asked me what I thought we should do. I advised him to sell the company if he could, and we would do everything possible to keep it out of bankruptcy. Brad agreed and he went to the board with a resolution to embark on finding a buyer.

In the meantime, it was business as usual and then some. Around the first of August, a consortium of several unions in Las Vegas embarked on an organizing drive in Laughlin. It was over 115 degrees when the union put informational pickets in place just outside our public entry way. We countered with promotional pickets of our own, walking just inside the property line at the entry way to the casino parking lot. Our picket signs read, "Strike Out Inflation with a $3.99 Buffet." We resisted union organizing that year, but eventually the union prevailed several years later when the big Vegas operators started buying in to Laughlin.

Speaking of buffets, as competition heated up, buffet price wars became common place on the River that summer. What started as a promotional gimmick to get early morning gamblers in the door, our $1.99 breakfast buffet was soon trumped by a 99 cent buffet at the Nevada Club. Before we could sample their product, the Colorado Belle lowered their price to $.49. When the dust settled, we were selling our breakfast buffet for $.24 plus tax…or for a quarter you could have a great buffet. Fortunately, we all came to our senses before the Labor Day crowd showed up.

CHAPTER 15

CRIME IN LAUGHLIN was pretty tame, when you consider that the Hells Angels toured through the area from time to time and everybody on the Arizona side of the river carried guns. Laughlin had one full time police officer assigned from the Las Vegas Metropolitan Police Department. Billy Moma was his name and he resided in the trailer park right there in Laughlin. Retired today, you will still find his name on one of the busiest street signs in Laughlin.

Billy knew everybody that worked in Laughlin and probably all the local customers and many of the transient out-of-towners as well. He was frequently seen chomping on his cigar while in uniform, hanging around the casinos and especially the sports book when we opened ours for football season in 1982. What we seldom saw Billy do was arrest anybody.

One evening, we were alerted to a potential slot cheater on the floor. This guy was working in concert with an employee to set up phony jackpots. We had seen their work on a review of a video tape from the surveillance room and we wanted to catch them red-handed. On that particular night, he was spotted on the casino floor along with his accomplice, who had just come on duty as a slot attendant. With no announcement, we temporarily closed all the slot change booths on the casino floor as this fellow and the crooked employee set up the machine. The $300 jackpot was paid in dollar tokens and the slot cheat proceeded to rack the coins in three containers and head to the closest change booth to cash out for currency. He approached the first booth only to find no cashier and the booth temporarily closed for service. He scampered across the casino floor to the farthest change booth, also finding it unattended. In panic, he headed for the casino cage as his last resort. As he put the three racks of tokens on the counter to cash out, two security officers cuffed him while his hands reached straight out holding the racks.

The security officers took him into the interrogation room and called Billy Moma and the Gaming Control Board to report the theft. For whatever reason, the security officers released the handcuffs and when they did, this guy bolted through the casino and out through the front door and into the parking lot. I happened to be having a beer at the bar with a customer and with all the noise and commotion caused by this guy, I took chase and tackled him in the parking lot myself. When the security guys showed up this time, the cuffs stayed on.

Billy Moma arrived on the scene about thirty minutes later and after two hours we finally had investigators from the Gaming Control Board show up to press charges. The agents did not look kindly on having to drive the 180 miles round trip to handle this little matter, and Billy Moma didn't look too happy either. Once we wrapped the paperwork up and the agents left with the slot cheat in tow, Moma pulled me to the side.

"Listen," he said, "we do things a little different here on the River. I suggest you go up and buy a few Riverside gambling chips and keep them in the security stand. When you get a clown like this in the future, you kick the shit out of him, stuff a few of the Riverside chips in his pants and toss the son of a bitch into the river. When they find him downstream, they will never trace it back to you."

While maybe it sounded like a good idea at the time, I was just glad that I never had to test the idea. By the way, I never did go down and buy those Riverside gambling chips. I later learned that Moma was just kidding me anyway.

Billy Moma was a good customer of our sports book. We had been fortunate to hire a guy from Omaha by the name of Fred Dettmer. In Omaha he was known as "Filthy Fred" for operating filthy dirty bars and gin mills. He was a family friend of Jackie Gaughan, the owner of the El Cortez Casino in Las Vegas at the time.

Stuart Sherman, my *Eye in the Carpet* was also from Omaha and he knew Jackie Gaughan. When I was looking to create a sport book at the Edgewater, Stuart called Mr. Gaughan and Fred was suggested as the perfect candidate. And sure enough, he was. Fred fit in with the rest of the river rats like he had grown up in Laughlin. He was fun to be around and all the employees loved him. We carved out a twenty foot counter at the far end of the casino and created the "Hole in the Wall" sports book and Filthy Fred became a legendary character in the Laughlin-Bullhead City region.

The Edgewater Sports Book took off from the start. It was the only book on the river at that time, and the action was generally small neighborhood bets. But then one day reputed crime boss, Anthony "The Ant" Spilotro, showed up with his brother and they wanted to bet thousands of dollars on football games. Fred had no idea who they were, but certainly liked the idea of all the action. On top of it all, "Filthy Fred" and Tony "The Ant" got along fine and enjoyed chatting with each other.

For the next four or five weeks, Spilotro and his brother continued coming down to Laughlin to place more bets. Fred was starting to get nervous, especially since the two brothers had won big two weeks in a row. Everything appeared to be on the up and up, but when you deal with these guys, you always seem to see ghosts, and Fred was seeing ghosts.

Then we received a telephone call from the Gaming Control Board: "We heard you are dealing to Spilotro in your sports book."

When we acknowledged we were, they instructed us to tape the two Spilotro's entire visit each trip, and photocopy every $100 bill wagered by the two brothers. The next week, the brothers beat us again and the photocopying was becoming a pain in the ass, to boot. Finally, I called Fred and told him we needed to tell the Spilotros that we didn't want their action any longer. Fred was naturally nervous about having to be the bearer of this news, but when the Spilotros showed up that next week to cash out their winnings, Fred bravely informed the two brothers of the company's decision to deny their future action. Tony says to Fred, " Yeah, we heard, Freddie. Don't worry, we don't hold it against ya! See ya later, Freddie!"

MY *EYE IN the Carpet* was also an alchemist. Stuart Sherman knows more about booze than anybody in the business. He knows what tastes like what. He knows what proof is what and he knows what specific gravity is what. Two items moved like mad in a Laughlin bar in those days. If bar customers did not simply ask for a "Quaalude and a water back," they probably were drinking either a "Kahlua and Crème" or a "Crown Royal and Coke." Stuart knew that no one could tell the difference between certain brands of liquor, especially when mixed with cream or cola. With our precarious cash situation, Stuart uniquely managed the flow of Crown Royal and Kahlua in a fashion that met the demanding expectations of the consumer but yielded a far better cost of sales percentage than was expected by our financial controller. The alchemy worked fine until our purchasing agent inquired how we could only buy four cases of Crown Royal and wind up selling ten cases. With our cover exposed and our cash flows improving, I suggested to Stuart that he discontinue the chemistry.

My new casino manager, (rest his soul) was a playful guy by the name of Dennis Robie. Nobody knew the casino table games better than Dennis and he was a real asset to the casino. He had been a pit boss for us when I worked at the MGM in Reno and he was well liked by the employees that worked for him. But as serious as he was about his job, he was the opposite in his play time. He straightened the mess out in the casino but he caused me problems on his off hours. One night I received a call from my director of security advising me that the Bullhead City Police had been contacted by the local Burger King that a car had just pulled through the drive-thru to pick up their *to go* order, and the pimple-faced attendant was confronted by a car full of six men and women who were totally naked, except for the bandolier of shot glasses hanging around the neck of one lady. If they hadn't been such good tippers, the attendant would have called the police more quickly. But he waited ten minutes before making the call allowing Dennis and his gang time to cross the Davis Dam and get back to the Nevada side of the river safely. Yet the Bullhead City police found no humor in the antic, and it made the morning news to boot.

On another occasion, my wife and I took Dennis and his girl friend for a long ride in the company cabin cruiser up on Lake Mohave. We had no business owning a cabin cruiser but there was no interest by any serious buyers when we finally placed it up for sale. Since we owned the boat, I occasionally had to take it out and charge the batteries. It was a wonderful day off in early May of 1982 and we wound our way all the way up the Colorado River to a location just below Hoover Dam. On the return trip, Dennis asked if he could pilot the boat. He seemed to know what he was doing, so I let him take the reins while I went below to fetch a sandwich and a beer. I suddenly looked up and out the cabin window to see the boat heading toward a cliff. Before I could yell at Dennis he ran the boat up on the rocks. After crashing around in the cabin, my wife and I scurried out to the helm to find Dennis bent over the steering wheel with broken ribs. I turned on the bilge pumps and looked over the side to see if we had taken on any water. I could not believe that we had not severely punctured the hull. I pulled the engine hatch door and was surprised to find that no water was in the bilge. Then, I looked down into the cabin and saw the water coming in from the bow. There we were, sinking in over 200 feet of cold Colorado River water, with only rocky canyon walls on both sides of us. I pushed Dennis aside and started the engines. I pushed the throttles forward and headed for the shore. All of a sudden I spotted a small creek bed between two cliffs and with as much speed as I could muster with the front of the boat plowing through the water with its half submerged bow, I luckily landed the boat in the "V" of the tiny creek bed, the only safe haven along nearly another half mile of sheer cliffs.

We finally flagged down a fisherman in a small boat and hitched a ride to the Willow Beach Marina where we waited for several hours for a ride back to the casino. In the meantime, I had to make the dreaded call to Brad Hill and tell him we sank the company yacht. With every dark cloud, there is a silver lining. Now I could take the insurance proceeds and use it for needed cash at the casino. After the salvage company recovered the boat and transported it to the boat yard in Las Vegas for repairs, the insurance company agreed to junk the remains and write us a check for the value. The ass chewing I took from the boss for sinking the boat bought us another couple weeks of payroll.

My new slot manager was a diminutive guy by the name of Carmelo Pecoraro. We called him the "Little Pecker." While it was only 1982 and computers were relatively scarce in the gaming business, Carmelo had his own DEC mini-computer and he used it to help us make the most out of the lousy slot machine product we owned. Carmelo was all business and always serious. He had spent many years at the Sands Hotel in Las Vegas and enjoyed a wonderful reputation at the time with the slot distributors. With his pull, we were able to get Bally's Manufacturing Company to finance 100 new Series "E" slot machines for us, which were the state of the art in 1982. We opened a dedicated section of the casino floor with these new machines on Labor Day weekend in 1982 and the machines took off like a rocket.

In the meanwhile, Brad Hill had entered into some preliminary discussion with several Las Vegas gaming companies who were interested in entering the Laughlin market and who might be interested in buying the Edgewater Casino. Showboat Casino and Circus Circus Corporation had shown the most interest, and Brad was hoping to get the two of them into a bidding war. Then Showboat dropped their efforts and the Circus executives decided to stall, hoping we would get more desperate to sell at an even more depressed price.

This is when Carmelo came up with an idea to expand the casino floor by creating a new large casino area in what was currently an open atrium adjoining the lounge. The "Little Pecker" discovered that if we enclosed the atrium on the second level and converted the show lounge into additional slot space, we could add another 200 machines. Furthermore, he had worked out an agreement with Bally's to supply and finance the slots and fund the construction costs for the floor expansion. When we announced our preliminary plans, Circus Circus finally negotiated a reasonable offer to buy the assets of the Edgewater. The deal was to close on February 3, 1983 and when it did, the deal marked the second wave of major expansion in Laughlin.

When Circus completed the purchase, they simultaneously purchased the adjoining Colorado Belle Casino along with the residential trailer park located south of the Edgewater and adjoining the Pioneer Casino. During the next three years, Circus Circus expanded the Edgewater Hotel to over 1000 rooms and tripled the size of the casino. They built a new 65,000 square foot casino and 600 room hotel named the Colorado Belle on the old residential trailer park and funded the sewer district that enabled all the casinos on the Laughlin strip to abandon their smelly on-site sewer systems. The Circus Circus developments spawned the construction of the Flamingo Hilton (now the Aquarius), the Tropicana Express, the River Palms and the luxurious Harrah's. From 1983 until 1990, Laughlin led the State of Nevada in percentage growth of gaming revenues. Unfortunately, as of this writing, the glow of Laughlin has receded during the last ten years as competition from Native American casinos in Phoenix and California have siphoned off much of their previous loyal business. Laughlin remains a value driven destination and is still a favorite place for water sports in the summer and a "snow-bird" haven in the winter.

Four weeks before the sale of Edgewater to Circus closed, I was called to Las Vegas by William Bennett, the chairman of Circus. He and his chief operating officer, Mike Ensign, met with me and more or less promised to keep me on as the general manager of the Edgewater. They wanted me to do my best to keep morale up and assure the employees that there would be very few changes, and any changes that occurred would be good. The first thing they wanted me to do was pay off all the outstanding vendor bills, which made the new environment sound very encouraging from the start. I went back to the property and promoted the heck out of the owners. Knowing the new bankroll would be infused into the company in just four more weeks, we paid off all the outstanding invoices from our available cash. Morale among the employees, the vendors and the patrons had never been so high and we were all championing the sale.

Then on January 31, three days before the transaction was to be consummated, I was summoned to Chairman Bennett's office again. I was anticipating signing an employment agreement and was trying to prepare to posture for the best deal I could make. When I arrived in Bennett's office that Monday morning, I was met by Mike Ensign who told me that Bennett had been called to Reno. He then sat me down and told me that they had decided to bring their own general manager from their Silver City Casino facility in Las Vegas to take over the operation and wanted to work out an exit agreement with me. Naturally, I was disappointed but also understood their reasoning to begin a cultural transformation at the Edgewater using someone who understood their policies and value system better than I. When I found out that the guy they picked to take my place was a fellow UNLV graduate and an outstanding manager, I realized that at least they were not trading down. My replacement was Bill Paulos, who went on to become a very successful casino owner in his own right and is today a multi-millionaire.

My only regret was in the way they led me on for a month, but I guess if they wanted to ensure a good morale and a transparent transition, the method they used worked quite well. During the four week period during which I anticipated staying employed with the Edgewater under the new ownership, I declined an opportunity to interview for a similar open position at Lake Tahoe. That is not to say that I would have secured the Lake Tahoe position if I had interviewed, but by the time the Edgewater sale concluded, the Tahoe position had been filled.

On February 3, I packed my car with the few belongings I had in my office and headed back to my home in Las Vegas where I would embark on the next journey in my career.

Section 5

GRADUATING INTO SENIOR MANAGEMENT — MY BIG TIME CHANCE IN ATLANTIC CITY AT THE SMALL TIME DEL WEBB'S CLARIDGE CASINO

AFTER LEAVING THE employment of the Edgewater on February 3, 1983, I loafed for a couple of weeks and then began looking for a new job. I was hoping to land something interesting in Las Vegas. Laughlin and Reno had been interesting enough and certainly educational, but I wanted to be part of the more "glitzy" big time that was only truly found in Las Vegas. I yearned for a return to my days at the Sands, but in the top position of general manager or president. Unfortunately, in late 1982 and early 1983 there had been a massive management consolidation in the Nevada gaming industry and there were quite a number of other good qualified people out of work who also wanted one of those dynamic "glitzy" jobs in Las Vegas.

For the past seventeen years of my life, I had now worked in seven different casino venues and had never spent longer than four weeks between jobs. This time I found it was going to be different. Four weeks went by; then eight. Circus Circus had provided me with a small severance check and I was schooled early on by my father to keep six months worth of expenses in the bank for a rainy day, but I began to panic as my bank account balance began to dwindle.

One thing you find out when you're out of work is that you have a lot less friends. However, fortunately, you also run into a few people you would never expect to be your friends. Two of these folks (rest their souls, too) will always be in my thoughts because they constantly called and checked up on me when I was down on my luck for the first time in my life. Leo Lewis, the general manager at the Sahara had taken a liking to me some years back, and he often called to provide words of encouragement and usually a lead or two for a possible job. Along with him was Jack Gallaway, the gregarious general manager of the Tropicana Hotel. I had never worked with either one of these guys and I only knew them socially and from a distance. Yet they both called me constantly. They knew I was getting discouraged and that I was even thinking about seeking a job in some other industry. They kept reminding me that time passes more slowly for someone out of work, but they also encouraged me that I was suited for this business and I just had to keep looking. Something would eventually surface.

In the meantime, I took a part time assignment selling *barter advertising* to casinos for a San Francisco entrepreneur I had met at the Sands Hotel several years before. Sales were slow, but I did sell some good barter to several Laughlin Casinos and one or two Las Vegas properties, enough to make a mortgage payment or two on my home. Then in June, 1983 the Teamsters Union Local 995 went on strike at the Desert Inn Golf Course. I made a call to my old friend, Bill Sears, in the Summa Corporations human resources office and told him I was available to scab for him on the golf course. They accepted my offer and I spent the next several days mowing grass, raking traps and irrigating the Desert Inn Course. I was pretty good at it I guess, because the grounds keeper told me that I was able to rake all eighteen holes of traps faster than it took three Teamsters to do it on a regular day.

Two weeks later, the front desk Teamsters went out on strike as well, and I was summoned by Bill Sears to move inside and help operate the front desk. It was exciting to be back in the hotel operation, even as a desk clerk and I decided to focus my search for a new hotel management job beyond the boundaries of Las Vegas. A search firm arranged for me to interview for the position of general manager for the Smith Family casinos in Wendover, Nevada. Wendover was a border town located on Interstate 80 at the Utah border. I drove my pickup truck the 400 miles north to Wendover accompanied by my old slot manager, Carmelo *Little Pecker* Pecoraro. The interview went well and the owners liked both Carmelo and me and were prepared to offer us a position. They asked us to give them an answer in a week. I drove home knowing I needed a paycheck coming in soon, though I dreaded moving my wife to Wendover. Laughlin had been tough enough on her, but at least we were only 90 minutes from Las Vegas.

As luck would have it, the next day I received a telephone call from Leo Lewis. Leo told me that Bill Dougall, the president of Del Webb's Claridge Casino Hotel in Atlantic City, was searching for a vice president of hotel operations. Leo thought that my personality would fit great with Dougall and that I possessed the qualifications that Bill was looking for. Bill Dougall had been in corporate purchasing for the Hughes Nevada Operations back when I started as a desk clerk at the Sands in 1970. I knew who he was but I doubted that he would remember me.

The thought of moving to Atlantic City was almost as foreign as Wendover. When I told my Dad about the potential position, he told me that the only thing good coming out of New Jersey was the Turnpike, and I had to be crazy to consider moving that far away. Nonetheless, I had never been to the east coast and thought I owed it to myself and my wife to explore the possibility. I contacted Dougall and arranged to fly to Atlantic City on July 5, 1983 for my interview.

I pictured New Jersey as a huge asphalt environment with nothing but ghettos, like I had seen in the Newark and Camden riots on television. I landed at the Philadelphia airport and was greeted by a uniformed driver who took me the sixty miles into Atlantic City in the biggest and plushest limousine I had ever seen. As we crossed the Walt Whitman Bridge and headed toward the Atlantic City Expressway, I could not believe how beautiful the roadways and adjoining environment were. How different from my advance perceptions. It was now evident to me why they call New Jersey the "Garden State," and while I eventually did discover some tough communities that more readily mirrored my initial idea of what Jersey would be like, I actually fell in love with the state.

I arrived at the Claridge Casino around 5:00 p.m. and checked into my hotel room. The Claridge was the smallest of the nine casinos then operating. It had 500 rooms and a 38,000 square foot casino with 900 slot machines and fifty table games. After I settled into my room, I went down for a tour of the property and was amazed at the volume of people. I had never seen a crowd of this size in a Las Vegas casino, even on a busy New Years Eve. Then I walked out onto the boardwalk in front of Brighton Park. The location of the Claridge was Boardwalk at Park Place, and now I knew why these two squares occupy their position on the Monopoly Board. Looking west on the boardwalk toward Ventnor in the direction of the Golden Nugget, there must have been over 100,000 people walking the boardwalk which appeared to be as wide as a four lane highway. Then looking east toward Resorts International Casino, an equal crowd of people packed the boards. Even at 6:00 p.m. in the evening, the beaches were still packed with people. The air was balmy and dry. The Chamber of Commerce had put on their best face for me to evaluate this new strange environment, and I was starting to feel quite comfortable here.

I met Dougall for dinner in the London Pavilion Restaurant and we had a very productive and enjoyable dinner. The following morning I met Dougall again for breakfast and then finished our discussion in his fifth floor office. His assistant, Ione Nichols, was guarding the door to his office and I recognized early on that she was not a person to be reckoned with. Dougall advised me that he would be making a final selection from the candidates he had interviewed within the next ten days and thanked me for my time and interest. I jumped into my limousine and headed back to the Philadelphia airport kind of hoping I was going to get the job, and kind of hoping I wasn't. With a little extra time before my flight, I talked the limo driver into taking me down to Smithville to look around and I started to picture where I might want to live if I did wind up moving to Jersey. I had lived in the desert most of my life, so the idea of having a piece of ground with big trees and lots of grass was kind of appealing.

I GOT BACK to Las Vegas and a week went by and I did not hear from Dougall. Time really seems to go slow when you're anxious for something to happen. Then on July 15, I received a telephone call from Dougall. He was sending me an offer letter along with the New Jersey Key license application, which was almost 100 pages long and would require many hours to complete. Mr. Dougall suggested I complete the license application and arrange another trip to New Jersey with my wife to submit the completed application to the gaming authorities and conduct some house hunting while I was in the area.

I had mixed emotions about leaving Nevada. This was my home for many years and I really wanted Nevada as my permanent home. While no suitable career opportunities were now present, I felt that Nevada would rebound from the temporary 'funk' and eventually the opportunity I was seeking would surface. I decided to take the job in Atlantic City on a temporary basis and keep my options wide open in case a suitable position in a Las Vegas casino hotel surfaced. I headed back to New Jersey, this time with my wife, to look for housing. I submitted my key license application to the Casino Control Commission office and then embarked on a tour of available rentals with a local real estate agent. We ended up renting a nice older home on the ocean in Margate with a nine month lease. It was completely furnished including linens, china and silverware. I decided not to sell my Las Vegas house, but instead rented it out to friends so I could move back into it on a moment's notice. I packed all my goods and furniture and had them stored in a Las Vegas warehouse. Everything I needed for my temporary employment in Atlantic City fit inside my 1978 Camaro with a Uhaul rack on the roof. I figured I would work in Atlantic City for six to nine months and during that time I would find a suitable career opportunity back in Las Vegas so I could return home and get my stuff out of storage.

We pulled out of Las Vegas on August 29, 1983, and headed across the country for our new adventure. When we pulled into South Jersey on September 6, the Chamber of Commerce was not so hospitable this time. The temperature was almost 100 degrees and the humidity was over 90%. On top of that, the house we rented had no air conditioning. Accustomed to 11% humidity in Las Vegas, we almost passed out as we hauled our goods into our new home. Tossing and turning in the sweaty sheets with the noise of the ocean surf pounding on the shore made for a terrible first night's sleep, as I prepared for my first day on the job the following morning.

MY FIRST DAY on the job at the Claridge was like all my other "first days on the job." There is always anxiety that first day. You don't know where you're going. You don't even know where the Men's room is located. Except for Bill Dougall, I did not know a soul at the Claridge. It was evident from my first day on the job, that Dougall was admired by most of the employees at the Claridge and he filled the position of role model, mentor, partner and friend for a large number of people in that organization. He was one of the few guys in my life that filled all four roles for me as well. I still felt that way when I attended his funeral in 2006.

I met Mr. Dougall for breakfast in the Hyde Park Coffee shop at 8:00 a.m. that very first morning on the job. What was going to be a private introductory meeting with my new boss was immediately interrupted by one of the most audacious people I had ever met. A genuine character in his own right, George Duberson, a close friend of Dougall and the director of engineering for the Claridge introduced himself and then sat down at the breakfast table with us, as if he had been invited. I had never witnessed someone taking over a meeting and monopolizing a conversation as George did that morning, and I soon learned that this would be a common occurrence for as long as George worked at the Claridge. He handed me his personal business card that read, "Don't Aggravate Me!"

I also learned during that first breakfast meeting that George and his old partner had originally owned a small boat yard in the marina section of Atlantic City. They apparently paid a little over $6000 for the property back in 1968 and George operated the boat yard and performed routine maintenance on the many boats that were stored there. In 1979, George and his partner sold their boatyard for $8,000,000 to a Los Angeles tycoon named Lou Walters who partnered with Holiday Inn to build the first casino hotel resort in the marina section of Atlantic City. For George, it was like hitting the lottery. He and his wife, Vicki, went from middle class living to millionaire status overnight, and George would constantly let you know about his new status in his bellicose manner. Yet George remained a hardworking "wrench" even with his new found wealth. He was a clever mechanic and knew his way around construction as knowledgeably as anyone I ever met. When George sold his marina property to Walters, Dougall moved in to develop and manage the project for Walters. Dougall took a liking to Duberson and hired him on to be the manager of his engineering and construction department at the new Marina Hotel. George managed the construction of the first casino parking garage in Atlantic City.

In early 1982, Harrah's bought out Walters and replaced Dougall as the manager of the Marina property. Dougall immediately signed on with the Phoenix based gaming company, Del Webb Corporation, to take over the management of their fledgling Claridge Casino. Dougall's first order of business was to bring George Duberson along with him to the Claridge.

As a quick aside, the Claridge was opened in 1981 as a partnership between the Del Webb Corporation and a Connecticut paving contractor by the name of Frank D'Adario. Frank was also known as "Hi Ho" D'Adario, and the new casino project was named the "Del Webb's Claridge Hotel and Hi Ho Casino." Quite a mouthful to be certain, but Frank D'Adario was adamant that every advertisement and collateral brochure mentioned the "Hi Ho" casino. He even demanded that the restaurants serve only "Hi Ho" crackers by Sunshine…No crappy Nabisco products for Frank.

The Claridge Casino was the smallest of the Atlantic City Casinos. It was constructed on a tiny 1.8 acre footprint over one block north of the boardwalk off Brighton Park and away from the natural flow of the heavy boardwalk foot traffic. The old Claridge tower was totally gutted and refurbished up to modern 1981 code. A 250 room hotel addition was added in a manner that was seamless and looked to be part of the original building, first constructed in 1931 and patterned after the Empire State Building concept. Because of the tiny footprint, the casino of the Claridge was by necessity built in layers…. In fact, when the Claridge Casino first opened its doors in 1981, it featured six different levels of casino floor space. To compound its impediments, was the fact that it only had five small elevators that had to service eight floors of public space and 24 floors of hotel rooms. The restaurants were on the third and fourth levels and the convention facilities were located on the sixth floor. The health club, swimming pool and hair salons were located on the eight levels. Vertical transportation is generally not the preferred method for gaming patrons to travel through any casino, but especially when they had to deal with the famous Claridge "Annual Elevator" service.

With this aside out of the way, you now have a brief idea of the physical facility with which I was about to become associated. We finished our breakfast and Dougall invited me up to his office where he was having a staff meeting and would introduce me to his team of managers and executives.

The members of the executive team were all pleasant people but the person who stood out the most was Dougall's secretary, Ione. It was evident from the beginning that she ruled the roost. She was like a pit bull at the entry to the president's office and nobody….and I mean nobody, could get through that door without her permission. With a great deal of respect and admiration, I fell in love with Ione from day one and we are still friends today.

After the staff meeting, I was ushered to my new office, just steps away from Dougall's. I was taking over for a long-time Del Webb Hotel executive who was being transferred to Laughlin, Nevada to become the general manager for the company's "Nevada Club Casino." This fellow was going to spend several days going over some of the nuances of the hotel environment at the Claridge for which I would soon be responsible. In addition to inheriting his office, I also inherited his secretary, Diane. This lady was a talented African American woman who I grew to trust and depend on, and she immediately grasped my style and became my proxy.

That afternoon, I called my first staff meeting and handed out to each of my subordinate managers a very lengthy due diligence list of information and documents I was seeking from them. The purpose of this exercise was threefold. First, I wanted each of them to provide me with a consolidated summary of their particular part of the hotel operation based on my specific questions, so I would have a quick glimpse of how they managed their area of responsibility. Secondly I wanted to see how they could respond to meeting a tough deadline. I was asking for quite a few materials and written dialogue from them, and I was only giving them four days to deliver the requested items to me. Third, I wanted to see how each of these people communicated in writing. It was a good test of their business writing skills.

Dougall called me at about 6:00 p.m. and invited me to have dinner with him in the London Pavilion Gourmet restaurant. He had apparently received some kind of nasty report on the conduct of the food and beverage manager and he was hoping that I might have someone in mind to bring into the operation from Las Vegas that could fill the position. Likewise, Dougall was not very pleased with the quality of the hotel rooms operation and thought that the manager he had in place may not be up to the task of running a high volume casino hotel.

Being on the job for only one day, I asked Dougall to allow me some time to fully evaluate everybody that now reported directly to me, which included the hotel manager and the food and beverage manager that he had doubts about. I told him that I needed several days to get my hands around the policies and procedures that were driving the present operation. I also advised Dougall about my due diligence exercise that I had issued to each department head and suggested that my research from those findings would help me decide the strategies and tactics I would deploy to achieve both his goals and mine. He was satisfied with my approach, but said he expected an action plan within four weeks and no later.

To my pleasant surprise, every single department head reporting to me completed their assignment on time. As I expected, some of these folks were not great business writers, but every single one effectively communicated their answers to my questions and they all supplied the "show and tell" documents that I needed to evaluate their operations. Most surprising was the food and beverage manager, a guy named Barry Cregan. Contrary to Dougall's perception of him, I found him, not only to be an exceptionally talented person in the area of food and beverage management, but a non-stop workaholic who loved digging into details. This was a guy I had to salvage.

Likewise, the hotel manager, George Fetter was a well known hotelier who had been around Atlantic City for many years, dating back in its heyday and he certainly knew the hotel business. He also had political connections in town and his brother was the general manager at the prestigious Seaview Hotel and Country Club. Fetter did not have the intestinal drive that Cregan possessed, but in my opinion he ran a generally smooth rooms operation, that after my diligence only needed to be tightened up a little bit....and occupancy had to be increased through more aggressive over-booking, which Fetter had resisted before my arrival on the scene.

Even though these two guys satisfied my needs, I knew they were still perceived by Dougall as managers that needed to be replaced. I felt replacing them was the wrong move and would be doing the Claridge, Dougall and me a disservice. Then it struck me. Duberson was the key. Dougall respected his judgment and would listen to George more than me during my first few weeks in office. After all, Dougall barely knew me.

I rounded the three of them up for dinner, Duberson, Fetter and Cregan. All three of them were somewhat reluctant to open up to me, but they bonded together in a form of self-defense. As the evening wore on, and wine flowed, we all began to talk about the business and how we could work better as a team to make the experience for our customers more enjoyable and provide a better place for our employees to work. Duberson left dinner with a newfound respect for Fetter and Cregan, and especially for Cregan, who soon became a special close lifelong friend of George's. During the next two weeks, I persuaded Dougall to leave these two guys in place, and we embarked on a mission that improved quality, efficiency and pushed hotel occupancy to the highest level of any Atlantic City Casino.

In the spring of 1984, my lease was up on my rental property on the ocean. Time had gone by so fast and I was enjoying my work so much that I totally forgot about my initial plans to return to Las Vegas as soon as employment conditions improved for me. The boss had given me a big raise and turned over the entertainment department for me to manage along with the hotel operations.

I decided I would postpone my plans to return to Las Vegas and continue for a bit longer in Atlantic City. I rented a different home on the bayside in Margate this time and finally moved all my belongings from Las Vegas to New Jersey, and began to think of the East Coast as my permanent home for the first time. I was really into my job and I was especially enjoying being part of producing Broadway-style shows for the Claridge Palace theater crowds, and my personal time off spent in New York City and Philadelphia couldn't be better. I had become good friends with all my department heads, especially Duberson and Cregan. Dougall's secretary, Ione, and her husband, Gordon (who headed up our transportation and parking department), had become very close to my wife and me. I also had formed wonderful relationships with the vice president of human resources, Peter Tiano, the casino administrator, Paul Burst, and the head of public relations, Glenn Lillie. We all worked hard together and we played equally hard together.

Then in June 1985, Dougall called me into his office one morning and told me he had just resigned. Just like that. He decided he did not want to put up with the New Jersey gaming regulations and Atlantic City politics any longer, and he was going to head back to Nevada. The announcement was a major blow to all of the management and staff at the Claridge, who had all come to love and respect Dougall, who was regarded as a very paternal boss. A change in top management was worrisome to all, because it almost always meant major changes in department heads, as well. As I said earlier, the new broom always sweeps clean, especially in casino operations when there is a change in top bosses. In my mind, after meeting with Dougall, I just knew that all the great relationships and friendships of the last two years were soon to be in jeopardy.

That afternoon, Dougall called me to his office again, and this time he told me that he had recommended to the Del Webb Chairman in Phoenix, that he should promote me into the position of president. I was dumbfounded. I was 37 years old and not sure I was ready to be president. I told Dougall this and he assured me I was. Then he told me that if I was offered the job and refused it, the company would probably promote the CFO into the position. If that happened, I probably would be out of work anyway, so why not take a shot at the new job.

The next day, James O'Brien, the head of gaming operations for Del Webb Corporation from Phoenix showed up in my office and presented the opportunity to me. On June 15, 1985, I became president and general manager of the Claridge.

SERVING AS PRESIDENT of the Claridge was certainly a very enjoyable part of my career. Looking back, it seems that, often, the time in our lives in which we believe we were the most vibrant, productive and mature was around the age of forty. I was at the Claridge when I hit forty. It was at this age that I learned to work better with regulators, politicians, bankers and unions. It was in this position that I met some of the most memorable people in my lifetime. It was at this age that I got myself into some legal troubles. But it was in this position that I matured as an executive.

Like the Edgewater in Laughlin where I had previously worked, the Claridge was physically impaired as well as being financially handicapped. Soon after the Claridge opened with Del Webb Corporation and D'Adario as partners, Webb sought to buy D'Adario out and did so through a unique financing scheme that was popular on Wall Street at the time. The Claridge was then financed as a tax shelter under some strange tax laws in the early 1980s that provided tax benefits for big losses in the partnership structure which had been created by the Wall Street boys. The Claridge had been financed in a way that leveraged the tax codes at the time and benefited the investors through the losses. However, a year later, the tax laws changed and the investment for the 405 limited partners became a liability to most of the investors. Unfortunately, while the official name of our casino was Del Webb's Claridge Casino Hotel, the financial media usually reported us as the "financially beleaguered Claridge Casino Hotel."

Because of our financial situation, we were not able to expand or compete effectively with the bigger premium facilities in town. However, shortly after my appointment as president, we enjoyed a few months of very good results. We were able to convince the home office in Phoenix that it would be possible to expand the Claridge gaming floor by over 12,000 square feet, if we could secure the air rights from the city over Park Place, the street that separated our main casino building from our parking garage.

In July, 1986 we opened our new expansion to the public, and while we still had the smallest casino in Atlantic City, we now had the horsepower to take advantage of the peak business cycles that, with our smaller floor, we were heretofore constrained. The new expansion afforded us with a new steak house and entertainment lounge to augment our already wonderful coffee shop, gourmet room and buffet.

The expansion was a mere twenty million dollar project but the "hoopla" and publicity around its grand opening made it feel like we were opening the casino for the first time. Glenn Lillie, our talented public relations executive had dozens of celebrities and entertainers present along with the press to cut the ribbon in the vestibule that connected the new expansion with the original building. As the ribbon was cut, the giant wrestler known as KING KONG BUNDY threw out a set of giant dice onto the new casino floor and the new casino games opened with much fanfare and media coverage.

The Celebrity Cabaret lounge became the talk of the town and headliner lounge personalities that frequented our competitor casinos in town were clamoring to play the new venue. Celebrity entertainers including Billie Daniels, Buddy Greco, Pat Cooper, Sal Richards, Jackie Leonard, The Platters, Drifters and Coasters all frequented the stage of the intimate new room during the next five years.

We engaged Jack Avrett and his New York advertising firm to develop a new campaign for the Claridge that would distinguish us a safe and comfortable place to gamble. In the new campaign we promoted our new casino with a cartoon character that was based on the persona of a unique character, Eddie Lawrence who was famous for his many comical routines about the "Old Philosopher". "Hi Ya, Bunky!" became a common phrase among the employees at the Claridge as we all mimicked the contents of over 145 distinctly different radio ads that were narrated by Eddie Lawrence to promote the Claridge. Bunky was depicted as a cartoon character that looked like Einstein, and the character adorned newspaper ads, billboards and magazines all over the east coast. Bunky was the Claridge mascot (similar to the Philly Phanatic) and it was commonplace to see him walking the floor of the casino or out on the boardwalk. Bunky was used as a good will ambassador for Atlantic City, and he was even on the cover of a magazine with two other key Claridge sports representatives, Mickey Mantle and Sparky Lyle.

Bunky also came to my rescue with a small hamburger shop we operated at the Claridge. We had previously named the place 'Wally's Burgers'. In designing the logo for Wally's, we inverted the McDonald's Arches and used the upside down "M" for "W"allys. It sounded like a good idea until a member of McDonald Corporation's board of directors visited the Claridge one day and noticed our use of the Arches in Wally's name. We received a cease and desist order and worked out an agreement with McDonald's to change the name and eliminate the use of the McDonald's golden arches. Eddie Lawrence agreed to let us use the name "Bunky's" and we converted the burger joint to the new name. Out of spite for the big corporation, though, I had our graphic artist design a plastic toothpick to stick in all the hamburgers. The Toothpick was topped with a "B" for Bunky, but the two loops in the "B" were created out of the McDonald arches. McDonald's never caught on to that one.

We always enjoyed pushing the envelope when it came to trademark infringement. Right after we developed the industry's first electronically read player rating card which we aptly named "Comp Card," our initial print advertisements and outdoor billboards all had the message, "COMP CARD, Don't come to Atlantic City without it!" If you are old enough to remember, back in 1986 American Express was using the trademarked slogan, "Don't Leave Home Without it." Within a week, lawyers for American Express contacted our attorney and demanded we discontinue the ads. We argued with them and they gave us two weeks to comply with their demand. We never told them, but our kick off campaign was ending anyway. We just wanted to see how far we could push them. These big companies all spend big bucks to protect their trademarks, as they should, but it was always great fun to see how far we could push.

1986 was a great year and we all felt good about the progress we had made, that is, until the New Year dawned. 1987 was not as much fun.

Our new expansion met expectations until the Showboat Casino opened its doors in the spring of 1987, and we began to experience a downturn in business. Then, in June, 1987 we were served with two petitions from the local Teamsters Union and the Local Electrical Workers Union, each representing the claim that they should be the bargaining agent for the Claridge table games dealers. Up until this time, no union had ever successfully organized table games dealers in any casino in the country. While I had good relationships with all the unions that represented Claridge Hotel employees, I did not intend to have the Claridge be the first casino in the USA to have unionized dealers--- not on my watch. The focus of management went from trying to market the property to trying to win an election to remain non-union.

My team of dedicated executives moved into the hotel and conducted meetings, hundreds of them. Around the clock we talked with dealers both one-on-one and in small group meeting in an effort to educate them to see the benefits of not seeking a third party representative to speak for them. After a grueling campaign and a bitter exchange of words between supporters on both sides of the issue, we prevailed in the election with almost 70% of the dealers siding with management. We did not take the win for granted. We recognized that we had issues to deal with or there would never have been an action by the union organizers in the first place. Following the election, we made several key management changes in the casino and improved overall benefits for all non-union employees. We went out of our way to bring the dissenters back into the fold and employee relations became much better than before the union campaign started. In the end after the battle scars healed, I believe most of the dealers would agree.

In 1988, Del Webb announced they were getting out of the casino and leisure business and would concentrate their future business activities around their core retirement community development division. They sold their Park Service resorts to ARA of Philadelphia and contributed their ownership shares in the Claridge and their Lake Tahoe property back to their limited partner groups. They sold the Mint Casino in Las Vegas to Binion's Horseshoe and their Nevada Club in Laughlin to Steve Wynn's Golden Nugget Corporation.

As part of the divestiture in the Claridge, Del Webb Corporation was required to provide the remaining entity with some banking guarantees as we headed out on our own. The remaining operating company was actually a small group of privately placed shareholders, most, though not all of whom, were also the limited partners. The surviving Claridge Company received the blessings of the new Jersey Casino Control Commission, and the new board of directors named Shannon Bybee as chairman and CEO. I remained on as president and general manager and our primary focus was on paying down debt.

At the same time, we brought on a new chief marketing officer who had recently headed marketing at Caesars Palace in Las Vegas. Robert Renneisen had prior experience in Atlantic City at the Tropicana before heading west to Caesars and he had a very good grasp regarding what made the east coast customer tick. Along with our New York advertising agency, Bob developed and implemented a very successful marketing campaign for the Claridge around the theme "Smaller is Friendlier." Promoting the Claridge with The Old Philosopher and "Bunky" had been a successful campaign, but unfortunately the campaign identified the Claridge as a place for lower-end clientele. Bob Renneisen felt we could upgrade the image of the Claridge by appealing to the creature comforts of people who desired smaller, less noisy and more intimate surroundings.

With the opening of the Trump Taj Mahal Casino Hotel just a few months away, the competition was only going to get fiercer as the customer-pie was divided into more pieces. The massive Taj Mahal gave the Claridge the opportunity to demonstrate truly how much smaller and intimate it was compared to the big places in Atlantic City. The ad campaign was very effective from the first day it hit the air waves and print media. Glenn Lillie, the Claridge PR executive, was a master at pulling in free articles and much commentary regarding the new image of the Claridge. Customers began equating "small" with *FRIENDLY* and conversely "large" with *unfriendly*. The campaign was equally successful with the employees of the Claridge. They actually began to believe that they were friendlier than the employees in the larger casinos, and when they believed it they actually delivered better service.

When the Taj Mahal opened in 1990, the only Casino that did not lose market share was the Claridge. It had successfully carved out a niche of the market that actually preferred the diminutive property with its seven gaming levels, because of itself and not in spite of itself. In fact, 1990 was the most successful year in the Claridge history. We achieved our highest annual cash flow and paid our first mortgage debt down to a very manageable $20, 000,000 balance. The success of the Claridge in 1990 created the segue for the next phase of my career which I will cover in the next section of this book, but for now, more on my experiences at the Claridge.

As I said, I was fortunate to build some great friendships among the many fine people I worked with at the Claridge and in Atlantic City. It was also during my tenure at the Claridge that I encountered some of the most memorable people of my career. Some of these people were nice ....and some were not so nice. It is only appropriate that I identify some of these interesting people who were very unique characters in my world at that time, nice or not.

CHAPTER **5**

THE MOST FAMOUS of these people was Mickey Mantle. As I was growing up in North Dakota as a kid back in the fifties, Mantle was my idol, along with Roger Maris, who reigned from Fargo. I was a Yankee fan through and through. I couldn't play baseball very well myself, but at age ten, I owned a Mickey Mantle autographed Wilson glove and a Mickey Mantle engraved Louisville Slugger. I admired Mantle all my life and, even after I moved to Nevada, I followed his life after baseball and I even paid to watch Mantle hit golf balls in a long driver contest at the Paradise Valley Country Club outside of Las Vegas back in 1979.

I remember during my first job interview with Dougall that he had briefly mentioned that Mickey Mantle was a personal friend of his and that Mantle was doing some promotional work for the Claridge. Dougall had previously worked for Del Webb and he knew Mantle from the days that Webb had been the owner of the New York Yankees. Prior to moving to New Jersey, I had read that Mantle and Willie Mays had both been exiled from baseball by then-Commissioner Bowie Kuhn because they had taken on promotional relationships with two different Atlantic City Casinos. However, I had no idea of the scope of Mantle's arrangement for services with the Claridge. You can imagine how excited I was when I learned that Mickey Mantle was the director of sports promotions for the Claridge and he actually had a written contract to provide 120 days of appearances annually for the company. I could hardly wait to meet him.

That day came three weeks after I started work. In late September, Dougall had arranged for a promotional "roast" of Mantle during a party for high rollers that was held in the Claridge Palace Theater. Tom Dreisen and Frankie Avalon narrated the roast, and Mickey's fellow roasters included Bob Feller, Cletis Boyer, Ernie Banks, Whitey Ford and (now, the late) Roger Maris. After the event concluded, Dougall took my wife and me backstage to meet Mickey and the other celebrities. Mantle and Maris signed a baseball for my wife, and I remember her refusing to let Frankie Avalon sign the ball, telling him it would destroy the value. The event turned out to be one of the last times Mantle and Maris appeared together before Roger's death from cancer in 1985 at age 51. I don't know what the value of that baseball with the "M&M Boys" autographs on it might fetch today, but all I know is when my wife and I divorced in 1993, before she grabbed the cash and her jewelry, she grabbed that baseball and locked it in her safe deposit box.

Because Mickey was obligated to appear on our behalf for 120 days a year, Mickey and his wife Merlyn were frequently seen around the Claridge by the customers, locals and the employees. Mickey participated in charity softball games and often visited local hospitals to look in on sick kids. He was the consummate ambassador for the company… that is, when he was sober.

Much has been written about Mickey's booze problem. It never seemed to amaze me how much vodka Mickey could consume and still hit a golf ball straight. Unfortunately, with a snoot full of booze, Mickey could not keep his personal conduct so straight and he was known to get downright raunchy and disrespectful when he had too much to drink. Nonetheless, the press loved Mantle and they often overlooked his poor conduct and only focused on his accomplishments. However, the more he drank as he became older, the harder it was for us to shield his negative antics from the public.

Shortly after I joined the Claridge, we also signed on a retiring Cy

Young award winning relief pitcher named Sparky Lyle to work with Mantle, assisting him in promoting the Claridge to gamblers. We also hoped that Sparky could help us harness some of Mantle's behavior and help limit his drinking during working hours. Mickey and Sparky worked well together although Mickey always referred to Lyle as his gopher. They were a "one-two punch" with high rollers and we had a constant demand for their appearance at charity events throughout the Tri-state region that served as our primary customer feeder market.

Mickey and Billie Martin were lifelong friends and Martin was frequently seen at the Claridge hanging out in the bar with "The Mick." One Saturday evening, Mickey, Billy and Sparky were huddled in the London Pavilion Bar around closing time when Glenn Lillie and I were leaving the restaurant. They invited us to join them and we sat around mesmerized by the many stories they recounted. We locked the restaurant but kept the bartender on for Mickey's sake. About 2:00 a.m., Mickey excused himself to visit the restroom. As Mickey departed to attend to nature's call, Billy started telling some tall tales. The time went by so fast that we forgot all about Mickey. Suddenly a casino porter came in and pulled me aside. He said it looked like Mr. Mantle had passed out on the stairway leading from the restroom to the bar. Billy adjourned the meeting and Sparky helped Glenn and I usher Mantle to his suite and into bed.

On another occasion we took Mantle down to Baltimore to help us host a Casino Charity party at the Pimlico Racetrack for a popular annual Baltimore area event called "Save A Heart." The chairman of the event was a big gambler at the Claridge Casino and many of his friends at this event were potential new customers. The trip from Atlantic City to Baltimore was made in a Super Bus with Mantle and about fifteen other casino hosts and executives. Of course the bus was fully catered with an array of food and liquor and a great looking waitress to serve us all. Before we hit the Delaware Memorial Bridge, Mantle was toasted. We checked into the hotel at noon and put Mantle to bed hoping he would get a good afternoon's rest and be ready to greet the thousand or so guests at the special event scheduled that evening. About 2:00 p.m.,

I had arranged to meet a good customer in the hotel lounge. When I walked in, there was Mickey holding court with a half dozen beautiful young ladies. Unfortunately the noisy commotion of holding court was not appreciated by the Bar Mitzvah celebrants in another section of the lounge, but Mickey didn't really care. "What's the little prick doing in a cocktail lounge, anyway?" he asked.

Eventually we were able to get Mickey to leave and prepare for the party. The party was a huge success and the charity casino raised several hundred thousand dollars. Mickey was well behaved that evening---that is, until we headed in for a special dinner party with fifty of the most prominent people associated with the charity. Among these dignitaries was Brooks Robinson, and everybody knows that Robinson was revered by Baltimore fans in the same way that Mantle was held in esteem by New York fans.

Mantle and Robinson were friends, but that did not stop Mickey from being determined to steal Robinson's toupee. The Mick was standing in the reception line at Pimlico Racetrack next to our PR man, Glenn Lillie. Mantle was bobbing and weaving as he spotted Brooks Robinson surrounded by a gaggle of fans all gathered around. Mickey drawls to Lillie. "Hey Glann, here comes that asshole Brooksie. I'm gonna knock that shitty lookin wig off his haid." Glenn quickly replied to him, "Mick, we are in F-----g Baltimore. That would be like tugging on Superman's cape and Superman will not be amused. Mick retorted, I don't give a shit, Fug 'em! Then it got interesting. Brooks spotted Mickey and saw him with that familiar drunken countenance and anticipated what prank Mickey might attempt to perform. Robinson, in his wisdom, knew the best way to calm the situation down. He walked up to Mickey and asked, "Hey Mick, how are your boys doing?" Mick always felt much love…and guilt about his sons, so that kind of question always sobered him up. Mantle then abandoned his plan to snatch the Baltimore star's wig and instead calmly replied to Robinson's question with, "Oh, they are alright Brooksie. How are your guys?"

But then Mickey sat down at our banquet table and immediately placed his hand on the derriere of the daughter of one of the Baltimore dignitaries. Mantle did indeed grab quite a nice handful and I thought all hell would break out. The young lady turned around just about ready to slap the Mick when she caught herself. Through gritted teeth she said, "Mr. Mantle! If it were any other man than you I would have smashed you, but I know that my father and grandfather would kill me if they ever heard that I had punched Mickey Mantle," Everyone seemed to laugh it off, including the young lady. I don't know, but maybe she was a closet Yankee fan.

Another time that Mickey almost embarrassed me occurred when a big player from New Brunswick, New Jersey asked me to set up a room reservation for his company's travel manager, a pretty young lady named Kathy. I won't use her last name because that would definitely embarrass her. It was a Saturday afternoon and I was in my office at the Claridge catching up on some paperwork, when Kathy called me and invited me to meet her in person and have a drink with her. We agreed to meet in the Bombay lounge on the third floor of the tower. The Bombay Lounge was a quiet and very remote piano bar that was ideal for conversations and business meetings. I met Kathy at the entry of the lounge and escorted her to a booth across from the bar. The lounge was dimly lit and there was only one other person besides the bartender in the room and he was sitting silently at the bar. As I sat down with Kathy in the booth, the fellow at the bar turned around and stated, "Does your wife know you are screwing around with a beautiful woman?" It was Mickey Mantle. I laughed his comment off and invited Mickey to join us. When I introduced the Mick to Kathy, she was infatuated. She pointed out that she was a diehard Yankee fan and her father had idolized Mickey Mantle all his life. Kathy exclaimed that Mickey was all her Dad ever talked about when she was a kid. She told us she could hardly wait to get back to New Brunswick to tell him she met Mickey in person. Mickey said, "I'll do even better than that. I'll autograph some baseball cards and balls for you and you can take them back to your father." Kathy was ecstatic.

Mickey produced a handful of special Claridge logoed baseball cards that had his portrait on the front and his lifetime statistics imprinted on the back. Mantle autographed and personalized the baseball card for Kathy's father and did the same with a brand new baseball as well. Then he specially personalized and autographed another baseball just for Kathy, herself. As he handed her the ball, he grabbed her naked thigh with his right hand. Startled, she jumped just as she read the inscription Mickey had penned on the ball…. *"Dear Kathy. I would like to F..k you very much! Mickey Mantle"*… I was very embarrassed but Kathy laughed it off. In fact, I talked to Kathy recently and she still has the infamous ball. She won't give it up for anything.

On the New Year's holiday in 1985, we decided to offer a complimentary coffee station and a free breathalyzer test for people departing the Claridge Casino following our New Year's party celebration. Glenn Lillie decided to get us some advance publicity and invited the press to come in and observe a staged use of the breathalyzer with Mantle in the picture. The press showed up in the early morning of December 30 to take their picture of Mickey blowing into the breathalyzer. We were promised the picture would be on the front page of the Atlantic City Press on the December 31 morning edition. Mickey came down from his suite and blew into the device registering a .13 that early in the morning. At least we knew the breathalyzer was working fine.

For one of our more prestigious special events, the Claridge hosted an old timer's celebrity golf tournament with some of our best gamblers. We invited seventeen of the well known baseball players of Mickey's era to join him and Sparky Lyle for a two day best-ball golf tournament. Some of these famous ball players of the fifties and sixties included Moose Skowron, Gil McDougald, Lew Burdette and Whitey Ford. The eighteen baseball legends including Sparky Lyle were grouped with three casino guests, making up eighteen foursomes each day. Mickey Mantle was designated to tee off with every foursome on the short par three tenth hole. This enabled each foursome to have a photograph taken with Mickey and their respective team, and they also could use Mickey's drive for their team effort, if it was the best shot.

The problem with our format at this tournament turned out to be the location of our hospitality tent. We had located it adjoining the tenth tee. With ten to fifteen minutes or so lapsing between each foursome arriving to tee off with Mantle, Mickey had just enough time to grab another vodka tonic. Seventeen foursomes later Mickey had knocked off close to a fifth of Vodka. The amazing thing was he was still hitting the ball straight. In fact, he was always within fifteen feet of the hole on every drive and over half of the foursomes in the tournament used Mickey's drive as the best ball, even the last one in which he matched his eighteenth drive with his eighteenth shot, of vodka that is. As I said earlier, Mickey could hit a ball straight no matter what he had to drink. The problem with this particular high roller event occurred at the end of the tournament when the television cameras showed up.

Glenn Lillie was being interviewed on camera talking about all the baseball celebrities that had attended. Glenn, being an old radio announcer himself, was the consummate PR guy for the Claridge and he knew his baseball statistics better than the sports writers themselves. Glenn's goal was to keep Mickey away from the microphone and he was doing a pretty good job of it. Then the assistant PR lady stuck her nose in the process. She decided to line up a photo shot with Mickey hitting a baseball with his pitching wedge. The television camera operator happened to be good looking young woman. With her camera lens aimed at the face of the golf club with the baseball in front of it, she zoomed in for a real close picture. As she did, Mickey hit the ball with the pitching wedge in a nice arc that shot right between the camera girl's outstretched thighs. It was a great shot, but just one inch higher and it would have been a hole in one. Again the press was kind to Mickey. No mention of his cheap shot and nothing but a great article with a nice shot of Mickey's pitching wedge just nudging the baseball on the grass.

The coup de grace involved Mickey Mantle's reinstatement back into baseball. Bowie Kuhn had ousted Mickey and Willie Mays, both of whom became casino hosts for Atlantic City Casinos in 1983. When Peter Ueberroth became baseball commissioner, he immediately arranged to reinstate both of these superstars back into baseball. It was decided by the commissioner that he would announce the reinstatement at a special press conference in the Waldorf Astoria Hotel on the afternoon of March 18, 1985, where Mickey and Willie would meet the sports writers. Several members of our marketing team went to New York City on Sunday evening to meet Mickey for dinner and to be there to support him at the press conference the following day. The Claridge had a New York City field office in the Lexington Hotel, located cater-corner across the street from the Waldorf, so we made arrangements to stay there with Mickey. When we arrived in New York City, we were notified by the desk clerk that Mickey had missed his plane in Dallas and would not arrive until eleven o'clock that evening. We had dinner and waited as long as we could but getting tired, we retired to our rooms before Mickey landed.

Mickey came looking for us and then headed to the bar in our hotel lobby. Being after 11:00 p.m. on a Sunday evening, the bar had already closed. That did not deter Mickey. He knew the Big Apple better than most and he knew the *Bull and Bear Lounge* at the Waldorf Astoria was still open. Apparently after quite a few drinks he met some girl at the Waldorf that wanted to see Mickey's World Series Ring. Mickey told her he had left it on the night stand in his hotel room but if she had the courage, she was invited to go across the street with him to his hotel room to view it. She accepted his invitation and away they went.

As Mickey sheepishly told us the next morning at breakfast, while the girl admired his championship ring, he went into the bathroom to relieve himself and get into something more comfortable. As he slipped out of his clothes and was standing in the bathroom with nothing on at all, he heard the hotel room door open up. Peering out the bathroom door, he saw that the young girl was departing along with Mickey's World Series Ring and a couple thousand dollars in cash. He raced out the door and chased her down the hallway where he watched her race down the fire stairway. Not able to keep up with her, he headed back to his room only to find his hotel room door locked and there he is standing in the nude. Mickey called the front desk and told them he had stepped out of his room to look for a newspaper and the door closed behind on him. The clerk sent a security guard to his room and let him in. As Mickey is telling us this story, he has a great big smile on his face and he is actually amused. We admonish him to keep the story quiet. We tell him that if the press picks up on the story, Ueberroth may change his mind. Mickey agrees. For the rest of the day, we stayed very close to Mickey and we were pleased that he was taking the press conference very seriously. We had lunch in the Waldorf and Mickey drank iced tea with his meal. When we arrived at the press conference, Mickey was totally sober and was the charming shy guy everybody remembered from his early Yankee days in New York.

As Ueberroth sat in the middle seat on the dais, Mantle joined him on one side and Willie Mays sat on the opposite side. As the technicians were adjusting the microphones and cameras, Mickey blurts out to Ueberroth, "Hey Peter, you'll never guess what happened to me last night." Yep! He told the commissioner the whole story. Laughing like hell, the commissioner reinstated Willie and Mickey back into baseball nonetheless.

Mickey was very tough on his wife, Merlyn. She was not happy that Mickey was working for a casino and she allegedly blamed the Claridge for much of Mickey's bad behavior. In fact, Mickey's employment contract with the Claridge was a lifeline for him. Unlike in today's professional baseball, salaries and endorsements were nothing back then. When Mantle retired from the Major Leagues, he was making less in salary than his first year employment contract at the Claridge. He had never saved much money during his career. Mickey always thought he would die young like his father did, but now he was worried he would outlive his savings, He wanted to live well in his retired years. The controversy over his disbarment from Major

League baseball kept his name in the press for years. His eventual reinstatement led to the opening of a New York restaurant in his name and a new income stream from baseball memorabilia and autograph signing shows that became popular in the late eighties and early nineties. That being said, Merlyn still was unhappy with his arrangement at the Claridge. Merlyn knew that Mickey had a roving eye so she traveled often to the Claridge with him because she wanted to keep her own eye on him. The two of them argued frequently while staying in their Claridge Hotel suite. On one occasion, Mickey shoved Merlyn out the door of their suite while she was attired in only a skimpy negligee. Then Mickey called the security office and reported that a hooker was trying to get into his suite.

Mickey only had two real jobs in his entire life: "Number 7" with the New York Yankees and director of sporting events for the Claridge Casino. Mickey Mantle had never been fired in his life. But finally, in the fall of 1977 after an event in the Claridge elevator in which he inappropriately touched a female guest, this writer had the unpleasant distinction of giving my childhood idol and good friend his first and only pink slip.

After Mickey departed, Sparky Lyle took over the reins of the Claridge Casino sporting events department. Sparky frequently invited old Yankee and Philly player friends into the Claridge and before he decided to go back into baseball as a minor league manager, we aptly named a new bar we built, "Sparky's Dugout."

Sparky introduced me to Tim Kerr, the hockey great who played for some time on the Philadelphia Flyers. On several occasions when running around Wildwood bars with Kerr, I had the pleasure of impersonating Bernie Parent, the famous Flyer's goalie. I was told that I resembled Bernie Parent, and whenever I was seen with Kerr, it was assumed I was Parent. It was fun but it was annoying. Tim would just tell me to sign my name "Bernie" when asked for an autograph, and the people would eventually go away. After those occasions, I have more empathy for celebrities who become annoyed and frustrated by overzealous fans and the paparazzi.

The best way to see the Yankee stars was in person at Yankee Stadium. Glenn Lillie had become close friends with Stanley Kay, a well regarded entertainment creator and producer. Kay was best known for managing Maurice Hines and other great artisits of the time. Kay was a musician himself, and he produced several Atlantic City shows. Glenn Lillie met him in Atlantic City and forged a wonderful friendship with Kay. Stanley's claim to fame from my standpoint was his close association with George Steinbrenner. Steinbrenner had made him the entertainment director for the New York Yankees and he held that position until Stanley died in 2010. With Glenn's love of baseball and my infatuation with the Yankees, Stanley Kay became our hero. Kay arranged for us to frequently watch the Yankee ballgames from George Steinbrenner's sky box and we always dined either in the clubhouse restaurant or with the players and their families, all compliments of the New York Yankees. Meeting Steinbrenner personally and having my picture taken in Steinbrenner's office on the big love seat shaped like a baseball glove was almost as exciting as meeting Mickey Mantle for the first time, and Stanley Kay made it all possible.

SEVERAL MONTHS AFTER I joined the Claridge, Bill Dougall added the entertainment department to my list of responsibilities. The Claridge had a very intimate 600-seat theater that was a favorite of celebrities who liked to be right up close and personal with their audience. There was not a bad seat in the house, which was known as the Palace Theater. The first show I watched in the Palace Theater was the Lennon Sisters. They were engaged for $50,000 for the weekend. Their opening act was a young comedian named Billy Crystal. I think the Claridge paid him $7500. Imagine what Crystal would cost today?

Except for Billy Crystal, who was an exception, most of the acts the Claridge had been booking were not competitive with the larger casinos in Atlantic City. While the Claridge could not afford to attract the stars of those times like Frank Sinatra, Lionel Ritchie or Linda Ronstadt, I knew we could identify acts that were still within the Claridge budget---stars that would still have excellent name appeal and be worthy of our premium customers. During the seven years I had the opportunity to book the headliner acts at the Claridge, I was very proud of the diversity of acts we were able to attract. Best yet, we were able to achieve near capacity occupancy for each and every show we featured, of course with a flop here and there.

Atlantic City casinos created a renaissance for star entertainers. In the 1970s, Las Vegas casinos began moving from star entertainers

toward production shows, where consistent costs and show room occupancies could be achieved better than with an expensive headliner
act. The new entertainment concept put a damper on the stars that
were used to playing the Las Vegas night club circuit for big bucks.
Then Atlantic City casino hotels opened with big showrooms.

The William Morris Agency in New York City headed up by Lee
Salomon represented the major talent, and Salomon peddled the best
and most costly stars to the biggest gaming companies which included
Resorts International and Golden Nugget at the top. Salomon sent his
second in command, a wonderful guy named Marty Klein, to represent
the lesser stars that might be booked at the smaller joints, such as the
Claridge. Unfortunately, Marty Klein was seldom able to pitch any of the
best acts in the William Morris stable to play in the Claridge show room.
As I took over the reins of the entertainment department, I decided that I
would look for talent agencies that might appreciate the business of the
lowly Claridge more than Salomon did at the Morris Agency.

Ed Micone, a sharp young man from New York City who later
became director at Radio City, showed up on our door step from the
ICM agency and brought us an interesting array of new talent opportunities. Likewise, D.J. McLaughlin from the APA agency in Nashville
set us up with a bunch of upstart country acts that were just becoming the rage in the mid-eighties. Our reliance on second level star
acts from the William Morris Agency was over. We kicked off the
country music program with the likes of Waylon Jennings and Ronnie
Milsap. TG Sheppard opened for Johnny Cash, and then we booked
the most expensive act the Claridge had ever landed, Anne Murray.
The entertainers who played the Palace Theater were so well treated
by the Claridge entertainment and PR staff that the word went out to
the headliners in the business. We were regarded as a classy place
to work, even if we were not the biggest and best known casino in
Atlantic City. We finally landed Barbara Mandrel, which would have
been the biggest act to ever play the Claridge. Unfortunately, Mandrel
was involved in a serious automobile accident just a month before
her engagement, and she never returned to the night club circuit.

Other noteworthy acts we booked included Laura Brannigan, known for her rendition of "Gloria", and Philadelphia jazz great, Herbie Hancock, to name just two. My dear friend, Al Martino known for his role as Johnny Fontaine in the movie, "The Godfather" became a frequent showroom act and also did a stint or two cooking his fine Italian food for some of our better players. When the Claridge renovated its gourmet room in 1988, we re-themed it to upscale Italian cuisine and renamed the restaurant, "Martino's."

While the new live entertainment policy proved to be popular with our higher end guests, the showroom was only used on weekends. The star performers were way too expensive to engage for more than one or two performances on weekends only. As I mentioned earlier, the Claridge was on the cusp of developing the gaming industry's first electronically read player rating card, aptly know as "Comp Card," and this new technology enabled us to understand more about our huge database of customers than ever before. With several hundred thousand active customers in our list of customers, we needed more than hotel rooms and restaurant offerings to entice our customers into the Claridge. Our research told us that many of our regular customers enjoyed live star entertainment, but because so many of them only visited Atlantic City Casinos during the middle of the week, they seldom had an opportunity to enjoy a show with a star entertainer. Several of the other casinos in town had experimented with variety shows and lounge-type burlesque shows, but almost all of these were considered low budget after-thoughts by casino customers.

Then one day, I had an opportunity to meet Maynard Sloate. This character was an old Las Vegas professional musician who had played the drums in the band at the Tropicana for years. Maynard loved Broadway musicals, and in his last fifteen years he had produced tab-musicals for the Union Plaza Hotel in downtown Las Vegas. A tab musical is a "90 minute" shortened version of a full Broadway style musical. A full scale Broadway musical generally runs longer than two hours and includes an intermission. That length of a show is just too long for a casino showroom.

The concept of this type of show for the Claridge was intriguing to me, especially if we could recruit recognized celebrity talent to star as the lead in the shows we produced. Sloate and I discussed my idea and we agreed that the concept might just work. First of all, most of our customers came from the New York or Philadelphia metropolitan areas surrounding Atlantic City, and even those who had never attended a Broadway musical knew what they were. Secondly, Maynard Sloate was in touch with many recognized entertainers who he knew would love to take a shot at a live acting role. Many of these stars were slightly over the hill as a standalone act, but still had valuable name recognized prominence when promoted as the lead in a musical. Third, Maynard knew he could purchase the rights for older Broadway musicals at very nominal prices, thus making the production of such shows very affordable. Using Actors Equity Union dancers and actors accompanied by live band members who often doubled as extras in the cast, the concept theoretically sounded like it would work and Maynard Sloate was the right guy to pull it off for me.

When we opened our first musical as a pilot, we tested our new concept with a very inexpensive musical named "I Love My Wife." We hired Joey Travolta, the brother of John Travolta, to star in the leading role. Of course Lee Salomon of the William Morris Agency and his friend, noted entertainment columnist, David Spatz publicly declared the concept as flawed, cheap and doomed for failure. I was named the "Casino Cowboy" for shooting from the hip in my new role at the Claridge. After all, how could a cowboy from Nevada understand the East Coast mentality in just a month or two in Atlantic City? Yet, Spatz was not surprised to hear that brother John Travolta flew his own jet plane into Atlantic City to have dinner with his brother, Joey, and then watch the show. John loved the show and the audience loved having John in the showroom.

The inexpensive first musical was an unqualified success. We performed two shows a night with only Monday off. For less than the cost of an opening act on a weekend, we were able to produce twelve shows. Our success led us to be a little bolder for the future productions. Our second musical had a budget of $40,000 a week, almost three times larger than the pilot. We decided to do a re-make of "Sugar," which was the Broadway version of the famous movie, "Some Like it Hot" that had starred Marilyn Monroe, Jack Lemon and Tony Curtis.

Maynard thought it would be fun to hire football great, Joe Namath to star in our production of "Sugar." Namath had just done a television commercial for a panty hose manufacturer, and it was known that he wanted to get into acting and singing following his retirement from the NFL. Namath signed on to star in the Tony Curtis role and the show was a huge success, nearly selling out every seat, and eight shows a week. Namath was a fair actor but a mediocre singer. Nonetheless, the crowds loved him and the following year, we signed Broadway Joe up again to star in "Bells are Ringing."

George Maharis, co-star of an early television series "Route 66" starred in "The Best Little Whorehouse in Texas," and by the end of the first year of tab musicals, David Spatz started to write nice things about the Claridge musical concept and the William Morris Agency started to pitch potential stars for future musicals we had planned. All in all, Maynard produced 23 musicals for me while I served as the president of the Claridge. The star power of these musicals included the likes of Elke Sommers, who starred in "Woman of the Year"; Phyllis Maguire, who headlined the Tony Award winning musical, "Applause"; Billy Daniels, who danced up a storm in "Bubbling Brown Sugar"; Theodore Bikel, who starred in "Fiddler on theRoof"; Lainie Kazan, who headed up "Hello Dolly"; Clint Holmes, who starred in "Pal Joey"; and Donald O'Conner who headlined in "How to Succeed in Business without Really Trying," just to name a few.

The Broadway Musical concept is a mainstay of many Las Vegas Casinos today. Of course with their bigger budgets and larger seating capacities, these casinos tend to purchase the newer shows, but even the newer expensive shows have been trimmed back to fit into 90 minutes. That is the length of a show that entertains a gambler but still leaves time to gamble.

THE FIRST DAY I went to work at the Claridge, Bill Dougall admonished me to steer clear of a local night club on Atlantic Avenue called Anacopa. Dougall told me that many of the members of the Philadelphia and Atlantic City organized crime family, and specifically Nicky Scarfo frequented this night club and being seen there by gaming regulators could get somebody in trouble. I understood the gravity of guilt by association and told Dougall I would heed his warning. After work that evening, Barry Cregan called me and invited me out for a drink and an opportunity to meet some of my colleagues. I accepted his invitation and met him at the front entrance of the hotel where we decided we would walk to the most popular cocktail lounge in town. Yep. You guessed it. We were all going to meet at Anacopa.

As we neared the entry of the night club, a big black limousine rolled up. I said to myself, "Man, I hope that's not one of them mobsters." Then a big guy gets out of the limo, grabs the doorman from the night club and throws him against the vehicle slapping him around a bit. This guy was really irritated over something. I said to Barry, "Who the hell might that be? Is it Nicky Scarfo or one of his gang?"

Barry looked more closely at the big guy who was slapping the doorman around, and remarked, "No, that's Arnie Fleishman. He's the president of the Playboy Casino. But don't worry; he's a close friend of mine. And no, he is not part of organized crime. Arnie is just a big Jewish guy that likes to kick ass every once and a while."

As we headed into Anacopa, heeding Dougall's advice, I stayed clear of everybody that was not associated with the Claridge. When Nicky Scarfo passed by, one of the guys pointed him out but I made certain to never personally meet him that night. Arnie Fleishman was as close to a bad guy that I wanted to meet that first evening in Atlantic City. I knew he possessed a New Jersey gaming license.

Several months later, I was introduced to Scarfo at some social event and I found him to be a very cordial person. Neither Scarfo nor any of his reputed henchmen ever made any overtures to me and I am certain they didn't even care who the hell I was. Then, years later, at the Saloon Restaurant in Philadelphia, I met Scarfo's associate, Ralph Natale. I was having dinner with Al Martino and a Philadelphia friend of mine named Joe Moderski. Obviously, Joe knew Natale and he introduced us. A couple of weeks later, I brought my girl friend and her family into the Saloon for a birthday dinner, and Natale saw us and sent over a bottle of champagne. He seemed like a genuine nice guy and I thanked him for the kind gesture and never thought any more of it. A few weeks later on December 30, 1997, I learned what Dougall had warned me about several years earlier when I joined the Claridge. Be careful of guilt by association.

I was awakened at my Smithville home by a 6:30 a.m. telephone call. It was an agent from the FBI and he said that he and his partner were anxious to talk with me. Not wishing to aggravate these two guys, I invited them to come by my home which was only five minutes from the donut shop from which they were making the phone call. They rolled up to the front of my house in a little government owned Chevy Cavalier. I let them in the house and offered them some coffee, but they declined. They had me sit down at my kitchen table and they started in on their questioning. "What is your relationship with Ralph Natale? How long have you known this guy?"

I was stunned by their questions and still wiping the sleep out of my eyes, I replied "I don't know a Ralph Natale." That is when they produced a photograph that showed me with Al Martino shaking Ralph Natale's hand at the Saloon Restaurant several weeks earlier. Then I recalled, "Oh, you mean Ralphie. I met him at a Philadelphia Restaurant several weeks ago while dining with friends, but I have no idea what he does. With his presence in the Saloon, I figured maybe he was a part owner in the restaurant."

Then they wanted to know what I was doing palling around with Joe Moderski and Al Martino? I advised the FBI agents that both Martino and Moderski were friends that I had met in the casino industry years ago, and we often dined together. I told the FBI agents that I was even planning to have dinner with Moderski the following night at the Bellevue Stratford Hotel to celebrate New Year's Eve. I then asked them if dining with Moderski would be a crime and they told me, "No, but do you want your boss or the gaming regulators to know you're hanging around with a pal of a gangster?"

I did go to dinner the following night with my friend, Joe, but I made it a point to stay out of the Saloon Restaurant from that day on. Incidentally, years later, my friend, Joe Moderski was eventually indicted for various crimes and income tax evasion. Scarfo and Natale were both gentlemen when I met them. They behaved like you would expect them to after watching the Godfather movie. They were family people and they were nice to their friends. Fortunately for me, I never had the occasion to cross any of these guys or do business with any of them. They both seemed like nice people, regardless of their rap sheets.

But there was a man I met early in my term as president of the Claridge that turned out to be a very bad guy. I mean a real bad guy. His name was Oscar Harris and a Google search on the internet will give you a real run down of his background and the terrible crimes he committed.

When I became president of the Claridge in 1985, I immediately spearheaded a project to expand the size of the Claridge casino. At that time, Oscar Harris was the director of economic development for the city of Atlantic City. When casinos were first legalized in New

Jersey, all licensed gaming operators were required to purchase at least fifteen percent of their goods and services from certified minority companies. Oscar Harris was well aware that with the opening of the first several casinos, there were very few minority owned suppliers with the types of goods and services the casinos required to operate their businesses. So he took it upon himself to fill the vacuum. With a few trusted friends, Harris created an array of services under different minority companies that he controlled so he could undertake the harnessing of as many service and product agreements for himself with the casinos as he could muster.

He had a talent service to sell the casinos live entertainment acts. He owned some billboards that he would lease for big rent charges to the casinos. His advertising agency would place media advertisements for the casinos in return for an 18 percent commission. He had a chemical distribution company to sell the casinos profitable cleaning supplies. He owned a commercial laundry capable of cleaning the hotel linens and uniforms. You name the service or products that an Atlantic City Casino might require, and Oscar Harris had a company to provide it. Furthermore, Oscar was not shy about using the *race card* and constantly reminded the casino operators of the fines we faced if we failed to meet our minority purchasing goals.

Harris had been successful in landing a very lucrative contract with the Sands Hotel to provide linen cleaning and laundry services and we heard that he was going to try and leverage his prestigious city position to land a contract with the Claridge, too.

But his biggest enterprise was Ebony Construction Company, a mid-sized general contracting service. As you would guess, the moment after we announced our planned expansion of the Claridge Casino, we were contacted by Harris asking for a meeting. In an attempt to be politically correct, I agreed to a meeting, but I also made certain that I had the Claridge General Counsel and our company construction manager present at the meeting. I also instructed my assistant, Ione to leave the door open between my office and hers so she could transcribe the contents of our conversation. I had my suspicions about this guy and I was taking no chances of being trapped alone with him. Harris had a reputation on the street of screwing anyone standing in his way, including his own mother if she was in his direct path.

As we suspected, Harris arrived with his most trusted confidant, Robert McCurdy, and immediately began his sales pitch for every service he offered, reminding us that we were required to buy from a minority business. After giving him reasons why we couldn't use his advertising services or cleaning chemical company, he pitched us on his laundry services. When I challenged his laundry pricing schedule, which was more than double what we were paying our Wildwood New Jersey Laundry service, he finally got to the primary reason for his meeting. He wanted the contract to be general contractor for the Claridge expansion project. We knew he lacked adequate insurance coverage, so when we asked him if he could arrange for a twenty million dollar bond, he called me a bigot. He accused the Claridge of not living up to its good faith requirements to hire African American employees or using enough minority services.

Getting angry about this false accusation but not wanting to show my emotions, I jokingly reminded Harris that the Claridge had just opened the Broadway Musical, "Bubbling Brown Sugar" starring Billy Daniels along with an all black cast and orchestra, so how could he call us bigoted? Harris then rudely asked me, "What do you think? That us 'N-----s' can only sing and dance?" To which I abruptly responded, "Nope, I attended auditions with the show's director in New York City, and I can tell you from watching those auditions that not all black people can sing or dance." Then I added, "I also played sports in college and have frequently been in locker rooms with a lot of African Americans. I can also attest to the fact that not all blacks have big dicks, either!" With that last exclamation on my part, the meeting was over.

As luck would have it, several weeks later I received a notice to appear before the New Jersey Grand Jury in Trenton. The Sands laundry contract had become the subject of a potential extortion investigation, and the Claridge meeting I had with Harris and McCurdy was on the prosecutor's radar. Fortunately, I had wonderful transcribed notes from the meeting and witnesses, so it was easy to testify. When I told the jury about my response to Harris asking me if I thought that African Americans could only sing and dance, all twenty three people on the jury nearly fell over laughing. The three African American jurors laughed the hardest. I never did volunteer to tell them about my locker room observations, though, and the prosecutor never asked.

Of course, my testimony at the Grand Jury prompted an investigation by the New Jersey Division of Gaming Enforcement to see if I may have violated the law by not immediately advising the division about Oscar Harris's attempt to extort the Claridge. After several hours of grilling, the investigators finally accepted my response that I never felt threatened by Harris and did not consider our meeting to be an act of extortion on his part. They finally noted that we never did any business with Harris and he never used any influence to impede the Claridge construction project. I never even considered Harris a mini-mobster, let alone a full-fledged organized gangster.

Harris was eventually convicted of stealing funds from the city of Philadelphia for a project he was working on to rebuild the houses destroyed during the MOVE confrontation in 1985. Later he and McCurdy were sentenced to fifteen years for operating a scheme to pass $17,000,000 in fake money orders to pay off mortgages and other bills. Harris and his co-conspirators were members of a separatist group that asserted the United States laws did not apply to them and they need not pay income taxes.

CHAPTER **8**

THE NEXT YEAR, I got myself in a jackpot and almost lost my gaming license. The incident I will relate in this chapter ranks as the dumbest thing I have done in my life, and demonstrated to me how one quick moment of anger can almost ruin your life and your career. If I could turn the clock back, this is the one incident in my life that I would do over.

The date was April 15, 1986: Tax Day. On top of celebrating the filing of our tax returns on schedule, the Claridge executive team was also having a party at Grabel's, a popular local gin mill of that day to celebrate the successful launching of our company's new players club. During the party, the owner of the bar turned on the television sets so we could all view the story of President Reagan sending in the F11A Fighter jets to bomb Muammar Gaddafi and Libya.

The party was still going strong at midnight, but I had an early morning flight to make in Philadelphia in order to attend a management meeting the next evening in Phoenix, so my wife and I departed for our home. Having come to the party in separate cars, I left first but could see my wife in the rear view mirror following me. Suddenly I saw blinking red lights in the mirror and realized that a police car was pulling my wife over. I circled the block and when I came back around to where my wife's car was stopped, I witnessed the police officers taking some liberties with my wife's bra and blouse. I was enraged but knew better than to confront the officers while they were arresting my wife. I watched as they shoved her into the back seat of their squad car and then followed them to the police station. While there was certainly no emergency with the arrest of my wife, the driver of the police car must have thought there was. He raced through the streets of Atlantic City with his red lights flashing while running every stop light on Atlantic Avenue. When I arrived at the police station, I observed the two officers escorting my handcuffed wife through the rear doors of the station house. I parked my car in the regular parking lot and walked into the police station through the front doors.

I encountered a female officer at the office reception window and demanded to see my wife. I told the officer that I wanted to post bail and take my wife home. The officer left the window and went back into the offices to talk with another officer. When she returned, she advised me that my wife was not in the station house and instructed me to leave the station myself or face the consequences. That is when I started to raise my voice and begin using profanity. About that time the two arresting police officers came into the lobby and demanded I leave. They told me that I could not see my wife and that she would be detained for several hours. I could hear her crying in one of the back detention rooms and that is when the 'Rambo" in me came out. I drilled one cop with my right elbow and the other one with my left as I scrambled to reach my wife.

For a supposedly smart guy, I wasn't so smart right then. I should have known that there were more than just these two police officers around. After all, this was the police station. Like flies around a manure pile, police officers came out of the woodwork from everywhere and jumped on me. I was handcuffed and carried off to a holding cell like a suitcase. Screaming for a lawyer, the cops just kept looking at me and yelling, "Sorry, casino asshole. You will get your phone call when we say so."

I screamed back demanding they get the mayor on the phone for me. Then I demanded they get my city councilman on the phone. They just looked at me and again said softly, "Sorry, casino asshole."

Finally about four in the morning, Jack Scott, the director of security of the Claridge Casino showed up to vouch for me so I could be released on summons. Jack was a retired Atlantic City cop, himself. He was obviously appalled at how the police had treated me, but I had raised so much hell with my temper and behavior, that the arresting officers who I had shoved with my elbows had no recourse than to protect their own asses as well. I had made loud and serious allegations about how they had treated my wife during the arrest and then threatened my own lawsuits against all of them. Looking back years later, I could hardly blame the two cops for the actions they took and the charges they lodged against me.

I left the police station and drove home. Now I had the painful and embarrassing task of calling my boss in Phoenix to tell him what had transpired. They probably should have fired me on the spot; but, for whatever reason, the Del Webb Corporate executives all stood behind me. In fact, the chairman of the board helped me arrange legal counsel and by nine o'clock in the morning, I was sitting in the law offices of Joseph Fusco, the former Atlantic County prosecutor discussing my avenues for defense. I was anxious to bring counter charges against the police officers and was even thinking of bringing a law suit against the city for brutality against my wife. Telephone calls were coming in from people in the neighborhood near Grabel's Lounge who were willing to testify that they saw the police officers mistreat my wife during her arrest.

In the meantime, the early morning edition of the Atlantic City Press hit the pavement and the radio and television stations started blaring the story of my arrest. The leading story on early morning television and radio boldly announced "Claridge President Assaults Police Officers" with the secondary story declaring, "Reagan Bombs Libya." The small town press corps found my arrest more important than National Defense.

Then I received the bad news from my lawyer. Assaulting a police officer in New Jersey is an indictable offense. In New Jersey, anyone under indictment, regardless of innocence or guilt, is prohibited from holding a gaming license. If the charges held up and I was indicted, I would lose my gaming license and be suspended from my position at the Claridge Casino. This was a game changer. I quickly realized I had to alter my aggressive stance and start working on a plea deal. Finally in the end, the two police officers agreed with the county prosecutor to reduce my charges to three misdemeanor disorderly-persons counts, and I agreed to plead guilty. The two counts of simple assault against the police officers were understandable, but the third count of obstruction of justice was puzzling to me. Just because I called out for the mayor and my city councilman while in the heat of anger did not seem to me to be using political influence. Nonetheless, I accepted all three charges and was sentenced to thirty hours of community service and fined $2105.

While I initially held a great deal of animosity and contempt for the two police officers following my sentencing, during the following year I was courted by several community leaders including the chief of police to take over the presidency of the 200 Club of Atlantic and Cape May counties. This was an organization that raised funds that were dispensed to families of police officers killed in the line of duty. I accepted the position and spent the next five years building the reserve funds for the organization. During my term as president of the club, I also had to experience the pain of visiting the families of three fallen police officers to offer our organization' condolences and financial support. My leadership of the 200 Club helped heal my bad feelings about my April, 1986, arrest experience, and reminded me of what an important and dangerous role police officers play in our society. I guess the Atlantic City Police Department buried the hatchet toward me, too. In 1992, they presented me with the Keys to the Atlantic City Jail. Not the keys to the city, though---just the jail.

CHAPTER 9

IN THE FALL of 1989, three senior executives of Donald Trump's Casino organization were killed in a helicopter crash sixty miles north of Atlantic City. The tragic accident happened just six months before the scheduled opening of Trump's third Atlantic City casino project, the Taj Mahal. Trump lost his organization's chief operating officer along with both the Taj Mahal president and the executive vice president of the Trump Plaza Casino.

Trump replaced the deceased executives with remaining members of his executive team, but the new management lacked the strategic knowledge and natural intuition of the team that had perished in the helicopter accident. In April, 1990 the Taj Mahal opened its doors in what would be heralded as one of the sloppiest openings of a major casino development in history. Within two hours after the doors opened, the New Jersey regulators had closed most of the slot operations down because of irregularities in the coin handling procedures. The press was brutal and Donald Trump was embarrassed by the state of affairs at the Taj Mahal. On top of that, his chief rival in the industry, Steve Wynn, had beaten him to the draw by opening his own mega resort, the Mirage, four months earlier in what was considered a very smooth opening. The feud between Trump and Wynn was aggravated by the sloppy Taj Mahal opening.

Trump publicly lambasted his management team and began

making kneejerk changes to his leadership team. Within two weeks, he had hired and fired three different presidents for the Taj Mahal before finally settling in on a transfer of the Trump Castle President, Ed Tracey, into the position of chief operating officer. Trump decided Tracey would become the person designated to lead the gaming operations for him over all three of his Atlantic City casinos.

Two weeks after the disastrous opening of the Taj Mahal, I received a telephone call from Nick Ribis, then an outside gaming lawyer, whose firm did legal work for both the Claridge and the Trump casinos. Nick and I were friends for several years and he told me that Donald Trump was interested in having me come to work for him at the Trump Castle as its president to replace Ed Tracey. I advised Ribis that it would be hypocritical of me to leave the Claridge, since I had campaigned to the Claridge employees that they should not consider leaving their Claridge positions for employment at the Taj Mahal when it was recruiting 6000 new employees to ready itself to open it doors. If within two weeks after the Taj Mahal opened I defected from the Claridge, I knew I would certainly leave in a bad light for me, at least in the eyes of the Claridge employees.

Ribis insisted that I talk with Trump and at least be informed about the opportunity and I agreed to a meeting with Donald. Trump knew I liked the Castle facility very much. A year earlier, I had written him a letter to thank him for bringing boxing matches to Atlantic City. He appreciated the letter and called me to tell me. In our conversation, I told him how much I liked the Castle Casino and that I thought it had more potential than it was generating. Now he was going to offer me an opportunity to try to extract that potential.

I met with Trump and Ribis in the new executive offices at the Taj Mahal and Donald offered me the position. Donald is very charming and very persuasive. He was only 44 years old at the time, but his name was magic and I knew that working for him would certainly feed my ego, even though I dreaded telling my employees and the board of directors at the Claridge. Trump would not take no for an answer and as he departed from the meeting, he assumed

I was on board. He told me to contact Ed Tracey and work out the arrangements. Someone leaked the word to the street and the press announced that I was leaving the Claridge to take the helm at Trump Castle. What Donald apparently did not do was tell Tracey about me. As directed by Trump, I called Tracey. From our first words, it was evident that Tracey was not prepared for my call, nor did he seem interested in having me take over management of the Castle. When I hung up the phone, I decided to turn down the opportunity. I called Tracey back about an hour later and advised him that I was not going to be a candidate for the position and for him to make other arrangements.

I denied the rumors that I was leaving that had leaked out in the press and made it a point that evening to be more visible than ever on the floor of the Claridge Casino. The next morning, my secretary, Ione called me on the intercom and said that Donald Trump was on the line. When I picked up the phone, Donald exclaimed, "Congratulations on your new position! When do you start?" That's when I asked him if he had talked with Tracey. I advised Trump that I had concluded from my conversation with Tracey that I would probably not be a good member of his executive team at the current time, and therefore I was going to stay on at the Claridge. Trump had Ribis call me to reconsider, but Ribis also came to the same conclusion when he heard my reasoning. A week later, Tracey appointed Tony Calandra as the new Castle president. A month later, Trump Castle missed its first bond interest payment.

While the opening of Trump's Taj Mahal had no negative effects on my business at the Claridge, it had a devastating negative effect on the business volumes at both the Trump Castle Casino and the Trump Plaza Casino. Customers who had been loyal to Trump at his first two casinos now wanted to be a part of his new and bigger casino at the Taj Mahal. Cash flows plummeted at the Castle more than at the Plaza and the new Castle president, as hard as he tried, did not have the experience to engineer any kind of a turn around. Trump eventually made his June bond payment at the Castle a month late, but he knew that if the current business levels persisted, the next payment in December would be almost impossible to make.

On Labor Day weekend in September, Ribis called me again and asked if I would reconsider my decision and take over the reins at the Castle. Again, I turned the opportunity down. My bonus target at the Claridge was going to be easy to make in 1990, and I was already planning how I would spend it. I saw no upside in moving to the Castle, just to feed my ego of working for Donald Trump.

Then my aging parents came from Nevada to visit me in New Jersey over the Thanksgiving holidays that year, and following our big turkey dinner, I received a surprise call directly from Mr. Trump. He apologized for disrupting my holiday but asked me if I would consider traveling to New York the next day to discuss what it would take for me to leave the Claridge and come to work for him. He would have a limousine meet me at my home at the time of my choice and he promised to have me back in Atlantic City by day's end. My Dad encouraged me to take the meeting and I made the trip north to New York City early the following morning.

The meeting went well. Trump ended the meeting by saying, "Put what it will take in writing and fax it to me when you get back home. I guarantee we will make a deal." I left the Trump apartment and headed over to Mickey Mantle's Restaurant on Central Park South to catch up with my wife, who had waited in the restaurant while I had my meeting with Mr. Trump. As I walked in to find her, I asked the hostess if Mickey Mantle might be around. Her usual canned line was, "Sorry you just missed him. He left ten minutes ago." I expected that response again. But to my surprise, this time she said Mickey was in the last booth at the back of the restaurant with some people. I thanked her and, along with my wife, we strolled to the back of the restaurant to say hello to Mickey. Mickey jumped out of the booth and gave us both a big hug. Then he introduced us to his friends still sitting in his both: "Meet the Wagners. Mrs. Wagner is a great lady and Mr. Wagner is the only prick to ever fire my ass."

We all laughed at his comment, but it was evident that Mickey was still hurt over his termination at the Claridge three years prior. Ironically, several months later I would run into Mickey several more times at Baseball Memorabilia shows frequently held at the Trump's Castle.

On the way home from New York City that night in the limo, I outlined a "wish list" of compensation and perk issues that I knew Mr. Trump would not agree to. I figured if I presented him with such an aggressive list, it would be his decision to turn me down instead of my decision to reject his offer. The four biggest issues I threw out on the list were items that I just knew would be deal busters. First, I demanded a salary that was double what he had offered me the past April; Second, I was adamant that I report only to Trump and not to Tracey or any other surrogate without my expressed approval; and third, I wanted a three year contract with one half of the entire base pay compensation paid in advance and placed in an escrow account under the care of my personal lawyer. Since there were many rumors on the street about instances of past Trump executives being "stiffed" for the remaining portions of their employment contracts' when they were terminated, I wanted to eliminate that possibility in the event my employment with the Trump Casinos did not work out as planned. After all, possession is nine-tenths of the law. And fourth, Trump would have to guarantee that he would make the December bond payment. I did not want to go to work with a company one step on the way to bankruptcy before I even started work.

I faxed the list of "I wants" up to the Trump office in New York the following morning. A few minutes later, Trump and Ribis called me on Donald's speaker phone and went down the list. "Item one, Okay! Item two, Okay! Item three, Okay! Item four, Okay" ...right on down the list they agreed with every single request. Donald ended the conversation with, "Okay, when can you start to work?" I sat there at my Claridge desk dumbfounded. What had I just done?

CHAPTER 10

SEVERAL DAYS LATE, but better than never, Trump made the December bond payment. In the meantime, I was working with Hugh McCluskey, my personal lawyer to finalize the terms of my employment agreement with Trump before I announced my resignation to the Claridge chairman of the board. I had vacation scheduled for two weeks over the Christmas Holidays and found that to be fortuitous for me. That way, for the next two weeks I would not be seen sneaking around the Claridge with the guilt of defecting from the organization I had been leading for the past seven years. I returned to New Jersey to usher in the New Year at the Claridge Player parties, and then tendered my resignation on January 4.

The resignation was not taken lightly. Shannon Bybee, the Chairman and CEO, was also a lawyer and he took the position that Trump was tortuously interfering with my employment contract. On the other hand, Bybee saw the opportunity for me to be one that could certainly further my career and he was anxious to strike some type of accommodation with Trump whereby the Claridge would be compensated in some way. From January 4 when I announced my resignation until January 16, when the Claridge and Trump finally settled on a resolution that allowed me to leave the Claridge with no dangling participles, my employment fate was dangling before my eyes. Finally, on January 16, the final agreements were signed by all parties and my payroll escrow account was funded by Trump.

Picture courtesy of Bill Borrelli Studios of South Jersey.
Graphics courtesy of Avrett, Free & Ginsberg Agency in NYC, NY

Section 6

MY JOB AS AN APPRENTICE — YOU'RE FIRED! WORKING WITH THE DONALD AT HIS CASTLE

"I'm Still The Opposite Of Donald Trump In Atlantic City, But

Opposites Attract!"

Remember, I'm the guy with the old Ford that used to run another casino on the boardwalk.

Many have asked me why I left the Claridge to run Trump Castle.

Well, first, it was the facility. While smaller may be friendlier, it can also be cramped. Bigger is definitely better when it comes to rooms, facilities, and parking.

And I didn't have to move the idea of "friendly" to the Castle because it was already here in a bigger and better way.

Actually, it's a perfect partnership of a proven commitment to friendly service and Atlantic City's finest full-service resort facility.

But most of all, it was the people I found enjoying themselves in the Castle.

The Castle crowd refuses to get old.

They see us more as part of a casual and youthful resort facility than a noisy crowded boardwalk casino—sort of a fountain of youth.

Since I don't plan to ever get old, I decided this was my kind of place, so I replaced the old Ford with a classic Corvette and drove on over to join the crowd that also refuses to get old.

If you plan on staying "39" forever, why don't you also drive over from the boardwalk and join me and the Castle crowd on the bay.

I look forward to meeting you.

Roger P. Wagner

Roger P. Wagner
President

TRUMP CASTLE.
CASINO · RESORT · BY THE BAY
The Castle Crowd - They Refuse To Grow Old.℠

Advertisement picture and graphics courtesy of Golden Nugget, Atlantic City

AS I WRITE this section of my book, I am being extremely careful to relate only those experiences that were common knowledge to the general public, including for the most part the Trump Castle employees and the people living in the local community. While there are many more stories I wish I could publish, my separation agreement with the Trump Organization prohibits me from disclosing any confidential business or personal information not already known by persons other than myself.

I showed up for work at Trump Castle on Thursday, January 17. I met Ribis in the lobby and he ushered me to my new office in what was known as "Mahogany Row," the nickname of the executive office complex at the Castle. Originally designed and constructed by Hilton Hotel Corporation before they were denied a gaming license in 1985, the complex had been smartly and uniquely located for easy access to hotel guests and the public, while at the same time being in the heart of the back of the house with wonderful access to the administrative offices, employee cafeteria and rear entrance, as well. The plush offices were adorned with inlaid wood floors and expensive mahogany file cabinets, book cases and custom desks and furnishings.

My new office was plush, yet comfortable. While the carpeting and wall coverings were of a thick soft material, I was surprised at how masculine the furnishings were, given the fact that the previous occupant of this office had been Ivana Trump, who was the president of the Castle for a short period of time from 1985 through 1987. She had reigned as Queen of the Castle until Donald moved her to the New York Plaza about the time Marla Maples came into his life in Atlantic City.

Joining me at the Castle that first day was my trusted and loyal administrative assistant from the Claridge, Ione Nichols. After over 30 years with one organization and the job security that went along with such tenure, she picked up and left her secure job to assist me in what turned out to be much more challenging than either of us had anticipated. Having Ione covering my back made the job easier and a lot more fun.

My first order of business that morning was to meet each senior executive and try to get to know each of them quickly. The first individual I met was the acting chief financial officer, an introverted fellow named Tom Venier. I liked Tom immediately and trusted him. It was evident that he cared for the Castle and he took his job very seriously. In fact, he was almost devoid of humor and it was rare to hear him laugh, although he would occasionally sneak out a sneering smile when somebody else made a funny statement.

Ten minutes into my meeting with Tom, I realized that financial conditions at the Castle were in dire straits, far worse than reported in the press, and certainly not the rosy picture Trump and Ribis had painted for me when I interviewed with them in New York. The company had been experiencing negative cash flow during the past three months of the slow winter season, and making the December bond payment had drained away any cushion the company had to weather the usually busy New Year's holiday weekend. Consequently, casino management was very cautious during that holiday period, intentionally avoiding invitations to the really big players, who if they were to get lucky and win big, would make it difficult for the Castle to cash out their winnings. As the Castle entered January, after a very modest New Year's weekend, it was running on fumes. Then to compound the problems, when Donald agreed to pre-fund half of my three year employment contract in advance of my employment as the new Castle President, over one third of the remaining cash on hand in the Castle checking account was transferred into my escrow account. Venier then informed me that we would likely not be able to make the payroll which would hit us on January 28.

I realized at that moment that some very drastic decisions were going to be required quickly, and that I would not have the benefit of spending a month or two getting to know my way around the operation as I was accustomed to do in previous jobs. I also recognized that when you make decisions on the fly, often you tend to regret quite a number of them later, when the dust settles. Nonetheless, I knew if we did not take a chance at throwing the baby out with the bath water, we probably would drown the baby anyway.

After meeting with the other key senior executives, I found that most of them were not even aware of how truly dire the situation was. The marketing people in particular, were off committing resources as if we were flush with cash. They had no idea that none of our vendors had been paid for months. My first day at the Castle ended in despair. *What the hell had I done to myself and why did I ever leave the Claridge?* I went home and opened a bottle of Crown Royal.

Even though it was Martin Luther King's holiday, the next morning I arrived at the office early. My first order of business was to call Ribis and inform him of what I had learned. He was working the holiday as well and he always arrived at his New York office before 6:00 a.m. Nick Ribis had a reputation for shooting from the hips when making fast deals. He was generally a good shot, too. Nick had a great sense of intuition and used this sense to quickly close many deals when he had an impulse to do so. I knew that if anybody could find a solution for our upcoming payroll problem on January 28, it would be Ribis.

An hour later, Ribis called me back and announced he had found a solution but we had to act quickly. It happened that Trump Castle owned a warehouse and automobile service complex in Pleasantville, New Jersey, where the Castle operated and serviced a fleet of over 60 limousines that were used by all three Trump Casinos. The employees were all on the Castle payroll, and the Castle billed the Taj Mahal and Trump Plaza for the shared services. Ribis had come to the conclusion that the Castle could sell the building and real estate to the Taj Mahal and the Castle would lease the facilities back long enough for the Taj Mahal to take over the limousine operations on their own. Independent lawyers were engaged by both casinos and the sales transaction was completed in three days, with the cash from the sale transferred to the Castle payroll account in time to make the payroll. The sale also gave us a little reserve cash and I instructed Tom to horde it and only dole it out with my written approval.

That afternoon, I called a staff meeting that included every management level person in the Castle organization who was earning more than $50,000. In the meeting I went over the financial picture describing in the simplest terms the grave disaster we had to avoid. I made it clear that without sacrifice and hard work on their part, the job security of all was in jeopardy. Then I announced that we were implementing a wage freeze across the board for all non-bargaining unit employees and first line supervisors effective immediately. Additionally, I was asking that every manager making greater than $50,000 in annual salary agree to take a 5 percent reduction in base salary, also effective immediately. I informed the team that when our Gross Operating Profits reached $30,000,000 on a trailing twelve month basis, I would restore their salaries and pay them all a bonus for the cumulative lost wages they had given up. Our general counsel had prepared a release form that every manager signed agreeing to the reduction in pay. With no objections or exceptions, all of the management people affected by the salary cuts signed the release and authorized their reductions in pay. I was the first to sign. I had been on the payroll less than a week and was already taking a cut in pay.

On January 22, I called a meeting of only the vice presidents on my team, and had the vice president of human resources distribute spread sheets to the team that identified every employee by their specific position and original date of hire with the company. I told them that we had to go through this list, line item by line item and pick out at least 300 employees who we could trim from the payroll.

While cash was limited, it was only fair to provide the affected employees with some severance. We agreed to a severance policy, which would have to be paid in weekly installments to the employees who were laid off. We considered the work records, attendance records and, of course, tenure with the company in determining who would go and who would stay. We informed the unions that layoffs were coming, and admonished everyone to keep the matter as confidential as we could. We decided to make the cuts on January 28, the morning after our Super Bowl Sunday parties. Of course, this was not something we could keep quiet very long. During the middle of the Super Bowl game, I was summoned to the house phone during our high roller promotion to be confronted by a reporter who seemed to have all the details of the forthcoming layoff; he just wanted confirmation from me. I told him that if he would delay reporting what he had heard by rumor, I would give only him the scoop on Monday morning after 10:00 a.m. He kept his end of the deal and so did I. My team made the layoffs the following morning, and the reporter was given the full story which he reported fairy and accurately in the Tuesday morning paper, the morning after the layoffs were completed.

The next day, we decided to terminate the shared services limousine arrangement and have each Trump Casino provide their own transportation services, which we all determined would be more economical if sub-contracted out to a third party company that specialized in transportation services. We communicated the 60-day WARN act notification to the 110 employees working in the transportation center, and began to wind down operations. All in all, 410 employees lost their jobs that fateful last week in January, 1991, but the quick cost-cutting moves we implemented fortunately saved the jobs of the remaining 2000 employees.

CHAPTER **2**

SUPER BOWL SUNDAY was a busy day for the Castle. The place was full of high rollers who had been invited in to watch the big game on a giant screen in the showroom, complete with champagne, great food, celebrity guests and a special half time show. The weekend would not have been complete without the attendance of Donald Trump and his new girl friend, Marla Maples.

Donald met with me in my office and we made small talk as we started to get to know each other. Several months earlier, Trump had opened the new Crystal Tower at the Castle, which was a 14-story hotel tower comprised of only 96 luxury suites. Trump was very proud of the new accommodations, which were touted as the finest array of suite products in one building on the east coast. He wanted to take me on a tour of the new building and show me some of the interiors of the finer suites, but I informed him that the hotel was full and no suites were vacant. Ten minutes later, I discovered that 100% occupancy was no deterrent to Trump when he wanted to inspect his suites. Up the elevator we went and headed straight for the top floor of the new tower. As we walked down the hallway he pointed out the tall ceiling and the expensive appointments, which he declared were personally selected by Ivana and himself. While he and Ivana had just celebrated their divorce 45 days prior, Trump always spoke highly of Ivana's business and decorating skills, and he often reminded me that the Castle had never made more money than it did when Ivana was the president.

Finally we arrived at the big suite at the end of the long hallway, and Trump rang the doorbell. The customer occupying the suite answered the door, and Donald said to him, "Hello, I'm Donald Trump and I would like to show my new general manager your suite. Could I come in and look around?" The customer yelled back to his wife in the adjoining bedroom that Donald Trump was there to see their suite, and she, of course, yelled back, "Yeah, right!"

As he is today, Trump was a magic celebrity. He was like Richard Nixon, in a way. Even people who did not especially admire or like him wanted to be around him. Everybody wanted his autograph and everybody wanted to shake his hand. I had never been around a boss who required bodyguards before, but it was evident why he needed them, just to keep the crowds at bay.

Donald Trump usually came to Atlantic City in his personal helicopter. Jet black, with the name "TRUMP" emblazoned in big red letters, it was like watching the sleek helicopter from the television series, "Airwolf" when it landed on the Castle helipad on top of the nine story parking garage that adjoined the Castle Casino. Until my arrival at the Castle, it had been the practice of all the senior executives to stand in a gauntlet at the entrance to the top of the escalator to greet Trump as he emerged into the hotel lobby after exiting his helicopter. I observed this practice on Trump's first visit to the Castle that Super Bowl weekend, and I also observed that each of the executives involved also were sporting dark suits and the same red neck tie that Donald always was seen wearing at the time.

At my next staff meeting, I suggested that if we had time to kiss Trump's ass by dutifully waiting in the lobby dressed as "Stepford Executives" waiting for the boss to show up, we were obviously overstaffed and I would be looking to make some additional cuts. The greeting-gauntlets disappeared immediately and Trump never seemed to even notice they were missing from that point on.

ON FEBRUARY 1, Nick Ribis called to inform me that Trump was going to be hiring Ribis to become the CEO of the Trump Casino Empire. Ribis wanted to make certain that I was going to be okay with the change in my reporting relationship from Donald directly to him. Nick was aware that my employment contract provided that I would only report to Trump and nobody else unless expressly agreed upon by myself. With Donald involved in so many other big development projects that made his casino organization pale by comparison, I told Ribis that I thought the organizational change would probably be a good thing for the three Atlantic City Trump Casinos, and I would cooperate in every way.

Ribis made two great moves in his first month as CEO. He hired Dennis Gomes and Kevin DeSanctis away from Steve Wynn's Las Vegas Mirage casino to take over the helms at the Taj Mahal and Trump Plaza respectively. Ribis also had a strong political presence in New Jersey and he was well known at both the NJ Division of Gaming Enforcement (the DGE) and the Casino Control Commission (the CCC), where he had represented Trump and Del Webb on many occasions during the previous fourteen years.

My first political crisis came about just days after Ribis's appointment when it was announced by the New Jersey Division of Gaming Enforcement that they had discovered an illegal loan made to the

Trump Castle by Donald Trump's multi-millionaire tycoon father, Fred Trump. The DGE investigation uncovered a clever subterfuge used by the Trumps to funnel enough cash into the struggling Castle operation that had made it possible for the Castle to pay its previous month's interest payment obligation, while also concealing the loan from the regulators and other creditors. The best part of the scheme was the collateral secured by Fred Trump placed his loan in first call position even before the First Mortgage bond holders..... CHIPS!

That's right! Chips.... Baccarat Chips....

When the story hit the newspaper, the public learned that Fred Trump's personal attorney had traveled to Atlantic City just days before the Castle bond interest payment was due. Along with a bodyguard, this attorney entered the Trump Castle Casino with a briefcase full of money and went straight to the Baccarat tables. The elder Trump's persoanl lawyer dumped $3 million dollars onto the baccarat table and requested six hundred $5000 gaming chips.

The transaction took quite some time to accomplish. The casino management had not expected a player to show up that day who might require a seven-figure chip purchase, and the Baccarat tables on that date had only a small inventory of $5000 chips in their tray inventories when the Trump attorney arrived in the pit. The elder Trump's proxy dumped the cash out of the briefcase and onto the table. The cash sat on the top of the table for quite some time as the dealer and the pit bosses carefully counted it before converting into chips. Finally, six hundred $5000 chips were transferred from the casino cage to the baccarat table and after the appropriate accounting paper work was completed and verified, the 600 gaming chips were tendered to Fred Trump's attorney and the $3 million dollars in cash were stuffed into the table's "drop box," a process that took quite some time. Usually large chip purchases are made by issuance of a marker transaction, which eliminates the labor of dropping thousands in Federal currency into the count containers.

The lawyer gathered the chips from the table and stuffed them into his brief case, never making a wager at all. He headed off to the casino cage where he secured a private safe deposit box, and proceeded to lock up all 600 chips. Then he left the casino as quickly as he arrived and motored back to New York City.

With this transaction completed, Donald had just received an interest free loan of $3 million dollars, which was enough to get him over the hurdle he needed to make his $11,000,000 interest payment and still leave plenty of cash to operate the casino through the upcoming New Year's holiday. The Trumps probably assumed they could cash the chips out, all or in part as cash flows improved, especially if the casino played lucky over the holidays. On top of that, the chips Fred Trump held in his safe deposit box had priority over the first mortgage bondholders.

When word of the illegal loan surfaced, the Casino Control Commission quickly moved to prevent Fred Trump from redeeming any chips without the Commission's approval. Ribis masterfully smoothed over the incident with the regulators, and eventually the Commission proceeded to fine Trump Castle only $85,000 for this indiscretion. It was certainly a black mark, but looking back I have to admire the ingenuity of the methodology used by Trump. On top of that, the $85,000 fine we paid was far more economical than any interest we would have paid on such a loan, had we even been able to find somebody that would loan any money under the dire financial conditions at the Castle that cold December day in 1990.

CHAPTER **4**

THE FIRST FIVE months at the Castle were fast and furious. Taking over a casino operation that had ended the previous year with just enough cash flow to make its last payroll left little room for error as we tried to engineer a turn around. Fortunately, the team of executives I inherited when I arrived on the scene was street-smart and also cared deeply for the Castle. They bought into the business plan I had drafted and we embarked together on implementing a strategy that was geared to making the Castle markedly different from the other two Trump casinos and positioned in the marketplace as a place for a younger-feeling clientele that might be turned off by the noise, smells and bustle of the boardwalk crowd. Leading the marketing initiatives was a cool-headed guy named Bill Dayton. Bill knew his way around Atlantic City and had been a successful marketing leader at Harrah's Marina Hotel, so he understood both the Atlantic City customer and also the kind of patrons that preferred the more subtle Marina district area of Atlantic City.

In addition to downsizing the payroll, which was completed during the first month of my tenure, we embarked upon a new advertising campaign that headed us toward the goal of setting us apart from the casinos on the boardwalk as well as the other two Trump Casinos. Working with his very talented marketing group led by a ninety-five pound advertising wizard, Jeanine Repa, Mr. Dayton spearheaded an effort to roll out the new promotional campaign with a date set for May 1, just 90 days after the big layoff. The new campaign would promote the new theme and a whole new array of casino gaming products, yet to be purchased. The one thing we had at the Castle that the new Taj Mahal did not have, was a "View of the Taj Mahal."

I engaged the services of my old friend, Stuart Sherman (remember the guy we called the "Eye in the Carpet", and I gave him carte blanche to work with the food and beverage team to re-structure the menus and develop a friendlier and more casual service culture in each of the restaurants. The previous regime had modeled the service and cuisine after some pretty stiff New York gourmet establishments, and we knew from our research that the new crowd we were aiming at attracting to the Castle would not feel comfortable in the current facilities. We were able to convince our lenders to allow us to spend enough money to convert an underutilized casino lounge into a VIP slot club for preferred players, and Sherman and our engineering crew made the necessary conversion from a lounge to a club in time to open on May 1.

We also brought in the services of the nationally regarded slot machine expert, Butch Witcher, to help us reconfigure a very out-dated slot floor and assist us in finding slot manufacturers who might finance new machines for us, even in our troubled financial condition. Witcher was at that time, and still today, is considered by many as one of the best slot professionals in the industry and one worthy of induction into the "Slot Guys Hall of Fame."

To ensure that the casino floor was balanced with the proper number and type of slots and table games, we were able to talk Ribis into letting us transfer a table games veteran, Richie Zapulla, back to the Castle to work with Witcher and Dayton as we developed the changes to the way we would operate and market the Castle beginning on May 1.

Through Witcher's contacts and cajoling, along with a little luck from a lull in slot manufacturing at the three biggest producers, we were able to procure six hundred brand new slot and video poker units to fit our renovation schedule. During the month of April, we faced terrible business disruption as we effectively changed out seventy percent of the existing castle floor configuration. We eliminated four entire gaming pits of over 36 games that were located at the front entry of the casino and replaced them with "high frequency return" slots and the largest array of video poker machines in Atlantic City. While poker bars (with liquor) were not yet legally permitted in 1991, we installed the first ever flat-top video poker bar with exciting signage encircling the bar enclosure to give it that Las Vegas look. The only thing missing was the bartender, who we added several years later when the regulations finally changed to permit poker bars. In the meantime, customers were still able to secure their favorite beverages by summoning one of the very beautiful and abundant cocktail servers.

While we eliminated 36 table games and used the space to install slot machines, we actually lowered the overall number of slot machines on the floor. When the Castle had opened for business in 1985, it offered over 1500 slot machines for play. They had initially been installed in very long banks with rather narrow aisle ways between the rows, and very few machines were equipped with slot chairs or stools. While it was well recognized that slot machines that were equipped with a comfortable stool would win more money than those without stools, previous Castle management had neglected to provide such an amenity. It was also recognized that customers prefer an "easy-to-navigate" floor layout where they can quickly find and easily get to their favorite machines and other desired service amenities. Wide aisle ways, diagonal passageways and good informative signage are important to achieving this level of comfort and Butch Witcher created a plan that met this objective. Financial analysis also pointed out that the slot machines located on the end of each bank of units usually won more than those on the inside of the bank. Therefore, where adequate space existed to spread machines out in smaller and more accessible banks, this usually equated to more revenue often achieved with less machines to buy or service.

During the month of April we were able to reduce expenses and weather the disruption caused by all the construction and relocation of gaming units on the casino floor. We made it through the month with positive cash flow and our construction initiatives were completed on time and on budget, quite a feat looking back at it now and knowing what the odds were against us.

The new product and the new floor were quickly accepted by the public and revenues soared. In June, Norbert Aleman, the showroom producer of the long running show La Cage at Bally's, was engaged to bring in a production show to the long closed King's Court Showroom. On July 13, 1991 we reopened the popular Viva's dance lounge that had been closed a year prior due to costs.

Nick Ribis had taken a liking to Barry Cregan when he was working for me back at the Claridge. Barry had since moved on in his career and was currently working at the Hyatt Regency in Chicago. Nick suggested that I should try to recruit him to take over the hospitality arm of the Castle and I agreed. I knew it was also time to terminate the consulting services of my friend Stuart Sherman, the "Eye in the Carpet" and I would therefore require someone qualified to take over Stuart's responsibilities. Having Ribis's blessings when I recruited Barry, made it far easier for me to implement some of the initiatives for change I had on my agenda---changes that I knew might fly in the face of what Donald Trump may want to continue. Cregan agreed to accept our offer and he joined the team just as we started to make our big improvements. Barry did so well that he was later moved to New York City by Donald and Nick to run the famous New York Plaza Hotel. When Donald sold the New York Landmark in 1994, he moved Barry to Atlantic City to become the president of Trump Plaza Casino.

With operations on an even keel and operating profits improving each month, we had enough resources now to notch our service quality up a level or two. To accomplish this quickly, I engaged a recent business colleague, Bruce McCormack, to lead a quest to achieve the best level of service for customers and fellow employees alike.

Bruce had been a Navy fighter pilot who had developed a consulting company that focused on organizational cultural development. I had seen his good work at the Claridge just prior to my resignation and I was determined to achieve the same results, only better, at the Castle. Bruce came on board and developed a department that reported directly to the president. We aptly named the department *service enhancement*, and its sole purpose was to coordinate between the operating departments and human resources---to constantly re-engineer and measure business processes, service standards and, most importantly, measure employee and customer satisfaction levels. This new department provided the developmental leadership training for the entire management team and set forth the specifications for a Masters certification program with Rutgers University that was available to company managers who were excelling and who we knew had potential to serve in our succession plans. The program really got its legs in 1992 and gross operating profits that year doubled from those of 1991.

In late 1991, I recruited my old pal and first business mentor, Spike Cook, to join my team as the vice president of hotel operations. Spike had just turned fifty years old and was diagnosed with macular degeneration in both his eyes. I knew how effective Spike could be in making the hotel operation at the Castle number one in Atlantic City, but I also knew that he could not live in the area and commute to work because of his eyesight. Then it came to me. We had a small suite on the 27th floor of the tower that was seldom used. It had a serious leak in the ceiling that had been caused by an original construction defect and the many attempts to fix it only ended in a temporary solution. After a repair, it seemed that the tower building would shift in the wind and a small leak would show up again after the next rain. It was nothing that was dangerous or unhealthy to a human being, but it was unsightly enough and leaked often enough that the suite was seldom used by the casino marketing people and the front desk agents only rented it as a last resort. Additionally, this suite was one level above the Trump apartment on the 26th floor, and we hesitated to have customers in it when Trump was staying at the Castle, since customers often were noisy and stayed up late, and the Castle Tower was known to have lousy sound insulation both between walls and between floors. Since Spike was functionally blind, the décor and water stains would not bother him and since Spike lived alone and spent little time in his room, he would never create a noise problem for Mr. Trump, one floor directly below him. It worked out great. Spike joined the team and part of his compensation became the suite. As the only executive who lived on property, he was available "24/7" to handle emergencies that frequently occur in an operation of this magnitude. Under Cook's direction and tutelage, The Castle was able to take over the number one spot in Atlantic City in hotel occupancy percentage, and became the first hotel operation in Atlantic City to ever garner the prestigious Mobil "Four Star" award.

EARLY IN 1992, Trump and Ribis successfully reorganized the financial underpinnings of the Trump Organization through a series of three separate Chapter 11 pre-packaged deals at each of the three casinos respectively. Original bondholders tendered their securities at a discount for new bonds that carried increased interest coupons. The financial reorganization provided all three Trump entities with some breathing room. The extra cash infusion brought about by the pre-packaged deals meant some neglected capital purchases could be made and some back bills could finally be paid. Best yet, it enabled all three casinos to more effectively advertise and promote their goods and services. Donald hoped that over the next two years, conditions would improve whereby he could finally take his company public and place it on sound footing once and for all.

The bottom line improved substantially in early 1993. As promised to my team of executives that day back in January, 1991 when I cut their wages, by June of 1993, we were able to restore everybody's wages and give them all a cash bonus equal to what they had sacrificed on that fateful day a little over two years prior. Except for Bill Dayton, who had moved on to open the most successful convention support company in Las Vegas, the entire management team that had accepted the pay cuts was still working for us. You can imagine the celebration that evening out at the "Captain's Lounge" on the marina deck. Their destiny had truly been in their own hands, but at the time we made the salary cuts nobody really believed it. That day we restored their wages, it sunk in that they had been responsible for engineering our turn around and they deserved the celebration....and celebrate they did!

The year 1994 was a good year for the Castle, but improvements in profit were coming about at a pace that did not satisfy Trump and Ribis. The one big negative of working for Trump was his lack of patience. Turning a losing company around and building positive employee culture that last for the long term take time to create and instill in the mindset of the employees and customers. Trump and Ribis would make frequent changes in management, especially in the marketing areas, always striving for the silver bullet that would jolt them instantly into greater success. In 1992 we changed out management and brought back the venerable Bucky Howard and his team. Bucky had been successful at the Castle when Ivana was President, so Trump and Ribis believed Bucky could replicate his past success again. We transferred Bucky back to the Castle from his post at the Taj Mahal and turned him loose. But times had changed. Competition was keener and smarter. When improvements only came slowly under Bucky, Donald thought it would be a good idea to bring Lowell Sidwell over from the Showboat Casino to bolster the effort. Lowell was the foremost junket operator in Atlantic City who had also at one time been successful at the Castle. Sidwell had a very strong network of junket operators throughout the eastern half of the country. Like Bucky, he found that times had changed and the new business he brought to the Castle was very costly and only marginally profitable. I finally managed to receive Ribis's approval to bring on a great executive from Harrah's, named Pat Dennehy. While I was not a Harrah's fan, I was extremely impressed with Pat's ability to motivate the work force and keep an eye on expenses. With Pat on board, our management team matured and was becoming stronger and more cohesive than ever, but that fact was lost because of the impatience at the Trump headquarters.

Trying to remember that "The Boss is not always right, but the boss is always the boss" was difficult for me when Ribis called to tell me that he and Donald wanted to make another change in marketing management. I balked at first but knew it was hopeless. Trump and Ribis were impulsive and would not take no for an answer. Consequently, we fired Bucky and hired on a well regarded casino marketing executive from the Caesars organization named Nick Niglio, who had a reputation for attracting "monster" baccarat players from Asia. Niglio brought with him a small contingent of his fellow employees at Caesars to assist him in his efforts to improve Asian business for the Castle.

I got along fine with Niglio and we became friendly, but it took us a while to become accustomed to each other's style. I had been around operations where we had to pinch pennies for a long time; and he, on the other hand, had been working for a company that spent money like it was sand in the desert. Niglio had a good following on his own but the colleagues he brought with him from Caesars had a hard time adapting to our tight financial situation. Within four months, I had fired all of them except Niglio. But Niglio, himself was producing some big players. They were so big that they destroyed the financial results in 1994. As I pointed out earlier in this chapter, 1994 started out very robust. For the first time under my administration, the management team was on target to receive one hundred percent of their bonus. With two days until the end of the year, Niglio called me to advise that he had an opportunity to bring a group of Asians into the Castle for New Years Eve. They were originally scheduled to go to the Showboat, but through one of his contacts, we could intercept them. The only condition to getting them to choose the Castle was our willingness to allow each of the Asian players in their entourage the right to bet $100,000 per hand in Baccarat. I spoke to Donald and Nick and they wanted to take them on. But, aside from Niglio, my team of executives was reluctant. This group of players had beat the Showboat out of $5,000,000 on a previous trip so there was no guarantee we were going to beat them either. Worse, if they beat us bad on New Year's Eve, we would fail to meet our financial targets and thus forego a large portion of our bonuses. Nonetheless, we were in the gambling business and we had the house advantage on our side so Donald and Nick were correct in wanting to deal to this kind of action.

The Asians arrived late on New Year's Eve. In fact, the ball had already dropped and most of the party revelers had headed either to the casino or on to bed. But the casino accounting day does not end at midnight. In fact, on December 31, we extend the accounting day until 6:00 a.m. the following morning on January 1. So with the Asians in the house, we told Niglio and our Asian hosts to do everything they could to stall their play until early morning, if possible, to avoid the possibility of them beating us in the last few hours of the year. However, the Asians were anxious to get into action and they sensed our attempts to stall them. When they threatened to leave and head over to Showboat, we ushered them onto the Baccarat table. In the next two hours, they beat us out of six million dollars and when the drop boxes were removed at 6:00 a.m. on January 1, 2005, we were six million dollars shy of our bonus target. Timing is everything and the timing of that Asian Group's play that night brought a lot of frowns to the management team who had worked hard all year to meet expectations, only to have their successes wiped out in the last two hours of the year. Ironically, by 10:00 a.m. on January 1, we had won our six million dollars back along with another five million dollars. January, 1995 casino revenues turned out to be the highest ever recorded in Trump Castle history, and that monthly record still exists today. The Castle (or Marina) has never seen a month like that since. To their credit, Donald and Nick decided to pay the team their annual bonus that year disregarding the big loss on New Year's Eve. That set up the start of a great year in 1995. In fact, 1995 was the best revenue and profit year for the Castle since its third year of operation back in 1987.

However, by mid-July of 1995, Ribis was getting antsy over Niglio's inability to get some of the big Asian players to pay their markers. This was one of the best revenue years for Atlantic City Casinos, but it started the biggest marketing wars ever witnessed by the gaming analysts as well. As good as business was, cash was still scarce because interest payments were still so large. With patience short, Trump and Ribis were starting to sniff around for some new marketing talent. Trump had met a couple of Caesars executives at a boxing match, and he told Ribis, "Now these guys look like casino executives." One of them looked like he came out of a James Bond movie, so I guess that was the stereotype of a casino executive in Trump's mind. Several weeks later, we moved Niglio to a position at the Taj Mahal and transferred Dennehy to our Gary, Indiana casino development. And in came the James Bond crew.

These guys looked like two "GQ" cover models. Mark Brown was hired to replace Dennehy as executive vice president and Larry Mullins was brought on to take over marketing. While a lot of fun, the gaming business is a cut-throat business and career ambitions make competition for the few coveted top jobs acute. It was evident from the James Bond team's first week on the job, that they had my position in their sights. The perfect storm was developing. I had my own personal problems outside of business that I knew troubled both Trump and Ribis. Then with the marketing wars developing in the city, the cost of competing was starting to erode the bottom line. Larry Mullin was known to be a very clever promoter of slot business and was pretty good at being an entertainment impresario as well. The problems with his promotional strategies were that they were very expensive. Brown had been a casino manager at the Taj Mahal before taking on a bigger role at Caesars and he had some expensive customers he started bringing over to the Castle.

With Ribis's insistence, the James Bond Team began to implement their programs in the last quarter of 1995. The product of their new programs was neutral at first and 1995 ended up with the best bottom line in eight years. However, the perfect storm already brewing before the arrival of the James Bond team began to become even more intense during the first six months of 1996. Between Roger King of King

World Fame, Kentucky Governor J. Y. Brown and sixteen other high rollers that frequented the Castle, we entered a string of six months in which the casino table games only won half of what we theoretically should have won with all the huge action we were getting. It was one of the longest streaks of bad luck I have had as a manager in my 30 years as an overseer of a casino. Yet, the expenses of taking care of these big players were as costly as ever. Add Mark Brown to the mix---a guy used to spending big dollars on players at Caesars---and the Castle's profits plummeted.

The perfect storm alright! Bad luck, higher expenses, lower profits and my crazy personal life; I could see the handwriting on the wall. If we didn't get lucky real soon, Trump's patience would run out. By June 30, 1996 the Castle was $20 million dollars under budgeted profit and headed to the most disappointing bottom line since I became president. I know what President George Bush felt like in his last year in office. There wasn't much I could do at this point except pray and hope Lady Luck would turn around my fortunes.

As no surprise to me, In October, 1996 Ribis relieved me of my duties as president, but surprisingly, did not replace me with Brown or Mullin. However, several years later, Brown replaced Ribis as CEO of Trump and Mullin went on to become the president of the newly named Trump Marina (previously the Castle). Like anyone in my position, I held some animosity at first, but, looking back, I realize it was time for me to go. Term limits are important in government and they are equally applicable in business as well. History has treated me well at the Castle and both Brown and Mullin went on to do a pretty good job replacing Ribis and me.

I CAN TRULY say that Donald Trump was a role model for me, from the first time I met him when working at the diminutive Claridge Casino, until my last day on his payroll. I would not trade one day of experience in his company, for it matured my career in so many ways. More importantly, I became involved with more mentors, partners and friends at the Trump Castle than at any other time in my career. As I said in the introduction of this book, business relationships, regardless of the career you select, involve four types of people who will affect your life. Role models help one select goals, but mentors, partners, and friends are the ones that make it possible to achieve them.

Donald Trump was a very unique individual and I learned a lot about business in general from watching how he manipulated the circle of financial gurus on Wall Street and the politicians in whatever state or city environment where he was conducting business. While I classify him as a role model, I would not classify him as a mentor. It was also a new experience for me to be around a casino operator who would frequently involve himself in some of the more mundane and irrelevant aspects of the casino business. On the other hand, he had little comprehension of the most important issues of running a casino operation that mattered to developing a successful business culture over the long term.

Trump was then, as he still is today, a very meticulous and extremely detailed businessman. His penchant for cleanliness and obsession for order is evident in his preference for architectural lines that are sleek, slick, shiny and easy to clean. When I arrived at the Castle, I was impressed with the cleanliness and high standards of maintenance. Even as the company was struggling financially, Trump demanded that the facilities reflect his reputation for quality, comfort and cleanliness.

As everybody knows, Trump's name is the most important thing to him. "TRUMP" is a famous brand, almost as well known as Coca Cola. Donald really didn't care what kind of press he received as long as it was on the front page and his name was spelled correctly in the biggest print-fonts possible. His name was emblazoned on every piece of advertising and promotional material and his name was backlit on the giant signs at the top of each of his casino towers and on the top of his marquee at every entryway to his casino front doors.

My employment contract was written with a clause that prohibited me from being required to fly in a helicopter. This was due to the terrible crash of a helicopter carrying three key Trump executives back in 1989. Since this was the most common way for Trump and his executives to travel back and forth to meetings either in New York City or in Atlantic City, I wanted to make certain I could go by limousine instead. Nonetheless, one evening after a meeting I attended in New York, Mr. Trump decided to take a quick trip to Atlantic City in his new helicopter and asked me to ride along with him. Reluctantly I went along with the idea; and we took the 100 mile trip on down to the Castle. As we neared our destination Trump instructed the pilots to circle each of his casinos so he could point out certain attributes and design elements to me. Trump was a master at building huge developments, he was well versed in many engineering aspects of high rise construction, and he enjoyed telling you what he knew. As we circled the Castle, Trump frowned when he noticed that two of the letters on the large Neon sign on the front of the tower building were burned out or not functioning for whatever reason. He was a stickler for having all the decorative lighting working perfectly and he was especially sensitive to having his name in lights. There I was in a helicopter that scared the crap out of me to start with, looking at a burned out set of letters that was obviously irritating my new boss. On top of it, the two burned out letters were the "T" and "C", which left the lighted letters reading "RUMP ASTLE" to someone driving by on the roadway below. Bankruptcy looming or not, overtime prohibited or not, when we landed, I summoned the director of engineering who woke up the foreman at the sign maintenance company, and they had guys dangling from the roof by midnight making the repairs. When Trump flew home later that evening, the sign was working and his name was glowing away, all "T-R-U-M-P" of it.

Trump was a very interesting individual. He was fastidious about having clean hands. If he walked through the casino and shook anybody's hands, he raced to the restroom to wash his hands. I even saw him head into the kitchen of one of his gourmet restaurants to wash his hands in the kitchen sink after shaking somebody's hand in the restaurant. I never saw Trump walk around in public without a bodyguard, but one Saturday afternoon, I was driving to my home in Brigantine and as I turned onto the jug handle off the White Horse Pike on to Huron Avenue, the major roadway that connected the Castle to Atlantic City, my wife pointed out that Donald Trump was driving the big Mercedes in the car just next to us. He was all by himself and the windows were extremely tinted, but one could certainly make out the profile of Trump with his famous hairdo driving the car. I phoned ahead to the Valet parking people to alert them that I thought I saw Trump driving his personal car toward the Castle and to be on the lookout for him. Sure enough he drove up into the Porte Cochere five minutes later. When I told Trump later that we had recognized him in his car, he was startled. When I told his security chief, he had words with Donald. After that, I never recall Trump driving his car alone again. Come to think of it, I never saw him in the front seat of any vehicle again.

DURING THE FIRST few months of my tenure at the Castle, Trump would visit and bring along Marla Maples, who was now living with him at least part time. Marla was a lovely girl, not only nice to look at, but very nice to be around. She was respectful to the employees and almost everybody liked her. Trump was smitten with her at the time, but Marla had one quirk that drove Trump crazy, and he was not shy in letting her or anyone around him know about it. Marla was constantly late for whatever appointment she made. She showed up at the beauty parlor late. She would arrive for her health club appointment and massage late. The staff at the casinos recognized that she would usually be late and just planned for it as part of dealing with the boss and his family. When she was late for her own personal affairs, Donald did not object. But when she was late for dinner, which was almost always, this seemed to embarrass Trump and rather than apologize to his dinner guests, he would lambast Marla when she finally showed up, usually thirty minutes late.

It was evident to all of us working at the Castle that Marla's family also made Trump uneasy. Marla's mother, Ann, was as beautiful as Marla, but she could sometimes be a little pushy and demanding on our resources. She was very good at leveraging her position as Marla's mother while Marla was in power. Her step-father was a quiet guy and obviously took orders from his wife. It was not unusual for Marla's mother to bring quite large entourages of her friends and other relatives up to Atlantic City from their home in Georgia, and it was very common for Marla and her mother to do this on a moment's notice.

Trump had an able assistant named Norma and she obviously fielded all the corny requests from the Maples family. Norma communicated great with my assistant Ione, and often I had no idea of some of the crazy requests. The two assistants just handled them in the normal course of business. But the most common request had a code name: "The Clampetts are coming." It seems that requests from the southern family were so frequent that Ione needed no other instructions than to respond to Norma's request to take care of the Clampetts in the normal fashion. In fact we had to be careful not to joke around about this because one of the new desk clerks greeted Marla's Step-Father as "Mr. Clampett" on one of his first visits to the Castle.

The Trump Castle originally was built by the Hilton Corporation but for mysterious reasons, Hilton was denied a gaming license to operate it. Trump bought the facility from Hilton in 1985 and opened it as the Castle. Donald Trump had a two story suite on the 26th floor of the main Castle tower, with the main entrance at the far end of the hallway. I asked him why he did not take the larger and more opulent suite that had been constructed by the Hilton Corporation for use by their general manager. The Hilton suite had been built on the eleventh floor of the tower because after the disastrous Hilton fire in Las Vegas back in 1981, Baron Hilton wanted a suite that was accessible by hook and ladder truck. The tallest hook and ladder truck in Atlantic City would reach eleven stories. Trump explained that he had to occupy the best suite at the top of the building. He always needed to be on top. That was his goal. He also seemed to have no fear of fire.

Anyway, when the Clampetts came to town, they had to be housed near Donald's suite on the 26th floor. Usually the calls from Norma to Ione would come at very short notice and on most occasions, the hotel was operating at or near capacity. *The Clampetts are coming* became so routine, that the front desk could clear the entire 26th floor in about two hours flat, making all the necessary accommodations available long before the Maples family arrived, even on short notice. I asked Spike how he did it and he said, "Easy. We just call everybody on the floor and tell them we have a utility problem and there will be no water for 24 hours. We move them and give them a special rate for their inconvenience and we've never had a problem." So be it with the Clampetts.

I lived about a mile from the Casino in a waterfront property in Brigantine. I had a boat and several jet skis and several times a month in the summer time, I would drive my boat to the Castle dressed in suit and tie. Opening my mouth at dinner with the Trumps one evening, I offered my jet skis for use by Marla and her friends and family. I figured they forgot about my invitation when the summer season went by. But a few weeks before Memorial Day the next summer, Marla called me and asked if the invitation was still open. How could I say no? Then Donald called me and suggested I rent six additional jet skis because the Maples entourage was going to be big. Marla's step-father was on his way north to become the head of the maintenance department at the New York Plaza Hotel, where my friend Barry Cregan had just taken over as the general manager. Marla's step-father was going to enjoy a long weekend in Atlantic City with his family before formally starting his new job.

Bright and early on Saturday morning, the Clampetts (I mean Maples) family showed up at my house in a series of limousines that lined the street in front of my home at 93 Lagoon Boulevard. Donald was not with them as he had flown to Miami to retrieve his newly painted Boeing 727 personal airplane. He was scheduled to fly it back to Atlantic City and then join Marla and her family at my house for a barbeque.

All the members of the Maples group agreed to sign a waiver for any accidents on the rental skis, and they all declined instruction from the marina owner on the use of the skis. Marla and her step-dad wanted to head out for some big waves that were coming in about eight feet high just off the Brigantine jetty. I asked her step-dad if he had ever jumped ocean waves before and he informed me that he was quite good on skis like this. He told me that he had used them frequently in a Georgia lake. As Marla, her father and I took off on our separate skis, Marla's bodyguard followed in a small Grady White skiff. We headed out of the Absecon Inlet toward the shoals to the south of the Brigantine jetty. The waves were so big that the bodyguard had to turn back. Marla and her step-father hit the accelerator and shot over the first huge wave they encountered. Marla's flight over the wave was smooth, but her step-dad's first ocean encounter ended in disaster. As his ski went over the top of the incoming wave, he failed to hold onto the handles and while his momentum kept his body going in an upward trajectory, his ski dropped from under him like a rock. As gravity took control, Marla's step-father fell pelvis-first on then edge of his Jet Ski.

I scrambled to his aid and saw that he was in terrible pain. While the waves were still smashing in over us, the undercurrent was carrying us farther away from the shore. Marla tried to round up the unmanned Jet Ski while I attempted to tow her step-dad to shore behind my ski. He was just too much of a dead drag to make any meaningful progress. The water was only 62 degrees and he was getting cold fast and probably shock was setting in. I instructed him to grit his teeth and finally managed to pull him on to the ski with me, while he was screaming in pain the entire time. I told Marla to head back in and catch up to her bodyguard. I knew he had a radio or cell phone. I instructed Marla to have him summons a Brigantine Beach patrol with a four wheel drive vehicle to take her step-father to the hospital. She said, "What about my father's ski?" I said to forget the ski. Just get the message to the Brigantine beach patrol.

Slowly but surely I was able to guide the water craft with my injured passenger to the Brigantine beach where the beach patrol met me and carried him off in a stretcher to a four wheel drive ambulance. I headed back to the jetty and looked for the unmanned Jet Ski. There it was, floating near the Jetty. I pulled it back to my home where I found all the other jet skis tied up at my dock, but with nobody from the Maples entourage present. Then I saw a note left on my kitchen counter thanking me for the hospitality. Everybody had left for the hospital.

About that time, Donald and his bodyguard showed up at my door. I explained what happened to Marla's step-father and Donald just laughed. I was surprised when Donald blurted out, "If her Old Man was a horse, they would just shoot him."

Then Trump added, "There will be one guy happy about this. Barry Cregan! Now he won't have to hire Marla's Step-Dad to run the maintenance department at the New York Plaza." I then asked Donald if he was going to head to the hospital, but he said he had an appointment to show his new plane to some players at the Trump Plaza and the hospital would have to wait. The hospital confirmed later that Marla's step-father had indeed, broken his pelvis.

CHAPTER 8

DURING THE FIRST few months of my tenure at the Castle, much was published in the media about Trump's financial mess. Donald even joked about it. He told the following story to a group of high rollers. "Marla and I were strolling down Fifth Avenue when we passed a bum on the sidewalk peddling pencils. She looked at the bum and said how sorry she felt for him. I told her to look at me. In my current state of wealth, that bum has $1 billion dollars greater net worth than me.'"

Donald Trump seemed to enjoy parties we held for high rollers that honored him. Extravagant birthday parties were held each year for him with themes that were every bit equal to his ego. Yet his speeches were almost always the same. He thanked his players for staying loyal even in the face of his bankruptcy. But the players never seemed to get tired of coming to honor him.

After the problem we encountered in which Fred Trump made the improper loan to the Castle by purchasing $3,000,000 worth of Baccarat chips, New Jersey Gaming regulators prohibited Donald from taking any cash out of the Castle Casino operation for any purpose. I had heard that a lot of wealthy people carry very little cash on them and Donald was no exception. As powerful a guy as he was and still is, I was always amazed that he would show up in Atlantic City with hardly any cash on him. He would hint to me that he needed some pocket change to use as tip money. Not necessarily wanting to shell cash out of my own pocket, I found that I could slip him several hundred dollars through his hotel account in the form of a "paid out," and that this type of transaction did not interfere with the casino prohibition. I never told him we could have legally given him more, because he would probably have asked for more. The amounts were so insignificant , but as required, on a monthly basis we would bill Trump for these incidental cash disbusements but I never looked to see if he paid them

Donald and Marla did not hang around the casinos much, but when they visited the Castle during the balmy summer months, they sometimes did enjoy spending an hour or so sitting outside Captain's lounge down on the marina deck. Donald would drink his soda while Marla would imbibe in an island cocktail. Obviously they attracted much attention among the hundreds of people who used the 600 slip luxury marina that adjoined Trump's Castle. When they relaxed on the Marina deck, generally two security guards would be posted, along with Donald's chief bodyguard, to ensure that people did not get too close.

There was an elderly Philadelphia doctor who docked his big 45 foot Bertram Sports Fishing Yacht in the Trump Marina. The Doc had named his boat "the Philly Siren" and he had Tee shirts and bikini panties embroidered with his ship's logo and he proudly distributed his textile products as gifts to his friends at the Castle and in the marina. One afternoon he raced up to Marla, successfully evading the security guards and the bodyguard, to award her with a specially designed pair of his logoed Bikini panties. Trump was not amused, although Marla seemed flattered, and I bet she looked great in them. Come to think of it though, I never did see the Trumps lounging on the Marina deck again.

Donald and Marla finally got married at the New York Plaza on December 19, 1993. The event was out of my league but I do remember coming down the stairs to the reception behind Howard Stern. What do you get billionaires for a gift? After finding where Marla was registered, I purchased some expensive wine goblets to add to her collection; not too many to bust me but not too few to embarrass me either. Marla was a classy and appreciative bride. I received a nice thank you note from her two weeks after the wedding.

BEFORE THEIR MARRIAGE, Donald was always on the lookout for fine women. Maybe that's why he purchased the Miss Universe Contest. At the time, I was going through my midlife crazies myself so Donald constantly talked to me about beautiful women when he visited my office. One day he called me and said he was coming in for the night. Being a boxing promoter for years at his Atlantic City casinos, he was fond of looking at the beautiful *Ring Girls*, who were employed to carry the big signs announcing the next round number at the fights. It happened that Harrah's across the street was hosting the "National Ring Girl" contest inside their showroom that evening and Donald wanted to attend it. He also wanted me to attend it with him. I heard it was going to be a cheesy event, but what could I do? "The boss was the boss."

I called my friend, Steve Rosen, over at Harrah's and told him that Donald and I wanted to attend the event. Steve had booked the promotion so I think he saw an opportunity to exploit the fact that Donald Trump would be in his Harrah's showroom watching this special event. We were ushered to the best booth in the showroom and flooded with extra good service. The event lived up to its advance billing: Cheesy to say the least, but Donald was the center of attraction for all the contestants. Following the contest, there was a short press party back stage. We had not been invited to the back stage party. Yet Trump decided he was going anyway. With his bodyguard blocking and leading the way, we forced ourselves back stage. The press was present and of course they had to interview Mr. Trump, so in the end I justified our gate crashing because I believed that Steve Rosen was getting his money's worth for the two free tickets he gave me. As the contest ended, I heard Rosen telling the girls that after the back stage party, they would all be invited to mingle with high rollers in the Harrah's lounge. However, while Rosen was planning for his lounge party at Harrah's, Donald was planning for his own party with the girls back at the Castle's Dance Club. As Donald mingled with all the contestants he told them all that limos would be dispatched to pick them all up at the Harrah's valet entranceway in thirty minutes. Rosen was livid. I kind of chuckled but I couldn't blame him. Most of the girls did show up at Viva's lounge and Trump held his own contest. Oh, did he enjoy good looking women. If memory serves me correctly, one of these girls hitched a ride back to New York City that night with Trump in his black shiny helicopter.

Donald may be rich and powerful, but he is still human. Like all of us he has his quirks. Many people talk about his germ phobia and how he hates to shake hands with people. His famous hairdo, while eccentric is certainly part of his personality. I have mentioned how he is impatient and spontaneous and the best example of this happened one day on the casino floor at the Castle. We were touring the casino as we always did when he came to town. The casino manager and slot director participated in the tour so they would be available to answer any specific questions Trump might have. The Castle Casino at that time had red colored walls and a white ceiling. The walls and ceiling were separated by soffits that were encased with bronze colored glass. Apparently Donald had just seen a building in New York City where the duct work in the ceiling was exposed and everything in the ceiling area was painted the color black. Donald noted to all of us that this new look made the ceiling appear to disappear. All of a sudden, he instructed us to paint the ceiling black. He said, "It will take at least two coats so get started on it. I want it done when

I get back on my next trip." We thought he was nuts but the boss is the boss. We started the project the next morning. With over 90,000 square feet of ceiling, all located over the top of 1500 slot machines and 80 table games, the project consumed a lot of time, money and resources. Ten days later we completed the project and I sent Trump a memo advising that we had completed his request to paint the casino ceiling black. It looked terrible but I didn't put that comment in my memo,

For whatever reason, Trump did not visit the Castle for a period of over four months. We were all starting to get used to the dark ceiling, when Trump announced that he would be in for a tour of the property. As we walked through the entry way of the casino, Trump stared at the ceiling and yelled, "Who the F—K told you to paint the ceiling black? This looks terrible!" Before I could reply, the slot manager blurted out, "You did, Mr. Trump. Don't you remember?" He got the words out of his mouth before I could kick him in the shins. Ten days later the casino had a white ceiling once again. This time it took us three coats of white paint to cover the black. In the end, we put out a rumor that the slot manager had to resign for coming up with such a stupid ideas as painting the white ceiling black. After all, we couldn't blame Mr. Trump.

When it comes to an ego, Donald can "trump" them all. He brags about his kids, but rightfully so. Donald has three children from his first marriage that are top notch. Ivanka, his daughter, is not only beautiful but also both politically astute and business savvy. She did not spend much time at the Castle, at least while I was its president. When she did come to town with her father, she was quiet, shy and very polite. Her physical looks and features are perfect and I assumed she would become a top runway model or cover girl. It has been fun watching her grow up and now perform on television shows and be interviewed for her political viewpoints.

Donald Trump Jr. was a great kid, too. Back in the summer of 1994, or maybe it was 1995, Mr. Trump, Sr. called and told me that he wanted Donald Junior to work at the Castle for the summer. I suggested that he might enjoy being a Dock Hand at the marina. It would be fun and Junior would be able to mingle with other young guys in an environment surrounded by lots of young girls and rich people with big boats and yachts. I told him that the pay was only $7.00 dollars per hour but there were a few gratuities involved. Donald liked the idea. He said, "Great! Put my son to work. Pay him the going rate and don't bump anybody out of their shift to accommodate him. I want him to learn how the common folk live and work, so don't do anything special for him on the job." Then after a pause, he added, "Oh and by the way, also rent him a Jeep Wrangler and give him a complimentary room on the 26th floor near my suite for the summer." The kid did a great job at the marina and his supervisors and colleagues all admired him. No wonder he is doing so well in business some seventeen years later.

I never knew Eric very well. My only encounter with him occurred one night when Donald and Marla were in town with all three of Donald's kids. The comedian, Jackie Mason, was performing in the ballroom theater of the Castle and Donald thought it might be fun to see the show. Donald invited me and my girl friend to sit with him and naturally we were all seated center-ringside in the front of the showroom where everybody could see Donald and Marla. Jackie Mason began his routine and while funny as hell for most of the audience, young Eric found the show boring. Out of the corner of my eye, I noticed that Eric was removing the match sticks from several books of matches left in the ash tray at our table and he was stacking them in the shape of an Indian teepee. As Jackie Mason was about to hit us with a "punch line," Eric struck a match and lit the entire teepee of match sticks he had built on fire. There at center stage we had a nearly one-foot high flame blazing away with Donald Trump frantically pouring a glass of water on it to extinguish the fire. The fire was funnier than Jackie's joke. Until the end of the show, Donald never took his eye off Eric again.

Donald bragged about his golf game, too. Again, rightfully so. Trump would play in various casino golf tournaments as our resident celebrity and he was always the best player in the tournament. Even if

Trump went six months during the winter without picking up a club, he could shoot in the seventies on his first round out in the spring. In 1994, Trump made a hole in one at a tournament he was participating in at Pebble Beach Country Club, and before he left California, we were instructed by the New York Office to place a congratulatory announcement on our electronic reader board at the entry roadway into Trump's Castle Casino for everyone to see. The story then circulated that after making that hole in one, Trump marked "zero" on his score card. Maybe that's how he always managed to score in the seventies.

CHAPTER **10**

ONE WEEK AFTER I accepted employment with Trump Castle, Donald hired Nick Ribis to be his CEO. Nick became my immediate boss. I had been a friend of Ribis for eight years, first meeting him when I joined the Claridge Casino in 1983. He had been the Del Webb Corporation's chief outside attorney for gaming regulatory matters, and we worked frequently together over the years. As I related earlier, just like Mr. Trump, Nick Ribis was an impatient and spontaneous individual and he was known industry-wide as a guy who could blow his temper. I had seen him in action several times. Nick is not a big guy, but if he is ever angry, you want to keep out of his way. When his adrenaline is pumping, Ribis could no doubt whip somebody's ass twice his size. At the risk of him coming after me to kick mine, I will take a chance and relate to you one of the most humorous stories that involved Nick's temper. I was not present, but the tale became famous as it circulated through the industry pipeline and I can only imagine that the final story was more graphic than the actual event, itself. Nonetheless, this story remains vividly imbedded in the memories of many Atlantic City employees many years later.

After I closed the Trump Castle limousine center, it was necessary for us to charter limousines, when needed, to transport high rollers, celebrities or our bosses around. One hot and humid afternoon in August, Ribis arrived at the Castle for a weekend of relaxation with his wife and two other couples that were family friends from North Jersey. Ribis summoned one of our charter limos to take him and his party from the Castle over to the Taj Mahal for a dinner reservation they had. After the party loaded into the limo and it pulled away from the Castle, Ribis yelled at the driver to turn the air conditioning down because it was too damn hot. The limo driver ignored his request. Ribis yelled at the driver again demanding that he cool the car down. Again the limo driver ignored his demand. Finally, Ribis yelled at the driver to stop the car. When the driver stopped the car, Ribis jumped out of the passenger seat and ran to the front of the car. He opened the driver's door and pulled the driver out of his seat, leaving him standing in the middle of the Atlantic City ghetto. Ribis jumped into the driver's seat and piloted the limo on to the Taj Mahal, himself. You can imagine the look on the doorman's face when Ribis got out of the driver's seat. It seemed the limo driver had recently tendered his resignation and this was going to be his last run. He evidently didn't care for Ribis.

Ribis called me and instructed me to fire the Limousine Company with whom we were contracting our charters. On short notice I was able to replace the limo company with another company operated by a close friend who was also my neighbor in Brigantine. The first day the new company was on the job, I went down to meet the owner, and wouldn't you know it......he had hired the same driver that Ribis had thrown out on the street the previous weekend. Needless to say, I asked the owner to get rid of the guy, if he knew what was best for his future business relationship with the Trump casinos.

CHAPTER **11**

THERE WERE MANY noteworthy high rollers at the Castle during my reign as king. Speaking of king, the most unique and crazy customer we ever served was Roger King. Along with his brother, Michael, Roger King was the creator of King World Productions, which had produced Oprah Winfrey and owned the syndication rights for Wheel of Fortune and Jeopardy. Roger was a lot of trouble to take care of but every casino in town wanted to book his business. He seldom won and almost always seemed to lose a million dollars or more on a visit. We had an edge over the competition because Roger King had a huge 60-foot-long ocean race boat named "Jeopardy," and whenever he had mechanical problems that needed attending to, he would bring the vessel to the Trump Marina. He always radioed ahead and the dock hands would meet him. He would jump out of his boat, throw the rope to the dock hands and tell them. "She ain't running too well, so get her fixed while I gamble." Based on the way Roger played in the casino, he always knew we would pick up his boat repair costs, which generally ran over $20,000 a trip alone.

Once inside the casino, Roger played relentlessly. He never slept but he partied hard in his suite with lots of booze and whatever else. One night he came down to the crap game in a sweat suit. He was high as a kite and kept falling down so the pit boss suggested he retire to his room and sleep it off. Roger agreed and stumbled toward the casino exit when he tripped over the drooping leg of his sweat pants and fell to the floor with his pants down around his leg. What a sight.... An older guy with his pants down and no underwear. Security got him up and out of sight but not without a lot of applause from the occupants of the casino.

Very late on one Tuesday evening, Roger was in the high limit slot area playing away at a $100 dollar machine. The casino was very quiet and nobody else was in the high limit area that night. About one o'clock in the morning after dumping more than $200,000 into the machine, Roger decided he needed a restroom break, so he handed a security guard a $100 token and asked him to make certain nobody played his machine until he returned. Anyway, after Roger finished his business in the restroom, he sauntered over to the Baccarat Pit and decided to gamble with cards for a while. As luck would have it, after guarding King's slot machine for over an hour, the security guard waiting for Roger to return, decided that Mr. King was not coming back. So the guard took off to another part of the casino. You guessed it. At about two o'clock one of the biggest slot players on the Castle player's list moseyed into the high limit pit and sat down at Roger's machine. Ten minutes later the lady hit the big jackpot for $160,000 and of course all the excitement got Roger's attention in the baccarat pit. Mr. King demanded that we pay him the jackpot and fire the security officer. We did neither so Roger left and we did not see him for months. Then one day, he called and I just knew his boat needed repairs again. He told me he would agree to stay with us if we agreed to two conditions. First, I had to pay him the $160,000 he felt he was cheated out of and second, he wanted to challenge me to a Crown Royal shot drinking contest in Captain's Lounge. That would be retribution for not firing the security guard. I agreed to the conditions and Roger showed up with his broken race boat the following Friday. We issued him a cash comp for his $160,000 and I joined him in Captain's Lounge for the Crown Royal contest. The following morning I was nursing a nasty hangover but the Castle was $2 million dollars richer.

Another great player was a guy named John Stalupi. This guy was a multi-millionaire who had numerous automobile dealerships in North Jersey. Like King, John Stalupi often showed up in his ocean racing boat which carried the moniker *Octopussy* on its stern. I guess he was a James Bond fan. However, unlike King, Stalupi was an astute player. He was tough to beat and he played with no fear of losing. I greatly admired this player and I always hoped that at the end of the day we could break even with him.

Evander Holyfield was another huge player. He would bet ten thousand dollars a hand in Blackjack and had no problem losing a quarter of a million dollars in a session. Unfortunately for Evander, his knowledge of basic strategy in blackjack did not match his boxing skills. He would often get knocked out of his bankroll in less time than it would take for a ten round fight.

My favorite player was a lovely lady named Betty Fey. Compared to King or Stalupi, she was small time, but compared to most recreational gamblers, Betty was a big spender. She was well liked by all the employees and casino bosses and she was good to the help when it came to tipping. She also was quite attractive. When I joined the Castle and announced my big layoff, her favorite casino host who had taken care of her for years was a victim of the terminations. She called me and introduced herself. I told her I would love to meet her and I walked down to the casino to meet her in person. There she was in a mini skirt and tall leather boots and she looked like a million dollars. When you see somebody like Betty today, you call her a "Cougar." Anyway, Betty was curious as to who would take care of her casino and hotel arrangements now that Paul, her favorite host, was gone from our staff. I told her that I would and from that day on, I was Betty's casino host. When I moved on to my next two jobs, Betty followed me and played at all the casinos where I was manager. I still stay in touch with her at least once a month.

Along with some great players, the Castle hosted many celebrities and featured many fine artists in our two showrooms. There are far too many to list, but my favorite celebrity to appear at a special event was Muhammad Ali. Age and boxing had slowed the *Greatest* fighter. He was shaking with Parkinson's disease obviously caused by seldom seen but frequent head trauma he suffered from his years in the ring. He was a humble guy and always generous with his time when he was around our players. He was a cultural icon and after meeting with him you knew why he was crowned 'Sportsman of the Century' by Sports Illustrated.

As far as stage entertainers go, my favorite was Al Martino. Certainly not known for the biggest box office revenues, but as you know from the previous section in this book, Al Martino became my dear friend and one of my favorite singers. His voice was magnificent and right up to his death in 2009 at age 82 he could perform "a capella" in a big ballroom with a booming voice that could not be matched. Al would work his butt off for me. I could get him to personally cook dinner for players in the Italian restaurant and then have him come out and sing a few numbers to the restaurant crowd. After dinner, he would head to the showroom to perform in front of 1200 screaming fans. The Philadelphia Italian crowd just loved Al. After I left the Castle, Al began touring Europe, doing 45 weeks a year of concerts. Yet weekly, I would get a phone call from him in France or Germany to see how I was doing or to tell me the latest dirty joke. I really miss that guy.

CHAPTER **12**

WITHOUT A DOUBT, my time at the Trump Castle was the most exciting time of my career. I met more unique people, was more closely involved in my community, and probably had the greatest positive effect on the business I was managing than at any other stage of my fun life in the gaming industry. While it wasn't my most financially rewarding exploit, it definitely was my most exciting. Some of the craziest people I have ever met or worked with came into my life while working in the Trump organization. It was also the time in my life in which I entered my "mid-life crazies." Yes, I said *crazies*, not *crisis*, although my ex-wife probably would disagree with my terminology. In this chapter, I will relate stories of some of the more interesting characters who made my mid-life so crazy at Trump's Castle.

After my divorce in 1993, I became involved with a beautiful Brazilian girl who was a talented choreographer and who was also producing shows for several casino venues in the United States and Aruba. She was a free spirit and absolutely fun to be with, unfortunately in a crazy way that probably was not at all good for my business relationships. Reigning from Brazil, she showed up in this country with a G-string bikini bottom sans any top. Her troupe of dancing girls all liked to dress the same way and they loved to go out on my boat dressed to the "T." That means topless in their case.

This lady had been introduced to me by Norbert Aleman, the

show producer of the Crazy Girls show at the Riviera Hotel in Las Vegas and who had been hired by me to create a production show suitable for the Castle. Alleman was a fan of Gentlemen's Clubs and thought we might be able to create a "toned down version" for the lounge at the Castle. Under New Jersey law, strippers are not permitted to go topless so the law forces a toned down approach to start with. My lady friend and Norbert put an advertisement in two newspapers advertising auditions for a potential strip club at the Castle, and we were inundated with applications. For the fun of it, we decided to hold auditions in the Viva's lounge, so we constructed a pole on the stage and draped off the exterior of the lounge to prevent any customers from viewing the audition. When word got out on the casino floor that pole dancers were performing in the Viva's Lounge, all hell broke out. The gaming agents flooded the room and I got my ass chewed out the next day from Ribis. We never did get fined, but my idea for a Gentleman's Club, toned down or not, was doomed before auditions were completed. My first crazy idea ended up with "Strike one!"

My second crazy adventure involved what I always called the "G-String Cruise." At the time I had a dear friend named Frank Tedesco who owned a 92-foot Broward Yacht that he kept in the Trump Marina. This guy owned the Academy Bus Line in New York City and he used his yacht to entertain clients. I had worked out a beneficial deal for the Castle whereby he would moor his yacht at our facility for free, in exchange for our ability to use his boat and crew for Premium level player parties. The deal was a win-win for both parties. However the best part of the deal was for me. Since the sailing crew lived on the boat, it was always available for use and I was invited by Frank to use it once in a while for my own personal recreation. My girl friend suggested we host a "G-String party cruise" as one form of personal recreation. She invited fifty dancers she knew and told them the only admission was the requirement of wearing a "G-String." Of course, I invited twenty of my buddies to tag along for the view. I love the view of the ocean, but nothing tops a view of the ocean and the view of fifty girls in G-String bikinis. When Ribis heard about the mooring relationship I had with Tedesco, he made me cancel it. Sadly, that was my last "G-String Cruise" and also *strike two* with Trump and Ribis.

The coup de grace involved a night of partying at Captain's Lounge on the Marina Deck. Several pit bosses and cocktail waitresses from the casino were off shift and out celebrating one of their birthdays. I was there with my girl friend, so we joined their celebration, and I bought the group several rounds of cocktails to add to the festivities. Shortly, the group of pit bosses and cocktail waitresses disappeared out onto one of the main marina decks and I did not go with them. I figured they were out to get a cigarette. But the next thing I heard was Castle security guards come running through Captain's Lounge and running out to the end of the marina. At the same time, I saw the flashing strobe lights from a Coast Guard skiff and a New Jersey State Police boat pulling up to the end of the dock. It seems my celebrating casino crew had hijacked an electric golf cart used by Marina personnel. Loaded with the six revelers, they speeded down the main dock way at top speed and plunged into the Atlantic Ocean, nearly drowning and, of course, totally destroying the electric cart. I really was not involved, but since I was seen buying cocktails for the partying crowd, I swung and missed for *Strike Three*.

OCTOBER, 1996, PREDATED Donald Trump's successful show, "The Apprentice," for which I named this section of my book. Today he would simply have fired me from Trump's Castle, but back then, with support from my long time friend, Nick Ribis, I was transferred from the Castle leadership position into a corporate role at the new publicly traded company, Trump Hotels and Casinos Inc. as the president of the new development company. My new role was two-fold. First, the new publicly traded company wanted to expand beyond Atlantic City to diversify its holdings and risk, so I was directed to work with the new corporate team to seek out gaming licenses in new jurisdictions as they were coming on. Detroit and Niagara Falls were the two most promising opportunities, along with a potential river boat casino in Gulf Port, Mississippi.

The second aspect of my new role was to serve as the interim general manager for the newly opened TRUMP Casino River Boat located on the south shore of Lake Michigan in Gary, Indiana. I served in this role until I could identify a full time general manager to take my place. When we failed to win the gaming license in Detroit and Niagara Falls, Donald and Nick decided to close the development office and my position was eliminated.

Section 7

BORN AGAIN AT AGE 51 – LEARNING THE GAMING BUSINESS ALL OVER AGAIN THE RIGHT WAY, FROM THE ICON, JACK BINION

CHAPTER **1**

THIS LAST SECTION of my book covers my career working with Jack Binion, an *icon* of the gaming industry's greatest entrepreneurs. After reading about the qualities that make this guy the "greatest casino operator," you will understand why I dedicated this book to him. Jack Binion knew how to run a casino for gamblers because he was a gambler himself. After 30 years working in the hotel gaming business myself, Jack Binion showed me the real way to run a gambling joint.

As a kid in high school back in the sixties, my pals and I would often cruise Fremont Street in Las Vegas on Friday and Saturday evenings. I was always amazed at how much busier the "Binion's Horseshoe Casino" was compared to the other bright lit casinos in downtown Las Vegas, also known as "Glitter Gulch." In those days, the downtown casinos were as popular as the strip casinos and were usually the choice of local Las Vegas residents who enjoyed gambling entertainment as their favorite pastime. Little did I know during my teen age excursions into downtown Las Vegas, that one day I would be part of such a fun industry.

The Horseshoe was owned and operated by a notorious gambler from Texas named Benny Binion. Benny Binion took no crap from anybody and that included the syndicate guys that ruled the strip casinos. The elder Binion once testified in a courtroom that he was innocent of hiring a hit man to kill somebody as was alleged by the prosecutor. Binion told the court that if he wanted somebody executed, he would do the killing himself. Benny Binion eventually served four years in Leavenworth Prison for tax evasion, but during his time in prison he successfully sold control of the casino to his long time friend, Joe W. Brown, who tendered the title back to Binion when his prison term was over. It was during Brown's short tenure as owner of the Horseshoe, when the famous *Million Dollar* display was introduced as a promotional gimmick for tourists to see and have their picture taken in front of. When Binion reclaimed ownership of the Horseshoe, he embellished the display by featuring one hundred $10,000 bills inside a giant bullet proof glass display inside the casino. The famous display served its promotional purpose for over 35 years. Millions of Las Vegas visitors and Horseshoe customers still have memories of their visits to the Horseshoe enshrined in front of the *Million Dollar* display.

As an ex-felon, the senior Binion was no longer permitted to have a gambling license in Nevada so he turned the operation over to his sons and he participated only as a consultant. Jack Binion became the president and his younger brother, Ted, became the casino manager

Benny Binion operated a casino that catered to every form of true and degenerate gambler. He believed that smalltime gamblers should be treated well and deserved complimentary privileges for their loyalty, just as those who bet big money. Jack and Ted carried that tradition on. The Horseshoe was famous for giving customers the best odds and permitting the largest wagers in Las Vegas at the time. It was common for high rollers who stayed at the plush strip resorts to grab a cab or convince their host hotel to provide them with transportation down to the Horseshoe Casino so they could get in on really high gambling action, not generally available to them at their own strip hotel casino. After Caesars Palace opened its doors in 1967 and began giving its better gamblers higher betting limits, Jack Binion made it known that he would let a customer make any size bet, as long as the player made the bet on the first play. It wasn't long after Jack Binion made the proposition public that a gambler came in and wanted to place a million dollar bet. Jack let him make the bet and the rest is history.

There were many legendary stories circulating at the time. One was about a player who came in with two suitcases, one filled with cash and the other empty but ready to take the winnings home. The player was intent on placing all of the money in suitcase number 1 on "Black" at the Horseshoe Roulette wheel. Binion took the bet and the player walked out several minutes later with both suitcases stuffed full of cash.

The most legendary Horseshoe gambler was and still is Archie Karas. Look him up on Google and you will see over 65,000 stories about Archie online alone. This legendary character was on the brink of busting the Horseshoe Casino and Jack Binion will admit today that he thought it might happen. Binion has often remarked that Karas had more "gambling in him" than anybody he had ever seen. According to Jack Binion, Karas was the type of gambler who bet with absolutely no fear of losing; and because he was willing to lose everything he had, he consequently had the greatest chance for wild success as well. Karas had no respect for money and did not care if he lost. If he did, he knew he would rise again. Stories recount that Karas had amassed over a million dollars playing "nine ball" in local bars around Vegas and then started taking on the biggest poker legends, most of whom hung out in the Horseshoe. He allegedly took his first million dollars and turned it into $17 million playing poker against the best professionals in the world.

Playing poker at the Horseshoe put him in close proximity to the craps game, where he found himself on a lucky roll that lasted for weeks. It was rumored that at one point, he had every $5000 chip in Binion's Casino cage and his goal was to win the keys to the Casino and the hotel before he stopped playing. Binion always said, "When a player can run a toothpick into a lumberyard, it makes him a tough and dangerous player." But eventually, Lady Luck has to rest and the odds turned back in favor of the house. Still, Karas was ahead of the Horseshoe for over seventeen months before he finally lost back to the house the entire $22,000,000 he had won, and then some.

I HAD BEEN around the Horseshoe as a kid but never knew any of the Binions. When I entered college at UNLV (then Nevada Southern University), Jack Binion was already a legend in town as the 30-year-old president of the Horseshoe. When I went to work at the Dunes in 1966, I often went downtown and played Keno at the Mint next door to the Horseshoe and would often play a little single-deck black jack inside the Horseshoe. Throughout that period I never met the Binions. Then in 1988, when I was working for Del Webb Corporation, our company sold the Mint Hotel and Casino to the Binions so they could expand the Horseshoe. Even during the sale, I never met Jack or any of his family. Nonetheless, I admired the way the Binions ran their business. They had a reputation for taking great care of customers and very good care of their employees. Jack Binion knew every employee and most of the members of every employee's family. If you were a good customer or a good employee, you were golden with the Binions. Conversely, it was well known in the community that cheats and thieves were dealt with in the most severe manner. It is rumored that what you saw in the movie, "Casino" when a casino dealer was found stealing, probably happened at the Horseshoe and may have occurred in other gambling joints in town, as well.

The most well known casino operator today is Steve Wynn. At about this time, he was the owner of the Golden Nugget Casino in downtown Las Vegas. Wynn plowed a huge amount of money into the Golden Nugget and created a luxury hotel resort in the middle of downtown Vegas. Overnight, he created a destination that attracted the biggest players, accustomed to staying only in a strip casino resort. The newly refurbished Golden Nugget was instantly successful and enjoyed the kind of player volumes never seen before in a downtown casino. Yet it befuddled Wynn to understand what made the Horseshoe, his competitor across the street, so damn compelling to high rollers. Wynn made the statement, "I sit in amazement looking out the window of my new luxurious resort facility to watch a stream of my players, all for whom I comped and paid airfare, traipse on over to Jack Binion's place to get in on their action. It never ceases to amaze me." Wynn has always admired Jack Binion and they are great friends to this day. The type of action that Wynn saw at the Horseshoe in those days is now peanuts compared to the gambling action the Wynn Resort is attracting in Macau, China today, but Wynn no doubt saw the wisdom in the Binion gambling philosophy then and carried it on to even greater lengths in his wonderful resorts today.

In 1989 after the patriarch Benny Binion passed away, Jack Binion became interested in expanding the company business into the new jurisdictions that were starting to pop up around the country. Jack had a suspicion that there was a lot of money to be made in riverboat casinos, and he wanted to be part of it. Jack began using Horseshoe money to develop the Horseshoe brand in Louisiana and Mississippi. On the other hand, his sister, Becky was unwilling to have family money diverted from Las Vegas and a vicious family feud evolved culminating in a nasty lawsuit between family members. The lawsuit was settled in 1998 with Jack relinquishing all but 1% of his ownership in the Las Vegas casino to Becky in return for a 100% stake in the riverboat casinos he had developed and opened in the South. Just as the lawsuit settled, Jack's southern management team resigned to take over the leadership of an upstart riverboat casino company. On the same day, Jack learned of his brother's murder on September 17, 1998.

WHEN I FINALLY met Jack Binion, I felt I knew him because of the legendary background of his company and style that is described in the first two chapters of this section of my book. In other words, his reputation preceded him.

I had been out of work for about seven months and was out in the yard on my riding lawn mower, having taken over for my gardener to conserve money. I was on the far end of my property, when I saw my girlfriend, Carolyn (now my wife), frantically waving at me. As fast as a slow moving lawn mower can travel, I headed back to see why she was so intent on getting my attention. I guess she hated being around an unemployed casino executive. She said there was somebody on the telephone who called himself Jack Binion, and that he had been refereed to me by my old friend, Gary Border. Carolyn had no idea who Jack Binion was and since she grew up and only lived on the East Coast most of her life, apparently had never heard of him. But she knew Gary Border, so she figured this guy on the phone must be a live one.

For the first time in 20 years I was intimidated to answer the phone. Working for the likes of Trump, Ribis, Danner, Kerkorian and the early day bosses never made me uneasy, but here I was about to talk with Jack Binion, the Icon himself. Well, I should never have been intimidated. Even from his opening remarks, Jack Binion made me feel important and at ease. I learned that his entire senior corporate management team had just left him for an opportunity with a new casino company, and he was looking to replace the team. He was hopeful I would consider talking with him about taking the role of chief operating officer for his riverboat casino company. Then he added that he was in the process of acquiring two additional casinos in the Chicago area and he had learned from my friend, Gary Border, that I had recent experience in that market. Apparently that appealed to him most; since, based on our conversation, I could tell that he was obvioulsy deeply immersed in his two casinos down south as a result of the defection of his key management team.

He asked me to meet him in Chicago the next day so we could get to know each other better and determine if a deal could be made. He said that since I seemed to know the town, I should make a reservation for dinner at my favorite Italian restaurant, and he would meet me there. I quickly suggested we meet at "Centro" on North Wells, my favorite restaurant during the time I lived in downtown Chicago working for Trump. We said our goodbyes and I got off the phone and started hopping around. Wow! Imagine that I might get to work for the famous Jack Binion?

I started to call around to book a hotel room and an airline ticket, and in the next ten minutes I became concerned that I might not make my meeting with Mr. Binion. I immediately discovered that the annual Chicago marathon was taking place, representing 35,000 participants along with their guests and spectators. Most of the hotel rooms seemed to be spoken for. I shifted my attention to finding an airline ticket and found every flight to Chicago booked solid. I began to panic. I wanted this opportunity but how could I call Mr. Binion back and tell him I didn't even have enough juice to get to Chicago? If a hotel room and airline reservation were going to be out of the question, could I even book a dinner reservation at Centro? I decided I'd better do that right away. First of all, it was a little presumptuous on my part to select the Centro restaurant on the fly for my meeting with Binion when I had not even been there for close to a year. Who knows, maybe it had gone out of business during my absence from Chicago. I called the Centro, and fortunately it was open. Then I was lucky enough to reach the bartender, Tony, who remembered me from my Trump days at his bar. I guess the generous gratuities were finally going to pay off. Tony checked with his boss, and we were confirmed for dinner. I learned later that the Marathon participants were not big spenders in the premier restaurants during this annual event, but I was not taking any chances. The restaurant reservations were in place.

I finally located a Days Inn with an address that seemed to be near Lincoln Park and I booked a room. Since Binion was staying at the Drake Hotel, I knew I could easily walk to his hotel. Now I had to secure an airplane ticket. In 1998 there was no Orbitz or Travelocity. In fact there was no internet access to the airlines in those days at all. The process was old fashioned: Call around to every airline. I could not locate anything that would take me from Philadelphia to Chicago, but finally I found a kind reservation agent from US Airways that helped me route through Baltimore. I was able to take a shuttle airplane from Atlantic City to Baltimore and connect with a direct flight to Chicago. I was so excited I could not sleep that night.

The next morning, which was a Friday, I flew into Chicago via Baltimore and took a cab to my hotel destination. It was an old, sparsely furnished hotel facility but with a good location. The rooms were very small and I had no idea how four marathon runners could all fit in one room, when I found the accommodations cramped for just one person. Yet, apparently many of the contestants were able to do so. I arrived plenty early and it was a beautiful October day in Chicago. My first task was to hike on down to the Centro restaurant to make certain it was still as clean and classy as I remembered it. Since it was not yet open for business, I peered in and determined that it was as I remembered it. I was hoping to see the maître d' so I could grease him up, but nobody was around. I just had to hope that the waiting time for our table would be reasonable and that the food quality would be good. I returned to my little hotel room and took a nap. I wanted to be as fresh and alert as possible for my job interview with Jack Binion.

Promptly at 7:00 p.m. that evening, Jack Binion and an exquisitely dressed lady exited a taxi cab and entered Centro. I immediately recognized Jack Binion from his pictures and got up from my seat at the bar and went over and introduced myself. We shook hands and Jack introduced me to his daughter, Peri, who I soon learned was the vice chairman of Binion's Horseshoe Gaming Corporation. The restaurant was busy but not jammed and the maitre d' seated us immediately.

Jack ordered a Dr. Pepper and Peri ordered an iced tea. Remembering back to my interview at the Sands Hotel with Richard Danner years before, where he informed me that he never trusted anybody who did not drink booze, I decided to order a beer, but only one. The dinner meeting went well. I felt comfortable with both Jack and his daughter and, fortunately, I had a lot of the right answers to the many questions they had about gaming in Chicagoland. Jack asked me to meet him in his suite at the Drake the following morning and we would discuss the next steps. We summoned the Maitre d', and Jack requested he call a cab. We shook hands and as they headed out the door, I saw Jack shake hands with the Maître d, as well (if you know what I mean). Under my breath, I said to myself that if I can get a job with Mr. Binion, this is going to be a real "class act."

Talk about luck. The dinner was spectacular and Binion's daughter loved the Centro. In fact it became her favorite Chicago eatery after we all moved to Chicago in 2000. Unfortunately this fine restaurant closed its doors in 2001 and it taught me never to be presumptuous again. After that experience, I always check first before committing.

CHAPTER **4**

SATURDAY MORNING I checked out of the Days Inn and took a cab with my small suitcase down to the Drake Hotel, where I met Mr. Binion for breakfast. Jack ordered iced tea for breakfast and I found out from our conversation that he did not smoke cigarettes or cigars nor did he drink coffee or booze. He told me that he was not a prude and had consumed wine and liquor when he was younger. He also said he did not object if people around him, including his employees, enjoyed these vices; he just abstained because so many members of his family had abused such drugs. His recently murdered brother, Ted, had been a heroin addict for twenty or more years. One of his sisters had committed suicide after a long bout with drugs, and several other members of his family had their own addictions.

After breakfast, we went up to Jack's suite where he telephoned David Carroll, his recently acquired corporate vice president of human resources, who at that time resided in Shreveport, Louisiana. On the speaker phone, Jack introduced me to David Carroll and he instructed David to have me meet with the departmental management at both of his casinos and to host two separate dinner parties so they could all become comfortable with me. This was a new experience for me. Never in any of my past interviews did I have to also pass the muster among the subordinate managers who would be reporting to me. It was apparent to me and David Carroll, that any one of these department managers could "black ball" me if they found me unacceptable to be the chief operating officer of their company. And since many of these guys had been around from day one and been part of building the Horseshoe Company from scratch, they believed they were entitled to call the Horseshoe, "*their*" company. David Carroll arranged for me to fly to Shreveport the following week where I met individually with each department manager personally and then attended a very nice dinner with everyone in attendance. The following day, I flew over to Memphis and repeated the same exercise with the management team at the Tunica property. It turned out that both management teams were satisfied that I would be an able leader and would not rock *their* company, at least too much.

Following the team interviews and property tours, Jack Binion called me from New York City and asked me to meet him for lunch in Philadelphia. He requested that I pick him up at the 30th Street Train Station and arrange lunch at some place nice. I picked the Palm Restaurant and he picked up the tab. It was refreshing to see a rich man like Jack Binion taking a train, by himself with no bodyguards, and pulling his own suitcase behind him like a common man. It was so different from my experiences with Trump and his executives over the previous eight years, and he was even more down to earth than the conservative boys from the Del Webb Corporation.

During the lunch meeting Binion apologized for making me run the gauntlet while touring his two casinos. His previous management team, led by the affable Paul Alanis, whom had just defected apparently had great ties and relationships with all of the property level management. Binion was gun shy that some or maybe even many of them might defect along with Alanis. Binion also explained that he wanted me to see the "good, the bad and the ugly" of his company, and my individual meetings and detailed property tour exposed me to these three elements. I told him how impressed I was with his facilities. I had expected to see "sawdust joints' that resembled the old Horseshoe and its neighboring casinos in downtown Las Vegas, and his two Southern Horseshoe Riverboat Casinos were of such quality that they could have easily competed on the Las Vegas Strip.

While the defection of Alanis and his team was a blow to Jack and the Horseshoe Company at that moment, everybody associated with Horseshoe including Jack Binion can be thankful that Alanis had been involved in the initial development of Jack Binion's Riverboat Company. While Jack Binion certainly brought the vision for a true gambling facility to the new riverboat casino industry, it was Alanis who brought a touch of class to the design elements that made the Horseshoe facilities stand out from all its competitors. Adding in the best odds, biggest jackpots, highest limits, best food and most liberal comps, and now the finest Class A live entertainment….there was no way the competition could even come close.

CHAPTER **5**

THE HORSESHOE CASINO in Las Vegas was famous for everything except a showroom. It was folk lore in Las Vegas as to why Binion's Horseshoe Club offered no live entertainment. Benny Binion had always declared that he was never going to blow his casino's profits out of the end of some musician's horn. Jack Binion carried that tradition on for years. It was an obvious paradigm shift for Binion and his family when Jack approved the addition of major sized showrooms for both of his new Horseshoe Riverboat Casinos in the South. While Jack never believed that the showrooms contributed a penny to the bottom line, the "Riverdome Theater" at the Horseshoe in Bossier City and the "Bluesville Showroom" at the Horseshoe in Tunica, Mississippi were the envy of all the other operators.

It was also well known folklore that Benny Binion and his wife, Teddy Jane, pounded into their children that the hired help cannot be trusted. In fact, Teddy Jane ran the casino cage and guarded the family fortune until her death in 1994. Jack and Ted ran the Horseshoe and every aspect of the gaming operation. Not until Jack separated from the rest of the Binion clan to operate his riverboat casinos, did he ever have to really rely on people outside the Binion family to set strategy or watch over the family bankroll. With Alanis at the helm and the two management teams that were largely put in place by Alanis, for the first time in his life, Jack Binion had relinquished some control and had to trust somebody outside the family to operate the gas pedal and steering wheel of his casinos. Even with his daughter, Peri, working as the cage manager in the Tunica Horseshoe, the strategic operation of the company was placed in the hands of an outside entrepreneur. Besides having live entertainment featured in showrooms of a Horseshoe, which would more than likely have made Benny and Teddy Jane Binion turn over in their graves, trusting outsiders to run the strategic aspects of the Horseshoe operation would have probably made both of them do flips.

In our lunch meeting in Philadelphia, Jack indicated that while I was likely qualified to be his COO, he was primarily concerned about my ability to lead four casinos. In my long career, I had never before had responsibility over multiple properties, and until Jack built his two Southern riverboat casinos, neither had he. Yet, I knew Jack was impressed with my East Coast casino credentials and my casino experience in Chicago would be invaluable to him and his company when he merged his new casino with the two he was buying in Chicagoland. He also told me that he liked the fact that I had worked for financially challenged companies for most of the past twenty years, and with that background, I knew how to pinch pennies especially in tough times. He understood from Gary Border that I was well organized and could design and construct a management organization that would provide his expanded company with a more corporate structure, but do it in a way that customers and employees would not discern. In other words, Binion's goal was to keep the Horseshoe organization perceived as a family run enterprise and I knew I was up to that challenge and mission.

However, what I sensed in my lunch meeting was a re-kindling of his distrust for outsiders that had been ingrained by his parents, and then proven accurate without warning by the defection of his trusted executive team. I wanted this job badly and I knew if I took it, I would have to work long and hard to regain the trust that Jack had lost in Paul Alanis. I could tell his ego was hurt by the Alanis resignation, but he hit me with the first of what we eventually now refer to as a "Jackism", when he declared, "I told Alanis that nobody is indispensible. If he thought he was, I told him to put his hand in a bucket of water. Now pull it out and see what kind of a hole you leave. The Horseshoe will get along just fine without you." Nonetheless, the management defections were an emotional hit to a guy that generally showed little emotion.

We ended lunch with Jack offering me the position. He instructed me to contact David Carroll and work out an employment agreement. I assured Mr. Binion that working for him did not require an employment contract, but he disagreed. That is when he pronounced to me the second "Jackism" of the day. He said to me, "Two people can only keep a secret when one of them is dead. Remember this when telling a secret. But an employment agreement cannot be secret. It has to protect both parties and their families for unforeseen circumstances." I already liked and admired this guy and I had not even gone to work for him yet.

I showed up for work the first day by meeting Jack in the lobby of the Horseshoe Hotel in Bossier City, Louisiana. I was introduced to the new company attorney, Dominic Polizzotto, who also was there on his first day on the job. We were led to several small visitors' offices where we both would begin our task of understanding the daily workings of the company. As I distributed a very detailed diligence questionnaire to the operating and marketing folks at the casino, Jack directed Polizzotto to join the company's technology guru, Jon Wolfe, and immediately head to Pasadena, California to dismantle the company office of the previous Horseshoe president, Paul Alanis.

After meeting with the management team and spending significant time in the weekly staff meetings of various department heads, I began to have a general understanding of the inner workings and the social networkings within the Louisiana property. By the end of my first week on the job, I headed east to Memphis and down to the Tunica Horseshoe to perform the same exercises with that staff. By the end of my second week, I headed back to my home in New Jersey to prepare for moving my residence to Las Vegas, where the main corporate headquarters was located. On Monday of my third week on the job, I set up my office in Las Vegas. However, I immediately learned that nobody really spent any time in the Las Vegas office. Unlike the corporate environment I had worked in for the past twenty years, I was back in the environment that I first entered when I went to work at the Dunes Hotel for the old syndicate guys.

Jack's office was about the size of a small bedroom in a tract home development. Jack did not believe in big fancy offices and he thought the casino manager's office should be the pit stand in the dice pit. Also interestingly, Jack did not occupy the largest office. He gave that to the executive who needed the most space to do his job. Jack did have some interesting pictures and plaques on his office wall and some of the slogans still stick in my head such as the one that read, "*My friends can do no wrong and my enemies can do no right*"; or the one that read. "*Sometimes you have to go out on a limb because that is where the fruit is*"; or the best one that stated, "*Luck is unexpected talent that shows up late in the game.*" I include these in my long list of famous "Jackisms" that you will hear me recite throughout this section of the book.

Jack Binion was a guy who, whenever possible, spent seven days a week in his casinos. His home and wife were in Las Vegas, so he occasionally used the corporate headquarters in Las Vegas, but except for ski season, he was generally found in one of his two Southern casinos. I said earlier that Jack did not drink coffee, use alcohol or smoke cigarettes. But he was addicted to his buffets and steak houses. In fact, you could spot him every day at noon in one of his buffets and at 8:00 p.m. nightly in one of his other restaurants. Jack expected the same from his corporate executive team. As a result, the corporate executives were scattered around with the chief financial officer and chief technology executive based in Memphis, the corporate vice president of human resources based in Shreveport and the senior marketing and operations executives located in Las Vegas. While this arrangement facilitated frequent visitations of key corporate people at the operating facilities, it also proved to impede the daily networking by the corporate team members, because we rarely were all together at any one time to discuss overall strategy and problem solving issues.

As we began the diligence activities to complete the purchase of the Empress Casinos in Chicagoland, it finally became evident to Jack that we had to centralize our corporate team in one location as the company was going to more than double in size, and we could no longer function properly out of suitcases. It was decided that, once we received licensing approvals from both the Indiana and Illinois gaming regulators, we would relocate all members of the corporate team to some location in the Chicago area. In the meantime, all of our efforts from my first day on the job were to prepare the company for the merger of the Horseshoe Company with the two casinos we were slated to purchase in Joliet, Illinois and Hammond, Indiana.

AFTER MY FIRST six weeks on the job at Horseshoe, I felt I had a pretty good understanding of the inner workings and financial status of all the operating departments in both of our Horseshoe Casinos. Unfortunately, my many years of working for financially troubled companies prior to my employment with Horseshoe, had provided me with a frame of reference for evaluating an operation that was entirely different than Jack Binion's. Anyway, I met with Binion and decided to show him how observant I had been in my diligence. I brought in copies of departmental financial statements for both casinos and had drawn big circles in red ink around categories of expenses which I thought represented big opportunities to reduce costs and improve profits. Complimentary expenses seemed unusually high and payroll looked a little bloated to me, as well.

Jack looked at me a little funny and for the first time he call me "Pardner." He said, "Pardner, my company ain't broke and I never made any money cutting costs for cost's sake. You are going to have to learn that I make my money by building revenues and investing back in my business. I desperately want to run an efficient operation, but I cannot create value by simply cutting costs. I make my money by growing revenues and stealing market share from my competitors. I know I over-comp and I purposely have about 1.3 service employees for every one that my closest competitor employs. You notice that I do not run a bus program or pay any junket commissions. My rooms are full of gamblers so I don't pay any travel agency commissions. I have always believed that if you are going to err and be wasteful, you do it on programs that benefit your customers. So Pardner, while I appreciate your efforts, I want you to continue to study the operation for another eight months. If you still come to the same conclusions, then we will talk." That is when he hit me with another Jackism: "Money is like manure; you need to spread it around in your company to make things grow!"

Now I had been studying departmental financial statements with a magnifying glass for over thirty years. I was pretty good at analyzing revenues and expenses at first glance. I had never been rebuked like this before, but Jack let me down in a graceful manner and his reasoning seemed to make sense. After all, his two casinos were out-performing the Grand Casino in Tunica and Harrah's Casino in Bossier City by double the revenues and triple the cash flows. In the Tunica market, the Grand Casino was twice as large and cost twice as much to construct as the Horseshoe. It was also five miles closer to Memphis than Jack's casino. Yet, the "Shoe" as it was called in the Memphis region was the casino of choice for most of the real gamblers and for almost 80 percent of Tunica casino employees who liked to gamble there after their work shift ended. When I joined the Horseshoe team, the Tunica facility was capturing 22 percent of the gaming revenue with only 11 percent of the casino floor space in the region. On top of that, it was generating a gross operating profit margin of 34 percent. Over in Bossier City, Louisiana, Jack had just opened a new 26-story luxury hotel tower and a brand new Riverboat casino, named "King of the Red." It was, no doubt, the finest riverboat facility in the country. Harrah's casino across the Red River in Shreveport was closer to both the local population as well as the major feeder market in Dallas and Fort Worth, Texas. Armed with its famous "Total Rewards" players club program, Harrah's was definitely a worthy competitor, but the Horseshoe with its liberal player rewards and better employee service, was able to capture over 170 percent of its fair share of the region's gaming revenues. As I left Jack's office that evening, I was on the verge of being "born again." I would never again look at a gambling operation the way I had before becoming mentored by the Icon.

Interestingly, nine months later, most of the cost cutting ideas I had on my original list to show Jack were now erased from it. Yet, as he promised, he would sit down to consider my ideas that remained if I was still committed to them. True to his word, three or four critical areas that required Jack's approval for change still remained on my list. This time he said, "Pardner, I now know that you know what you're doing at Horseshoe, so go ahead and make the changes." The changes I made probably were not items that generated huge improvements in profits, but they sent a message to my subordinate executives that Jack championed my ideas. I also now had the feeling that Jack was starting to trust my abilities and most of all, my loyalty to him, his family, and his company.

THE TWO HORSESHOE properties in the South operated like well oiled machines. It was so nice to finally be involved with an organization that did not require a huge bit of tinkering just to pay some past due bills. The Horseshoe was rolling in cash. The showrooms were featuring the likes of Don Henley, Ringo Starr, Jay Leno and Tim McGraw. The two casinos were hosting a huge array of million dollar customers. Jack Binion's Mid-South Poker Tournament was just coming into its own as a new event to rival the famous World Series of Poker. Jack, himself was the center of his own commercials and was becoming a celebrity in his own right all over Mississippi, Tennessee, and Louisiana. When asked by a member of the press why his smaller casino did so much better than his larger competitors, Jack answered by saying, "I use my facility twenty four hours a day while most of my competitors only use theirs for twelve or less." That proved to be a key to the higher profit margins we enjoyed at Horseshoe. We had lower odds and higher jackpots than our competitors. We gave away more comps and rebates than anybody in our markets. Our live entertainment was the best and most expensive in the region. But with a promotional environment that required us to use our facility around the clock, we were able to spread the costs of all our programs and higher payroll expenses over a full day, and at the end of the month we just generated more cash and better profits.

While most casinos had stringent policies for the issuance of complimentary services to its patrons, Jack Binion's policy was to empower his employees to make judgment calls and not be controlled by a computer or some rule set in stone. Many of you who frequent casinos know what I am talking about. You ask for a comp only to be advised that you need to play for another ten or fifteen minutes before you qualify. When you are a loyal customer and also hungry, that response will tend to piss you off. The Horseshoe policy was almost the exact opposite. The first time I observed it in person, I was afraid it was far too liberal and maybe uncontrollable. Yet, the public relations value of Jack's comp policies alone, were worth millions in free advertising. In fact, it was folklore in Memphis that Jack trained his casino bosses and hosts to use the "smell test" when deciding when to comp. When I first heard about it, I inquired, "What is the smell test?"

I was informed that it was Horseshoe policy to comp any customer who smelled like he had money on him. If a patron bought in with a hundred dollar bill, the pit boss smelled the money and immediately asked the patron if he would like dinner in the buffet. Sure there were some people that knew the policy and took advantage of it, but the volumes of patrons that liked the no-hassle comp procedures more than made up for the occasional guy that worked the system.

Free booze was another trademark at the Horseshoe. It is well known that liquor is the lubricant for free and easy gambling and therefore our rule involved a no-hassle policy for getting booze to customers. In the South, the customer liked long neck beer bottles and was not particularly happy drinking the more economical draft beer. Nonetheless, all our competitors poured draft beer. Not Jack. Bottled beer was more expensive. Bottled beer took up more space and required more employees to move it about. But that is what the customers wanted so that is what we gave them. Likewise, if a customer wanted a name brand liquor, that is what we poured him. It was a major violation of Jack's mantra to ever substitute an alternative brand to satisfy a customer's request. The casino bars in the Tunica casino were stripped of their cash registers, because the cost of auditing so little cash sales was not worth the effort. Ringing up comp booze sales in the cash register was just more red tape the customer did not need.

The Horseshoe training programs were easy to understand and simple to teach. They did not consume large amounts of time in boring classrooms, and they did not require the employees to learn "canned scripts." Jack Binion's service training followed the simple Golden Rule: Every employee could be himself or herself around a customer. Employees were encouraged to treat each customer as an individual, recognizing that each customer has a different set of criteria that makes them comfortable in a casino. The employees, as a team, all sensed that they were a surrogate Jack Binion, and they should act on behalf of the owner when dealing with each and every customer. Jack would constantly remind employees, "If you let a pissed off customer walk out the door, you better go outside and bring him back in or just keep walking out with him." Jack Binion was truly embarrassed when we screwed up a customer's visit. Yet he also knew that some of the best relationships with customers are forged through adversity. Therefore, he encouraged us to sometimes create small adversities for customers that we could quickly fix in such a glorified manner that both the effected customers and the people (including employees) around them would witness. Fixing these small grievances quickly and in such a glorified manner, cemented customer ties and continued to exemplify the customer service focus of Mr. Binion and his Horseshoe Casinos.

Jack also went out of his way to never let his family or his executives displace his customers. Unlike my days at Trump where we would vacate an entire floor of patrons just to take care of Marla Maples' family and friends on a moment's notice or even with MGM or Del Webb where the chairman of the board would demand the penthouse suite during a busy convention, Jack Binion proved to be the opposite. I recall my first visit to Tunica with Jack, where we learned that the Horseshoe was oversold and may be required to turn away some patrons with reservations. Binion and I gave up our rooms and rented accommodations at the Gold Strike Hotel next door. I also noticed that Jack never occupied a suite in his hotel, even when demand permitted him to do so. When his wife, Phyllis, traveled along with him, he would occasionally book a suite, but only if it did not displace a customer. Thankfully, Phyllis agreed with his policy and she was always a gracious guest, whatever room she occupied and regardless of the fact that she was also an owner of Horseshoe. But I guess that's why the employees all respected the Binions.

Every company has a culture. Some cultures are negative and some are positive but a culture of some kind always exists. A culture is developed and evolves based on the vision and behaviors of the leadership. Jack Binion had a vision that his casinos would create an environment for the serious gamblers where they could come and indulge themselves without apology and where there would be little if any red tape. Everybody understood that he successfully achieved his vision. Without a doubt, the culture at the Horseshoe under Jack Binion's leadership was the most unique ever to occur in the gambling industry. It has never been replicated, and the size and scope of the gaming operations today and leading into the future probably will never see the type of culture that led the Horseshoe Gaming Company to its rapid and successful merger with Empress Casinos and then its ultimate sale to Harrah's. Employees and customers alike all called Mr. Binion "Jack." Hardly anybody referred to him as Mr. Binion, and that just doesn't happen anymore in the current world of casinos.

AFTER MY FIRST three introductory months at Horseshoe, I found that my most important role was leading the merger with Empress Casinos. The deal to buy the Empress Company had been struck by Binion several months before I joined the company and it was the move that sky-rocketed the value of his company. Jack Binion understood the strength of the Chicago market and outbid rival, Caesars Entertainment for the right to acquire the two Chicagoland-based casinos of the Empress Company. Shortly after my appointment as COO of Horseshoe, our primary work focused on the operational due diligence necessary to develop a business plan to first merge and then operate the Empress Casinos under the Horseshoe umbrella. The Empress Casinos were highly profitable entities, but their culture was diametrically different from Horseshoe's. The Empress Casino in Joliet was the first riverboat casino to open in Illinois. It was inexpensively designed around an Egyptian motif that served its name. The pavilion area and casino public areas were constructed out of wood and I prayed we never would have a fire because there would be no chance to save it. As I feared, just eight years after we sold the Joliet casino to Argosy Casinos, a massive fire destroyed most of the pavilion lobby and restaurants causing the casino to close for 97 days. The second Empress Riverboat Casino was located in Hammond, Indiana on the border of Chicago and Indiana. This casino had virtually no architectural theme at all to support the Empress name, but being the closest Indiana casino to downtown Chicago, it happily enjoyed the highest revenues of any casino in Indiana. Neither Empress facility looked like a Horseshoe from an architectural standpoint.

But even more markedly different from the Horseshoe was the culture. The Empress Casinos were operated by their individual ownership group as cheaply as possible. Customers were accustomed to waiting for change and jackpot payouts. Comps were tight and food quality was just okay. The slot machines were five or six years old in the Joliet property and were just not at all competitive with its closest rival Casino, Harrah's, which was located four miles away in downtown Joliet. The housekeeping and maintenance of the Joliet facility, both in the public areas and the back of the house were acceptable but not up to Horseshoe standards.

The physical environment of the Empress Indiana casino was worse. The Empress Casino in Hammond was referred to by its own employees and by many potential customers who did not then patronize it as the "Ghetto Boat." The facility was dirty. The food in the buffet was not appetizing. The casino carpet was installed in three foot squares, allowing for small sections of the flooring to be replaced without doing the entire floor. With several winters of traffic and spotty carpet shampooing over the three years the casino had been open, the floors of the casino and pavilion looked tired and shabby. The back of the house was a disaster. It was embarrassing to take anybody into the employee areas where space was cramped, dirty, and supplies were in total disarray. In management's interest to be everything to every gambler, they had jammed in 1750 slot machines, a poker room and sixty table games on four floors of a small narrow-beamed riverboat. Banks of slot machines were long, and aisle space between slot banks was minimal. During busy times on the boat, it was next to impossible to get change, cocktail service, or a jackpot paid out if you were sitting in the middle of one of those long rows of slots. In management's attempt to cater to the bulk of their customer base, which was largely African American, a "FUBU" clothing store had been opened in the valet entry lobby of the pavilion. Most of the customers patronizing this shop were not gamblers, but tended to be younger folks arriving in gangs who merely milled around. The presence of this shop did little to improve the existing business but was a deterrent to the promotion of any Caucasian or Asian business.

Another impediment we quickly observed was the large number of idle people who would board the casino vessel and then sit at a slot machine stool for most of the cruise. In 1999 when we purchased the Empress Casinos, it was required by law that the riverboat casinos either cruise or simulate cruises. That meant that people could board the casino vessel at only set times, usually every two hours. If the boats sailed, customers had to stay on the boat until it moored. Whenever the Captain of the vessel or the state gaming inspector felt it was unsafe to sail, we were required to conduct simulated cruises. That meant people could only get on the casino vessel at the prescribed time, but people could get off at will. That was advantageous to actual cruising, but still inhibited spontaneous use of the casino. On weekends and holidays, the cruising schedules often created capacity crowds at the beginning of the cruise, and people hanging around sitting at slot machines without playing caused limited access to our slot machines for the new customers boarding. To compound the problem, it was learned that a sizeable number of the people hanging around were hustling customers for money or trying to steal credits left on a machine by a forgetful player.

Jack Binion had his nephew, Key Fechser, scout out the Hammond Casino from the perspective of a Binion family gambler. Jack wanted him to look for employee cheating, card counting and general "trouble" that a casino can often attract. Key was a mean looking rotund individual with a beard and a demeanor that just told you not to screw with him if you valued your life. Key had a reputation as the Binion family "enforcer" when Jack had operated the Horseshoe in downtown Las Vegas. Rumors have it that the cheaters and thieves at the Horseshoe always preferred a trip to the downtown detention center with a Las Vegas police officer over a short "off the record" meeting with Key in the basement of the Horseshoe Casino. It was said that Key was not afraid of anything or anyone.

Yet when Key returned from his surveillance of the Hammond Riverboat Casino on his first covert visit there to check out gaming operations, he told Jack he found it to be scary. In fact his exact words were, "This is the most dangerous joint I have ever been in without my gun!"

CHAPTER **9**

EVEN WITH KEY'S observations, when our operating due diligence concluded, we found it difficult to bring our findings and recommended course of action to Jack Binion because not only was our plan going to cost him a lot of money, but, worse, it would depress earnings in the short term. Once the purchase of the Empress Casinos was completed, Horseshoe Gaming Holdings Corporation would take on an additional $500,000,000 in debt giving the company a total debt balance exceeding one billion dollars and good earnings were important to support that level of debt. Nevertheless, we presented Mr. Binion with a business plan that had three expensive elements to it.

First, we proposed to spend upward of thirty million dollars in capital expenditures to bring the two facilities up to date and competitive within their market environments. Then we suggested that the company would have to spend over seven million dollars in training initiatives, especially at the Hammond facility where, for example, we found that the average time for a jackpot payout was over twenty minutes long. This length of time for an important slot customer service of this type simply was not going to cut it at a Horseshoe owned property for sure.

Empress had been the biggest Indiana Casino revenue generator and especially enjoyed being King of the pack among the five Northwest Indiana Casinos since the inception of legal gambling in the state. But as Jack would always say, "In the valley of the blind, the one eyed guy is King." The problem we foresaw was the fact that, less than one year before Jack closed his purchase of the Empress Casino, Harrah's Entertainment Company had completed the purchase of the Showboat casino in East Chicago, just next door to the Empress. For the first time since the opening of casinos in Indiana, Empress faced a serious competitor and Harrah's was improving service levels and stealing market share quickly. Harrah's moved so swiftly that it almost caught the Empress team off guard. As an example, Harrah's had improved its slot jackpot payout time to under seven minutes and the Empress management had either not recognized the improvement or had ignored it as a threat. With the sale of Empress underway, the old team was focusing on cutting costs to preserve cash and maintain profitability until the sale was completed.

Lastly, we suggested that to become number one in market share, we would have to liberalize our comps and reward systems and improve food quality and offerings. Furthermore, the number of employees on staff needed to be increased if we were to successfully improve the service levels and balance the workforce in each of the disciplines involved in the different cycles of service on the casino floor. By implementing this last recommendation, it would reduce operating profits by some ten percent the first year we owned the company. We argued that the short term cost would be overcome when we achieved market dominance, which we projected would take eighteen to twenty four months following the date we finally completed the merger. To magnify our concerns to Jack, we pointed out that the very first month after we purchased the Empress, Harrah's Casino took the top monthly revenue spot away from Empress for the first time ever.. Jack Binion had arrived just in time.

What I learned to value the most about working for the Horseshoe was our organization's agility. We were able to make decisions quickly. So many of the bigger casino companies tend to analyze everything so long that the opportunity being analyzed eventually fades away before any action is ever taken. This was not the case at the Horseshoe. While Jack Binion was known to vacillate on some decisions, when it came to talking care of his business, he could also make decisions on the fly.

The Empress merger was no exception. Jack listened to our reasoning and went along with our plans. We agreed that we would implement the Horseshoe business plan one month after we took possession of the company. While we had conducted months of operational diligence before taking control of the Empress operations, one always finds the unexpected after you take ownership and the extra month to validate our plans would be well spent. Since the closing was scheduled to occur on or before December 1, using that month before the end of the year to further evaluate the operation and ensure the company was well prepared for the events of "Y-2K" kept the Horseshoe merger team quite busy. We also used the month of December to set up temporary housing for our executives and began house hunting for the future residences of our corporate executives.

November 30, 1999 was the date finally determined for the actual takeover. The Indiana Gaming Commission had unanimously approved Jack Binion and the Horseshoe Company to own and operate the Empress in Hammond. However, the Illinois Gaming Board had different ideas about Jack's qualifications. Even though Jack Binion had held a gaming license for almost forty years in Nevada and had been licensed as an owner in Mississippi and Louisiana, the gaming board and its staff in Illinois did not like what they viewed as family baggage and some other ties that Jack had with close friends whom Illinois gaming staffers viewed with disdain. On top of that, the Illinois regulators seemed to want to right the wrong they felt occurred when Jack won a lawsuit against the Louisiana Gaming Board back in 1994. Nonetheless, in November, 1999 the Illinois Gaming Board approved Horseshoe Gaming Holding Corp to acquire and operate the Empress Casino in Joliet, even though it deferred the approval of its owner, Jack Binion, for a hearing to decide his qualifications later in 2000. In the November hearing, certain conditions were placed upon the Horseshoe including a requirement that Horseshoe move its corporate headquarters to Joliet. Joseph Canfora, the president of the Empress, was retained by Horseshoe as its new president to lead the operation following the merger.

CHAPTER **10**

THE TRANSITION OF ownership between the Empress Company and Horseshoe was seamless. Neither casino closed during the change over, although we coordinated the closing of the different levels of the casino vessels so that accurate accounting could be undertaken with state supervision. The change in ownership went so well that even the on-site agents for the Illinois Gaming Board were complimentary, much to the chagrin of their superiors. The Indiana regulators were as supportive as ever and I applaud them for their reasonableness and recognition that businesses operate with people and those people sometimes make errors. The Horseshoe corporate team was all staying in hotel rooms at the Joliet Empress Casino. The hotel was located some thousand feet from the casino pavilion and the rooms were average, maybe better than Motel 6, but probably not better than Super 8. This would be the last time the team stayed in the Joliet hotel rooms.

David Carroll, our vice president of human resources had identified executive apartments for our team located north of Joliet in the city of Romeoville. Shakespeare would have been proud of his namesakes: "Romeo and Joliet!" David had found us a very nice complex that catered to corporate executives desiring accommodations away from home that were more compelling than an extended-stay motel, but that fit within a reasonable budget for the company. For me, this arrangement was better than a hotel in downtown Chicago for a variety of reasons. First, it was closer to work and I could drive my rental car right up to my front door. Second, I could leave all my belongings in my room and travel back and forth to my home in Las Vegas or Atlantic City with nothing but a small brief case. Third, we had a nice kitchen, a stocked refrigerator and pantry, and even a clothes washer and dryer. But best of all, it was like a college dormitory. Having never experienced the dorm life in college, this was a first and also a lot of fun. I was paired up with Kirk Saylor, our CFO and we were the company's "Odd Couple." Kirk was a slob, tracking in mud and snow on his shoes, sitting around in his underwear on the sofa drinking his martini, and smoking a cigar while watching some TV in the evening. I was constantly running around cleaning up behind him or putting things back in the pantry that he left out on the kitchen counter. We were kidded all the time but we had a lot of fun and still talk about it today. Among the executive team, Kirk and I were known for the gallons of Vodka we stored in the freezer of our fridge. The other roommate pairings made sense as well. Jon Wolfe, our portly CIO, was paired up with another technology geek, and their freezer was stocked with ice cream. Gary Border, the chief marketing guru, was paired up with John Moran, the database manager. The aggressive and aloof Border loaded up on expensive wines, while his shy and deliberate roommate, Moran, kept the fridge full of Budweiser. This entire grouping of executives was located on the right side of the complex. Over on the left were our liberal friends. David Carroll, who paired up with David MacAlpine, stocked up who knows what? They operated the human resources department and were the employee advocates for the organization, thus explaining their political ideology. The collegial arrangement made for a very interesting five months as we implemented the Horseshoe plan at Empress Casinos. By May 15, everybody in the Romeoville dorms had finally found permanent housing and was moving their families from Las Vegas, Shreveport, Memphis and Atlantic City to the new headquarters in Chicagoland.

Moving the corporate headquarters to Joliet to satisfy the conditions of our gaming licensees proved to be quite expensive and disruptive to the Joliet Casino operation. Jack decided that rather than rent an office complex in the Joliet area, we would instead modify the office complex at the Empress Casino to accommodate our team. Over the course of two months, we eventually squeezed everybody in, even though I had never seen offices that small in the gaming business. I was chief operating officer and my office was ten by ten feet, but at least it had a nice window with a view of the Des Plaines River. We were just one office short when we finished up. Jon Wolfe, our CIO was coordinating the office moves and the computer installation and he told me he would find the missing office we needed. He told me to wait until the next morning and the problem would be solved. I came in the next morning to find one of the old Empress employees, a nice but annoying analyst named Matt Roobe waiting outside my office with a concerned look on his face. Overnight, Jon had moved this guy's desk out of his office into the hallway and moved the Horseshoe executive into Matt's office. As far as Jon was concerned, problem solved.

CHAPTER 11

OUR FIRST ORDER of business was to get the two casinos cleaned up from the front of the public areas to the rear of the house areas. Around the clock meetings were held with all employees at both casinos. Little groups of ten to twenty employees from every department participated in meetings that were always moderated by Jack Binion. Jack wanted to hear the employees' concerns and determine what tools they might be lacking to do their jobs. Then he spent time communicating his ideology for running a casino. Jack had a special knack for putting employees at ease. The new Empress employees had never experienced this type of behavior from an owner before, so they naturally were skeptical at first. But Jack knew how to impress them. For instance, at about 8:00 p.m., following the first meeting we held with employees in Hammond, we learned that the table games department was short of electric pencil sharpeners at the pit stands. After the meeting, we sent one of our accounting guys down to the office supply store and had him buy twenty electric pencil sharpeners. They were installed before we held the next meeting with table games employees. After that the dialogue between employees and Jack Binion became very open because they were now aware that Jack not only listened to them, but he also cared about them. It was not many weeks before all the employees were calling Mr. Binion "Jack," like they did at his two original southern casinos.

The two Empress casinos were famous for "sweating" the action at their table games. Whenever a big customer bought in, it was common for several pit bosses and games shift managers to hover around the table like crows on a fence post. These casino pit bosses were always worrying that the customer might possibly win some money. It was not uncommon for a floor supervisor to kick a dealer in the heel after a customer won a big bet, sometimes whispering in the dealer's ear, "Can't you win a F-ing bet?" Binion let the games people know from day one that he would not tolerate sweating the games. Well, some habits are hard to break. A few short employee pep talks just don't always do the trick. So the next time we witnessed an incident of sweating, we instructed the casino manager to suspend the pit boss and floor supervisors involved. I wanted to fire them because there is nothing like shooting the hostage to get attention in a crisis. But the suspension served its purpose. It sent the message that Jack wanted to deliver to the games employees, but also showed him as more compassionate than I might have been.

In the meantime, we were adding employees to the payroll, particularly among the cleaning personnel and the slot operations and cashiering employees. We brought in supervisors from our southern casinos to demonstrate the type of cleaning techniques we demanded in our operation. We wanted electrical utility closets free of any storage, and machine rooms were cleaned and painted so meticulously that they gleamed. The employee dining rooms were enlarged and cleaned up to reflect the same quality as the other cuisines in the casino. Comfort was a term that our customers were most concerned about, and yet comfort is defined differently by every customer. However, there are several common denominators in the definition of comfort. They include cleanliness and security. So as we cleaned the properties up, we also added one hundred additional employees to our security forces. We installed $300,000 of new lighting in the Hammond parking garage and $500,000 worth of closed circuit television cameras and monitors to improve the perception of safety.

As we increased the size of our cashiering and slot operations teams, we soon learned that turnover was stifling our ability to achieve our service objectives. We challenged the employees in both departments to help us develop systems that would reduce the steps in the cycle of service involved in each task they performed, steps they knew would improve service while also saving costs. Working together, the employee teams helped develop the proper training curriculum that began enabling us to move toward our goals. Within three months, we had achieved a slot fill and jackpot payout time of less than seven minutes on average, and we were finally competitive with our nemesis, Harrah's. By the end of six month, we had achieved jackpot payout times of less than four minutes at both Empress Casinos; and, remarkably, they were now beating the averages we had established for our two Southern casinos several years earlier.

The best thing to come out of this entire exercise was to see Jack Binion's shrewd observations of events and his response to our problem of turnover. Jack sat down with David Carroll and me to discuss an idea he had. Relating back to our early days in Las Vegas, he recalled that having a casino cage cashier job or being a slot attendant in a Las Vegas casino were coveted positions and were also considered to be career jobs.

"But looking at it now," he observed, "the riverboat casinos have mainly come about because of depressed economic situations in these new jurisdictions. The casinos were found to be a method to get people off of welfare and out of the unemployment lines. As such, the new riverboat casinos tended to pay only minimum wages or slightly better in these important jobs. People taking them do so as an interim step to a possible better position. They do not see these jobs as a career opportunity. We need to do something about that if we are to stop the migration and reduce the turnover."

We left that meeting with instructions from Jack to outline a potential plan that would improve the wages of these critical positions, and develop a career path for upward promotion that would slow turnover. Our mission was to establish an organizational structure and training program geared to make employees more prepared to take on additional responsibilities as they proceeded through a career path that worked best for them and the company. With input from cage cashiers and their supervisors, we began a program in the casino cages for cashiers to move upward into newly created positions such as lead banker and master banker. These new interim positions were designed to hone their skills and allow them to gradually take on additional tasks and responsibilities. Base wages were increased slightly, but the motivation to move through the system proved to be more rewarding. Jack's idea worked well almost immediately in the cashiers' cage, so we copied the concept in the slot department and security operations. Employee turnover was reduced substantially to the point in which the increases in base pay and the costs of promotions into the interim level jobs in each department were totally offset. Jack's idea, added to his willingness to experiment with his own money, enabled Horseshoe's to achieve its service goals at Empress within the company's first six months of ownership.

JACK BINION QUICKLY became a legend in Chicagoland. Because of licensing problems in Illinois, his picture was frequently on the front page of the Chicago Tribune. Unlike Trump, this was not the type of publicity Jack wanted on the front page. Nonetheless, it quickly made his name a household word in Chicagoland. Then we put him in his own television commercials as we introduced him in the Chicago area market as the new owner of the two Empress Casinos. But the elements that made him legendary among employees were his behaviors--- so different from the past owners to whom they were accustomed. Several of these legendary incidents stand out in my mind. On one of his first trips to the Joliet Empress about a week after we took over the ownership, the new president sent a limousine to pick up Jack at O'Hare Airport. When Jack spotted the limo, the driver opened the back door for him as he approached the vehicle. Jack threw his suitcase and briefcase in the back seat and then hopped into the front seat with the driver. All the way back on the drive to the casino, Jack solicited ideas from the limo driver on how conditions at the Empress could be made better for the customers and the employees. Jack wrote the driver's ideas down on a yellow legal pad, and instructed us to implement one or two of the ideas quickly, just so the word would get out.....and get out it did.

Jack also preferred to ride in the employee shuttle bus rather than the company limo. He was famous for walking around the casino with his yellow legal pad and he was constantly taking notes on employees' and customers' ideas for change. It was common and sometimes upsetting to the property management when Jack would walk the hallways of the hotel and grab six or eight housekeepers and invite them to lunch with him in the coffee shop. Nonetheless, these little informal rap sessions were important pieces of the Binion puzzle to create the culture that was second nature to Jack. Although Jack was brought up as a gambler, it seemed he spent more time in the hotel kitchens than he did in the dice pit on the casino floor. Great food was a Horseshoe Hallmark and Jack was the company's number one food tester. To Jack, the chef was more important than the casino manager when it came to meeting our marketing goals.

Jack flew in the back of the airplane for a long time on his many commutes from Las Vegas to his casinos, until one day he was walking through the plane and saw executives who worked for him sitting up front. Fortunately we were paying coach fare and sitting there because of frequent flyer mileage. Jack's secretary had signed Jack up for frequent flier benefits years before, but Jack had just not bothered to ever cash in on the benefits. But after that trip, he finally did fly first class from then on. Employees called him the "Quiet Billionaire."

Speaking of flying, as part of the acquisition of the Empress Casinos, Jack could have acquired the Empress Company airplane, a nice Cessna Citation. But Jack told the old owners of Empress that they could keep the plane, even though he received no discount in the purchase price of the company. Jack was content to have the Horseshoe company airplane read *Southwest* or *American* on its tail. But behind it all was his family history of Benny Binion spending as little money as possible on executive or employee frills, and a company airplane in Jack's mind was even less productive than showrooms with expensive entertainers…and he didn't care for them either.

Probably the most amusing episode in the Jack Binion saga of amusing events occurred during a series of employee meetings we were conducting at the Hammond Casino shortly after we bought it. The Empress Casino in Hammond did not feature a hotel, so we would often stay at the Ramada Inn, a small hotel located about two miles from the casino. Jack would usually take the Ramada shuttle bus up to the Empress, but on this particular morning, the shuttle bus was broken down. Not wanting to be late for the employee meetings he was hosting, he located the maintenance man from the Ramada and solicited a ride in the company pickup truck. Finding the front seat to be greasy and full of junk, Jack hopped into the bed of the truck and rode to the Empress up the main drag of Hammond and right up to the front valet entry of the casino in his suit and tie. You can imagine the look on the face of the doorman when he saw Jack Binion jump out of the back of that pickup truck. Before the employee meeting was underway, the story of Jack riding in Sanford and Son's pickup truck was all over the casino.

The employees all became fully aware that Jack Binion forbids the sweating of any game on the casino floor. After the suspensions of the casino employees I mentioned earlier, sweating at the Empress Casinos became a thing of the past. *Practice what you preach* was personified by Binion, when he joined us for coffee one morning in the buffet of our Hammond casino. Gary Border met up with us and informed Jack that the casino had just been beat by a big gambler for $3.5 million dollars the previous hour. With many buffet employees looking on, Jack did not even flinch, but just continued with his previous conversation discussing methods we could undertake to improve the buffet quality at the Empress Hammond. The loss did not worry him at all. He knew it was just a loan, because the player that won the money always came back. He had beaten us before, but never by that much. Sure enough, before the week was over, we had won all the money back from the big player plus another million of his own bankroll.

The employees all understood that when they screwed up, they embarrassed Jack. It was not uncommon to see Jack grab a book of comp slips and head out to the casino floor passing out comps to customers who he believed may have waited too long for service or a cocktail. Jack strived for perfection and, for him, embarrassment was an incentive to strive harder. Stories still circulate about opening day at his casino in Tunica where Jack ran around the casino paying jackpots out of his pocket because the staff could not keep up with the volume of business. He was even found making his wife, Phyllis, bus tables in the buffet and run cocktails to players on the casino floor.

And Jack would give you the shirt off his back. We were walking down a street in Chicago following a meeting with lawyers. It was a cool and balmy day. Jack noticed that our female accounting executive was chilly and he immediately removed his sport coat and covered her with it, even though he now had to walk the remaining distance in the cold, himself. Jack was just a different kind of casino owner.

AS WE CLEANED up the Hammond casino physically, we needed to also clear the dead beats off the casino floor. Using the surveillance cameras, I commissioned occupancy surveys for six straight weeks on the busiest cruises to determine utilization of slot machines. Our surveys indicated we could remove several hundred machines from the floor and still handle patron demand, provided we could eliminate the 'dead beats' from idly sitting on slot machine stools. When we convened a meeting of the security and slot department directors, my idea to establish a dead beat patrol was characterized as racist. So Jack suggested we take it to the employees and let them help develop a solution. Since 70 percent of our employees were African American and 70% of our customers were also African American, this constituency had to be as annoyed by dead beats as we operators were. Since it also appeared that 70% of our dead beats were African Americans, maybe the employees would have a solution. And they did.

They told us that, "Just like you white folks, we don't want to be hustled and we don't want to be pick-pocketed and we don't want to be annoyed by these clowns, either." With our employees' involvement, we implemented "Dead Beat Patrols" comprised of teams of employees from slot operations and security who all readily knew who the culprits were. One by one we moved them out.

As we did, we re-aligned and configured the four casino floors with fewer machines, opening up aisle space and access so customers and employees could move about more readily and patrons could finally easily access their favorite slot machines. We eliminated the poker pit, opening up even more comfortable space for the more profitable slot machines and as we did, we installed fancy, attractive casino carpet to replace the old worn out carpet tiles. As we completed the initial clean up and reconfiguration, we had actually eliminated three hundred gaming positions, yet casino revenues had not fallen one penny. Less was actually more!

With the first phase of our clean up completed, our marketing initiatives kicked in. Gary Border had identified a marketing executive from Atlantic City to take over the strategic initiatives for our Hammond Casino while Border concentrated on Joliet and strategies for the two Southern casinos. The new marketing chief, Phil Juliano, was a veteran casino marketing executive from New Jersey with years of experience in the highly competitive Atlantic City market. Armed with new ideas imported from Atlantic City, and with a newly reconfigured gaming floor with slot machine programs that had proven to be very successful in Tunica, Mississippi, we were ready to show Chicago how to run a joint. As everything kicked in, revenues began to decline and marketing expenses began to escalate. Juliano quickly realized that promotions that worked fine on the East Coast did not necessarily work in Chicagoland. To his credit, he shifted gears quite quickly and arrested the decline in visitor volume and restored market share of visitor trips to the casino almost overnight. But revenues still declined.

It soon became evident to us that the Chicagoland slot customer had a far different playing profile than the ones we were used to in the Southern casinos and our pricing policy was wrong. It was not loose slots that attracted the Chicago customer, but more the perception of time on the slot machine. We were giving too much away in promotions and our machines were too loose for us to maximize a patron's playing time to our advantage. We were advertising the loosest slots in Chicagoland so we had to maintain that image and be true to our promise, but we had to ratchet the win percentage up quickly to recoup the revenue declines we had experienced. We recruited Dennis Gentry, one of the foremost slot strategists in the industry today, to move to Hammond and take over the slot operations for us. Within 90 days, the Empress Hammond Casino was finally producing revenue numbers that qualified it for a name change to Horseshoe.

IN THE MEANTIME, over in Joliet we had initiated several big changes that immediately improved revenues. We increased table betting limits to $10,000, far greater than any casino in Illinois had ever dreamed of offering. We kicked in daily direct mail for our loyal customers to replace monthly promotional offerings used by the previous owners. The general manager and all the employees were seeing what the new business was doing to their reputations and pocket books, so they were enthusiastically jumping on our band wagon. Within two months, we were generating market share equal to Harrah's, which had led the Empress in monthly revenues by several hundred basis points for years. Our employment programs were working so well that Harrah's began soliciting our employees by driving trucks with "Help Wanted" billboards through the Empress parking lots. It backfired on them when Gary Border took a picture of the Harrah's truck in front of the Empress entryway, and placed a full page advertisement in the Joliet newspaper that read, "When Harrah's needs quality employees, they come looking at Empress Hotel Casino."

Harrah's was located in downtown urban Joliet while Empress was located outside the city on 300 acres of manicured and wooded land along the Des Plaines River. Harrah's was well established and had a lock on downtown, including all the billboards. Several months after we purchased the Empress, we were confronted with an opportunity to rent two billboards that would be affixed to the top of a six story office building located directly across the street from the Harrah's Casino front entryway. It would be impossible for a customer exiting from Harrah's not to notice the billboards directly across the street. Still pissed off from the mobile billboard incident in our parking lots, I told our advertising people to have the agency contract with the promoter of the two new boards and get them installed as soon as possible and with a very compelling message to Harrah's patrons. Our ad agency arranged for installation of the boards, which we found would be completed at 4:00 a.m. the following Saturday morning. We assumed this was the slowest time for traffic and for erection of a mobile crane to install the boards.

The boards were installed and the messages were wrapped on the board before the Harrah's casino opened for business that Saturday morning. As we hoped, they did their job. The general manager of Harrah's became enraged when he arrived at work. How could this happen without his knowledge? It turned out that he was not the only surprised party. The owner of the six story building was also surprised. In fact, he had no idea billboards were installed on his building and would never have given approval. The city building department had never been notified and proper permits were never pulled. Before the next business day was over, lawsuits filled the air from every party and, lo and behold, the bill board promoter fled and could not be located. Harrah's was demanding that we pay to take the boards down, but it turned out we never even paid to have them put up. Neither had our advertising agency in Chicago. The promoter had done the dastardly deed overnight and left town without collecting any fees from us or paying his crane operator and board installer. As the situation became testier, the Judge presiding over the legal claims put an injunction on any actions at all until he ruled. Consequently, the Empress Billboards stayed up for thirty additional days and in the end, we never paid a dime. The cost of the hoax was absorbed by the city of Joliet and the unfortunate building owner.

By June of 2000, the Empress in Joliet was generating revenues 34% greater than had been achieved the year earlier under former ownership. It was evident to everybody in Illinois that Jack Binion and the Horseshoe operation were going to be good for Illinois and Joliet in particular. Yet, during a week-long hearing at the end of June, The Illinois Gaming Board decided to deny Jack Binion a permanent license to operate his Illinois casino. When the hearing ended with such a terrible outcome for Jack after a grueling long day, Jack looked at the twelve very solemn people around the conference table in our lawyer's Chicago office and lamented, "Boys, we really screwed up this time. We have been in here all day and nobody made dinner reservations tonight. Where in the hell will a group of people this large get dinner reservations at this late time of day?"

Years later, in what is still regarded by the public as a bungled decision by the Illinois Gaming Board at the expense of Illinois taxpayers and gamblers, Jack Binion decided to take his lumps rather than fight it out in court. While Jack was excited about coming to Illinois every week and spending time in his casinos, he had no appetite for spending several years in and out of courtrooms trying to retain his right to operate in Illinois. Notwithstanding the fact that he had purchased an expensive apartment on the Gold Coast in Chicago and had spent millions moving his corporate team to the Joliet headquarters, he decided to work out an arrangement with the Illinois regulators that would allow him to make a graceful exit. Agreeing to never apply for a gaming license in Illinois again, Jack was permitted a reasonable length of time to sell his Joliet property and keep the profits if there were any. In the meantime, we were assured by the Indiana regulators that we were still welcome in Indiana and that state was actually looking for big things to come from Horseshoe in Hammond. They had already witnessed our ability to quickly improve revenues and now we were about to embark on a major capital improvement undertaking, something no other casino had recently done in any part of the state.

Negotiations over the Horseshoe's departure from Illinois lasted for several months and eventually culminated in Jack Binion's agreement to immediately move the corporate headquarters out of the

Joliet facility. And Jack also agreed to never again step foot into the Empress until it was sold. Jack and I met privately and I assured him I would be his surrogate and look out for his family interest in Joliet until the sale was consummated. The operations at the Joliet Empress would be run as if he was there daily, and I promised him we would not miss a beat.

Later that week, Jack and his board of directors decided to terminate the services of the new company president, Joe Canfora, and I assumed the duties of Joe without the title. Our corporate team immediately began searching for new office space to satisfy our agreement with the Illinois Gaming Board that we would exit our offices in the Joliet casino within six months. Jack really wanted us to move the offices to Hammond, Indiana so that our executives would not be paying Illinois Income taxes. Jack felt that if the state gaming regulators believed we were not worthy to operate in Illinois, then they certainly would not want to take our tainted income taxes and have it mingled into their income tax stream.

We argued with Jack about moving our office too far from Joliet, where most of our corporate staff lived. We told him that a move to Indiana would place such undue strain on many of them, and we probably risked losing half our corporate team. And the other half would be unhappy about a two hour commute to work every day. However, even with the risk of losing some of our staff, Jack was anxious to locate a suitable office building in Hammond just to get us all out of Illinois. He finally located what looked to be a suitable building in downtown Hammond just blocks away from city hall. Jack thought that the rent seemed a little steep for the downtown Hammond environment, but then he learned that the rent included armed guards who would walk our female employees to their cars when the offices closed each day. It sounded like a bargain until the night before we were due to sign a lease contract to rent the facility, three people were murdered in the Ramada Hotel parking lot just next door to the office building. The unfortunate murders of the three Hammond residents had a good ending for all of us in the Horseshoe

Corporate Office. "Murder Motel" as we called it from then on, fortunately killed the idea to rent the office complex in downtown Hammond, even for Jack.

In the end, Jack agreed to let us lease an office complex in a conveniently located business complex in the town of Tinley Park, Illinois. Rents were reasonable, space was generous and parking was wonderful. The office was exactly 25 miles from our Joliet casino and 27 miles from the Hammond Empress. Midway Airport was ten miles away and O'Hare was only thirty, making the office very convenient for our travels to Las Vegas and our Southern casinos as well. Best of all, downtown Chicago was only 25 minutes away (except during rush hour). The only negative about the Tinley Park location was the Illinois income tax. Still, it beat the hell out of the "Murder Motel."

CHAPTER **15**

WHILE WE WERE in construction at the new Tinley Park Office Headquarters, Jack struck a deal with Argosy Gaming Corporation who purchased the Empress in Joliet for $465 million dollars. We moved into the new corporate offices in May, 2001 and sold the Empress to Argosy in August 3, 2001. Considering that just eighteen months earlier, Binion had paid $645 million dollars for both Empress Casinos, which at the time were valued equally, the Horseshoe made a tidy $140 million dollar profit. The sale also enabled us to pay down our debt by over $400,000,000, giving us one of the strongest balance sheets in the gaming industry in those days.

Naturally the pain and embarrassment of losing the Illinois gaming license was excruciating and we knew it would have some serious negative ramifications on future license applications and renewals. Yet, the sale of the Joliet casino actually made the Horseshoe Company stronger. We could now concentrate all our energy in Chicagoland toward improving the profitability and the levels of service and quality of our newly branded Horseshoe Hammond Casino. We could now accelerate our efforts to turn the old Empress Casino into the most profitable Horseshoe in the country. The coup de grace occurred five months after we sold the Joliet Empress Casino to Argosy. Illinois decided to raise gross revenue taxes from 50% to 70%. When that occurred, Jack declared, "I'm going to change my name to Mr. Lucky!"

Then he changed my name to Mr. Lucky, too. He called me into his office and promoted me to president of Horseshoe Gaming Holding Corp. After two years, I had finally earned back the trust Jack had lost with the defection of my predecessor, Paul Alanis, and I was determined not to let him lose it again. That determination led to my most satisfying moment working for Jack Binion. While it only lasted all but eight hours, it is something I will always value about my relationship with him. About a year after my appointment as president, Jack was encountering some potentially damaging legal allegations that could have possibly caused severe licensing implications for the Horseshoe Corporation. On short notice, Jack summoned me to meet him for dinner on a Sunday night in downtown Chicago with his New York lawyer and Andy Astrachan, his financial advisor. In confidence, he told me about the allegations. Unfortunately when dealing with gaming regulators, perception is usually reality in their minds. Jack's lawyers acknowledged that it might take months to prove Jack innocent of the false allegations and during those months of legal turmoil, Jack might have to step away from his CEO role at Horseshoe.

The lawyers and Jack set up a contingent organization chart with an independent board of directors to be headed up by Andy as Chairman, and I was designated to assume the role of CEO. The morning following our dinner meeting in Chicago, Jack and Andy met individually with all of the senior executives to inform them on the potential course of events. I was to be named CEO that day. That was a trust of honor for me, not only from Jack Binion, but also of his wife, Phyllis, and his daughters, too. However, by the end of the day, Jack was informed by his lawyers that the allegations had been dropped and my reign as CEO was terminated. While short lived, I reveled in the trust and loyalty I had been able to build with my special role model in life.

DURING THE PERIOD of time we were trying to sell the Joliet facility and making plans to relocate our corporate headquarters from Joliet to Tinley Park, we were simultaneously engineering the re-branding of the Empress casino in Indiana. Jack had hoped to accomplish the re-branding within 12 months after our purchase, but we found the old culture we inherited to be far removed from what we had to make it, so we delayed the changeover. A brand represents a promise to deliver; and the Horseshoe brand was famous for delivering a great gambling entertainment experience for our guests, first time and every time. The executive team at Horseshoe was anxious to shed the Empress name. Yet, Jack convinced us that, until we could guarantee that the Hammond employees could provide the quality of service and products for which Jack Binion stood, it would be folly to spend any money promoting the name and brand change. On top of it all, the disposition of the Joliet asset and the move of the corporate offices were generating business disruption and some loss of focus by the senior executive team. We knew we were going to physically move the staff into the Tinley Park office building on the last weekend in April, so we decided to schedule the official grand opening of the new Horseshoe in Hammond for the second Tuesday in May.

The Empress had been transformed from a turquoise colored exterior to a white and gold building that reflected the décor of Horseshoe's two southern casinos. The interiors, an old Aquarius-nautical theme with accents of purple carpet and wall paper, were changed to the famous black and gold carpeting of the Horseshoe. Ceilings were raised and adorned with crystal chandeliers and the casino floors had been reconfigured Binion-style so that the tall slot machines were on the perimeter of the casino floors with the lower slots and table games located on the inside, providing a stadium view all the way across every floor. The new buffet was opulent and the ratio of protein to starch items was 70:30, the exact opposite of what we had inherited under the previous ownership. The old Lakeside Steak House was now called "Jack Binion's" Steakhouse with a new menu that incorporated all the favorite prime steaks featured on our Southern menus along with the many favorite entrees championed by our good customers in Chicago. Having the best Chicago steak houses as role models, we hired a wonderful Chicago Maitre d, a fellow who knew all the important customers and celebrities in Chicagoland.

Rick Mazer, the affable general manager of the Horseshoe, had originally opened the Empress. Rick proved to be a very adaptive individual who eventually bought into the Horseshoe strategies and tactics and led the successful transition to the Horseshoe brand along with his new marketing executive, Phil Juliano.

Rick Mazer knew every employee by name and every nook and cranny of the Hammond property intimately. Prior to Horseshoe, Rick had operated the Empress very autonomously and with little direction from the old owners. He constantly generated a good bottom line, but often did it in a way far different than Horseshoe standards. Rick Mazer was also commonly known as "Mr. Miser" by his employees and competitors. Rick was the architect of much of what we inherited in the Indiana riverboat, so he was somewhat defensive when we arrived on the scene and began talking immediately about changes we would have to make. He was especially taken aback when we said the FUBU shop had to go immediately. Rick adamantly defended the shop by saying that the Empress was "their casino," referencing the predominantly African American clientele that patronized the casino. Jack Binion liked Rick from the start. Jack always champions the underdog, and I think Jack sensed that his corporate team was ganging up on Rick, and maybe we were. We all wanted to make quick changes and Rick seemed to be resisting, although he always was cooperative. Rick was a politician. No doubt, he was the best lobbyist the company could have, whether it was in Hammond City Hall, the Lake County Courthouse or the Indianapolis Capitol building. Rick knew every politician on both sides of the aisle and they all knew and respected him equally. Jack did not want to lose this political "juice", so he coddled Rick; but, as he did, he also cajoled Rick into the Binion way of thinking. Within four months under Binion's tutelage, an outsider would have thought that Rick Mazer invented Horseshoe. Rick was now living and dying the Horseshoe mantra. The FUBU shop was replaced by a productive smoke shop. The herds of young gangs no longer milled about in the lobby and the place was immediately perceived to be safer. Table limits were raised and game-sweating ceased. The quality of food improved and the gratuities skyrocketed among the employees who worked for tips. By the time we were ready for the rebranding, Rick was ready to lead the charge and we were all proud of what he had accomplished.

The rebranding could not have been pulled off without the coordination of a top marketing mind. We had that in Phil Juliano. Phil was a lot like beer. He took a while to get used to, but when you finally did, he could be intoxicating. Phil lived downtown in Chicago and he palled around with some of the big players on a routine basis. He also knew how to communicate effectively with our ad agency. By luck, we had hired a Chicago ad agency to take over the campaigns at our two Southern casinos and they had cleverly utilized Jack Binion inside all of the television and print commercials. Working with the agency, Phil convinced the agency to develop a television advertising campaign that depicted the Hammond Casino as the closest casino to downtown Chicago. Using the new lighted Horseshoe facility with its 150 foot tall marquee sign, the agency digitally placed the Horseshoe Casino in a location that appeared to be within two miles of Navy

Pier in downtown Chicago. Working Jack Binion into the commercial, the campaign was instantly effective. The commercial debuted the day after our grand opening party was staged, and the stream of cars coming across the Chicago Skyway Bridge following the introduction of the commercial was overwhelming.

The grand opening party we threw to introduce the new Horseshoe Casino to Chicagoland was a spectacle in itself. Phil Juliano recognized early on that, next to New York City, Chicago is probably the most cosmopolitan city in the USA. Therefore the typical ribbon-cutting ceremony would not be considered much of an incentive-attraction for the "Who's Who" of Chicago to drive twenty minutes from downtown on a Tuesday evening for a speech by Jack Binion and Rick Mazer and maybe a glass of cheap champagne. No sir. This event had to have teeth. We all had a little vendetta in us that made us want to show the gaming regulators in Illinois how truly stupid they had been to run Jack out of their state, and there would be no better way to get even than for us to lure Illinois gamblers away from Illinois casinos and into our new Indiana Horseshoe Casino. This was going to cost some money though. The initial budget was $300,000 but we thought if Jack would approve the budget, we could make it appear to the media and public that we had spent a million dollars. The biggest cost was not in the party, though. We were going to make the party private and by invitation only. The state would not let us close the casino for a private party, so we were required to block off the pavilion and restrict loading of regular customers into the casino through a remote entry way. Consequently, we accepted the premise that the occupancy in the casino during the private party would be very low, and in the end it was. Jack approved the budget and the rest is history.

The mistress of ceremonies for our party was Ivana Trump. Her ex-husband owned and operated a competing riverboat casino five miles away in Gary, Indiana, and her inclusion in the party made for some interesting pre-party public relations noise and back and forth banter between Donald and Ivana in the press. Local celebrities such as Dick Butkus, Mike Ditka, and Ernie Banks were on hand to sign autographs and there was live music, cirque sole circus-style acts and gourmet food and beverages available to the invited guest on every level of the pavilion. Nothing was spared to make the evening a memorable event. The doors opened to the casino to coincide with the 10:00 p.m. cruise schedule and a majority of the 2000 invited guests flowed onto the new casino floor, many of whom were to experience the Horseshoe for the first time. The new Horseshoe Casino was off and running. The only negative we saw during the entire event happened when Mike Ditka left the casino late the next morning. As Ditka was waiting for his car in the valet lot, he was seen by the surveillance camera heading to the side of the building to relieve himself. We all had a good laugh watching the video tapes of Ditka smoking his cigar with one hand and tending to business with his other one.

When Binion purchased the Empress Casino in Hammond on December 1, 1999 the casino was generating about $18 million dollars of win per month on the average. Soon after the re-branding to the "Horseshoe," the State of Indiana modified the gaming laws that permitted open dockside gaming. We no longer were required to sail or even simulate cruises every two hours. The new laws provided unlimited ingress and egress from the casino floor at all times when the casino was open. The rebranding, along with the new dockside rules, enabled the Horseshoe to average over $26 million each month during the last six months of fiscal 2002.

Jack lived by the motto, "You gotta do one hundred things at least one percent better than your competition." To measure our success in achieving the goals of his motto, we actually developed a list of over 100 different things we did for our customers that we thought were important to creating and retaining their business. These specific items involved all elements of what Jack called the "**Four P**s of marketing." Keeping it simple for the customer and the employees, we prioritized our 100 different elements by the Four Ps as follows:

1) Products we offer which include slot machines, table games, restaurants, hotel rooms, showrooms;

2) Pricing of our goods and services such as room rates, menu prices, odds and payback percentages;

3) Promotion of our goods and services through the use of media advertising, comps, cash back bonuses and show tickets; and most importantly,

4) Presentation of our goods and services, namely great service.

By the time we re-branded the Hammond Empress to a Horseshoe, we excelled in almost every category we placed on the list as being important to the comfort and convenience of our patrons. Our only headache was parking. With our new name and improved levels of quality and service, we had outgrown our parking capacity almost overnight, and, consequently, our ability to grow our customer base. Now we had to convince Jack to build more parking. But what a nice problem to have, don't you agree?

CHAPTER 1

WHILE JACK WAS assimilating the Empress Casino into his Horseshoe Company, we were simultaneously expanding the operations and facilities at our two Southern casinos. The competition was putting a bull's-eye on Horseshoe as they began to develop promotions and provide new amenities to encroach on our market share. Bob McQueen, general manager of the Horseshoe in Tunica, took it upon himself to develop projections for expanding the Mississippi property for the third time. The highly successful Horseshoe was featuring 1500 slot machines and 70 table games in a 50,000 square foot casino that shared its barge-space with its popular Village Square Buffet. Each slot machine was generating over $300 per day each and it was impossible to get a machine on weekends after seven in the evening. Likewise table games were winning more than $2000 per unit each day as well. It was evident that more gambling space was needed, but it was also recognized that the buffet was a major attraction for the slot customers. Under Mississippi gaming law, casino games in Tunica can only be played in a room that sits on a barge or vessel on Mississippi River water. The simple solution was to move the buffet off the barge and expand the casino into the area currently containing the buffet. But not so fast. The logical area on land adjoining the casino barge in which to move the new buffet was occupied by the central plant that supplied all the utilities to the huge casino and hotel complex. For economic reasons, it had initially been placed close to the casino with nobody ever dreaming that business would get so good that the original location would put it in the way of progress. Jack was not excited about more construction. His last project had serious cost overruns and he did not trust the estimates. However, I learned early that while Jack hated to spend money on big unknown projects, he hated losing market share even more. In this case, his competitors were not doing anything significant to steal share from him, but the overall market was growing organically, and the Horseshoe was just too small now to grab our fair share of the growth. Since the growth was almost all on weekends, the only way to capture the business was to expand. Jack finally relented and the project was on. We would first move the central plant and size it so we could eventually add another 1000 hotel rooms if demand ever grew. We brought in $3,000,000 worth of dirt to bring the rear of our property up to the 100 year flood level and then expanded our valet and employee parking. When the central plant was moved, we constructed the most magnificent buffet ever conceived in any riverboat casino in the country. It featured 25,000 square feet of seating, with eight individual display kitchens and a center island bakery and salad emporium. Even today, it rivals the quality of any Las Vegas gourmet buffet on the strip and the Tunica dining facility is probably the largest in the country. As we moved the buffet into its new quarters, we quickly converted the old buffet to new gaming space. Twelve more table games and 600 new slots were place into action during the next four weeks. We opened the new buffet and casino expansion on Labor Day in 2001, on time and best of all, under budget. This was a first for Jack and doing it helped us get his quick approval with our next several projects. The expansion in Tunica, which cost $42 million dollars paid itself out within 12 months. The casino's annual cash flow increased from $55 million to $90 million during the first year following the opening of the new gaming space.

Over in Shreveport, we were facing a new competitor across the river. If you recall, my old nemesis, the Pratt family from Dallas, had purchased the Las Vegas Sands Hotel in 1980 and eventually sent me packing to Laughlin. Well, they were on the verge of opening their new Hollywood Casino on the banks of the Red River in Shreveport. The Pratts owned several riverboat casinos themed around a Hollywood nostalgia décor, and the fact that the Pratts lived in Dallas had our antennas up from the day they announced their project. Bear Sterns was the Pratt's investment banker and their financial guru, Jason Ader, was convinced that the Hollywood Casino would be a category killer. Jack Pratt, himself, was predicting that the new Hollywood would displace Binion's Horseshoe as the market leader within the first year.

In the fall of 2000, the country was entering into a period of economic recession but you would not know it in Shreveport or Bossier City. Unemployment was low and competition for good employees was as fierce as ever. If the Hollywood Casino was going to be successful, they would have to attract the best employees. The Horseshoe had the best employees and we knew we were at risk and would be the primary target of the Pratt organization as they geared up to open. There was plenty of worry among the Horseshoe's departmental managers because they saw the immensity of the Hollywood construction and they also read all the press, which was surprisingly very positive and supportive of Hollywood. That is probably because Shreveport only had one casino in its city while Bossier City, across the river, had three.

But all the hype and predictions of economic catastrophe for Horseshoe hardly entered Jack Binion's mind. If it did, he didn't show it. I only remember Jack calling me into his office and declaring, "Pardner, remember what Ronald Reagan did to the Soviet Union? That is precisely what we are going to do to Hollywood."

I said, "You mean we bankrupt them?"

Jack replied, "Yep, now go to work and get it done." That is when I heard another famous *Jackism* from him:

"People and companies can screw with me in almost any way they want and I won't get mad or troubled. There are only two things somebody can screw with to piss me off and when that happens I take no prisoners. Don't ever screw with my family and don't ever screw with my money. Everything else you screw with is okay."

If Jack Pratt thought he was going to screw with the Binion family's money by stealing the Horseshoe's market share, he definitely had another think coming. So we went to work on our plan. The first thing we did was start gearing up for the planned defection of employees over to Hollywood. We knew the grass is not always greener, but the lure of something new was going to be something we had to combat. We figured we would need to replace a lot of security officers, table dealers, slot operations employees and casino cashiers. We also knew that cleaning and housekeeping employees would be at a premium and we were always short kitchen employees, even without a new joint coming on line. Our goal was to hire and train approximately 250 additional employees to prepare us for the expected defection of our current staff to the new operator in town. We got a head start and new hires began to fill the ranks in every department of the Horseshoe.

As the hiring process began, we examined our employee bonus program. We normally gave out cash bonuses to hourly line employees during the first week of December each year so the employees would have the gift available to them in time for the holidays. However, we decided that since the Hollywood casino would be opening its doors on December 20, we would notify our employees that no bonuses would be paid until January 15, 2001, and to receive the bonus you must be on the Horseshoe payroll on that date. But to make the wait worthwhile, we advised the employees that the January 15 bonus would be double the normal amount. Likewise, we withheld the advance payment of executive bonuses for the management until the day after Hollywood opened to avoid making any payments to defecting managers.

Then, our marketing people piled on with a heap of direct mail incentives that were scheduled to hit the mail in constant drops every other day for three straight weeks beginning on the day Hollywood opened its doors. We were well aware that casino players from every casino including Horseshoe would visit the Hollywood and look the place over, so we had no preconceived notions that we could stop trial play to the new casino. But we knew that most players are driven by the promotional incentives they receive and ours were designed in a way that required them to play in the Horseshoe. They could not simply grab our offer and run across the river and spend it. We knew the Pratts had a very seriously leveraged balance sheet and they had forced an early opening of their new casino because they had to generate cash quickly to make ends meet. Binion knew this before he even used the Ronald Reagan and Soviet Union analogy. The Horseshoe had the financial wherewithal to push rebates and cash incentives till the cows came home, and Jack was prepared to keep the pressure on until it broke the Hollywood.

As the "A Team" used to say at the end of every television episode, "You got to love it when a plan comes together!" That is precisely what occurred during the next three months following the Hollywood Casino's December 20 opening in that first year of the new millennium. To begin with, instead of losing the estimated 250 employees we thought would defect to Hollywood, we only lost 30. As we came out of the busy New Year's Eve holidays, Larry Lepinski, the Horseshoe general manager was now 200 employees over-staffed. Larry was prepared to make some layoffs as we entered the first two weeks in January that are traditionally slower than normal and, with a new joint in town, anticipated to be even slower. Jack stopped Larry in his tracks. The Binions had never executed a layoff in the history of their casino involvement and Jack was not about to break that tradition in the first week of 2001. Instead, he had us examine all the positions where we were over staffed and made us estimate the amount of time it would take for normal attrition to bring the staff size back into par. We offered incentives to tenured employees to take their vacations during January and February and then we adjusted our operating budgeted profit downward by $2,000,000, to account for the additional payroll overruns we would absorb until the staff size could return to normal naturally through attrition. There were to be no layoffs, period. The word spread around the community like wildfire. In the meantime, the Pratts were laying off employees in droves as the "category killer" was falling like the Soviet Union in 1989. The Horseshoe paid out its bonuses and the marketing promotions kicked in as planned and took their toll on Hollywood. By April, just four short months after opening, The Hollywood was on the verge of bankruptcy. "You got to love it when a plan comes together!"

THE LAST DAY we owned the Joliet Empress Casino, I took the entire Horseshoe Corporate team (sans Jack Binion who was still forbidden from setting foot on the property) over to the property to say our farewells to the good team of people, who were the very next day going to become employees of Argosy Corporation. Following our farewell ceremonies with the staff, we attended our own farewell dinner in the private dining room of the Empress Steak House, the "Alexandria."

The acting general manager of the property was a fellow named Doug Ferrari and Argosy had agreed to keep him on to lead the operation for them. Ferrari fashioned himself as a food and beverage expert, having reigned from the Peppermill Casino in Reno, a casino well known for its great food and beverage operation. Ferrari constantly stressed this attribute in front of Binion and, politically, that was a fatal flaw on his part. Jack Binion was the Horseshoe food and beverage expert. The most talented Chef we had anywhere on our payrolls, even those who reigned from Cordon Bleu, would never challenge that fact. Jack knew what gamblers wanted to eat because he was a gambler himself. A mainstay on the desert line in his Benny Binion's style casino was bread pudding. Warm bread pudding made the way it's supposed to be made! Jack loved bread pudding and when we bought the two Empress Casinos, Jack was adamant that the two Empress general managers include it on the buffet line every day.

Yet Doug Ferrari detested bread pudding and thought it cheapened his buffet. Knowing that Jack could not come back on the property and, with his new job secured with Argosy, he decided to remove bread pudding from the buffet menu several days before the sale took place. He never dreamed I would show up on closing night, let alone stick my head in the buffet. After all, the sale was almost completed and why should I even care. He didn't know that someone had dimed him out and called to tell me that bread pudding was removed from the buffet line, with instructions never to be served on it again.

The Horseshoe Corporate executives and their spouses enjoyed a marvelous gourmet dinner in the steakhouse complete with fine wines and champagne, all compliments of our boss, Mr. Binion. The gourmet room staff went out of their way to treat us with great respect and I think they were truly sorry to see the company change hands again. They really had liked working for Horseshoe and had witnessed the wonderful changes that Jack had implemented in just two years, which had improved their workplace and even their community. Jack donated over $1,000,000 toward a city park in Joliet just one week before the sale was completed. As we finished up with dinner, the Maitre d' asked us if he could do anything special for us before we left. To bust balls, we told him that Jack Binion was hoping to have us bring back some bread pudding in a Styrofoam "to go" box, and the Maitre d' said he would be delighted to run to the buffet and fetch it for us. "Anything at all for Jack Binion," he declared. He returned several minutes later visibly shaken. Though we knew it, he did not know that the bread pudding was no longer being served. We thanked him for his efforts and forked over a really big tip for the great service we received in his restaurant. As we left, we asked him to make a notation in the daily food and beverage log. We said, "Write down in the log that Jack Binion was very disappointed bread pudding was taken off the buffet before ownership changed. That is very unfortunate!" We left it at that and the message was given.

CHAPTER **19**

BACK OVER IN Hammond, Indiana business was getting better by the minute. As part of the conditions of the sale of the Joliet Empress to Argosy, Horseshoe was prohibited for a period of one year to lease billboards within ten miles of Joliet or to solicit the database of customers who were sole customers of the Joliet casino. We had a whole year to develop a promotional effort to attack and attract that market and we started our planning immediately. In the meantime, we were beginning to face a serious dilemma. As I mentioned in a previous chapter, we had more customer-demand for the Horseshoe than we had parking spaces for their cars. Surveys and focus studies we had undertaken informed us that people were willing to pass us by on Interstate 90 and head on up Kline Road to Harrah's in East Chicago or Buffington Harbor in Gary, rather than search for a coveted parking space at Horseshoe. We had a remote lot with free shuttle bus transportation for our customers, but we knew that most guests hate that kind of parking. It is not convenient and it is generally not perceived as safe. Jack understood that we could not grow without more parking. It was our Achilles heel. As I also mentioned earlier, Jack lived by the mantra that our company had to do 100 things at least one percent better than our competitors, but when it came to parking, we had to be at least equal. Jack gave us a small budget to assess the costs of building an appropriate sized garage and we talked him into a bigger allotment so we could complete a full master plan. Since the cruise boat didn't cruise any longer, we had already broke out all the ballast tanks of the vessel and converted the tank space into 3000 square feet of additional casino floor space. But we were now at the limit. It was the proverbial yin and yang. If we fixed the parking problem, we would then not have adequate space in the casino. But we did know we had to fix the parking problem or we would risk losing market share, as our competitors found ways to make it easier for our customers to visit them. A new garage with adequate space for further expansion would enable us to determine just how big a casino we could eventually build for the demand we would generate.

The Horseshoe casino occupied a very small footprint of land tucked in behind a service road around the Hammond Marina and the Hammond Water Works. We had successfully negotiated a long term lease with the City of Hammond for half the parking lot of the marina, but we had to make some improvements on the leased land during our first five years of the term, or we would lose our right to keep it. We engaged the best casino architect we knew, the Brad Friedmutter Group of Las Vegas, and set forth incorporating our strategic long term objectives we wished to include in the design, even if they never occurred. Friedmutter and his team are the best. They can design in a vacuum over the telephone, if necessary and they grasped our ideas quickly and reduced them to blueprints and sketches within days. Jack liked the concepts but we were a long way from projecting any costs. Engineers and environmental experts were brought in to tell us where the booby traps were located, and as they did, we slowly watched the project costs explode. Jack had built his last parking garage in Bossier City just four years prior for about $10,000 per space, and the Tunica garage was built on a vacated cotton field for less than $8000 per space. But this was no cotton field. Our garage was to be built next to the shores of Lake Michigan in a location where high tension wires were located overhead. This we could all see without any expert engineers. But soon we learned that the big corn processing factory located several blocks inland from the lake had a huge oxygen pipeline underneath the proposed garage site and core drillings had also determined that there was an environmental hazard showing up, probably diesel fuel from some abandoned leaking tank buried somewhere on the site.

As the master plan began to come together, it was clear to all of us that a massive casino could be built on a barge in a way that nobody would know it was a boat. The new parking garage was being drawn in a way that enabled the current casino vessel to be serviced easily, but also provided for the conversion to a barge facility with a capacity never seen before on a water foundation. We were in the design phase at the same time as the Afghanistan bombing began following the 9/11 tragedy, and named our proposed casino project the "MOAB," after the daisy cutter bomb designed for the Pentagon called the Mother of all Bombs. Our MOAB would be an acronym for the Mother of all Boats.

Jack let us continue to plan, draw and design, but it became clear that he was not prepared to put $300 additional million dollars into the Hammond facility. So we pushed for approval of the parking garage, whose cost was now elevated to reach almost $60,000,000 (or over $30,000 per space). This increase in cost was the result of our requirements to relocate high tension electrical transmission lines and underground oxygen lines along with the construction of new seawalls around the marina and a mandate to remedy the leaking diesel problem using the little expensive workmen who show up in the white plastic suits and headgear.

For over a month we kept going back and forth with Jack and he would not commit to the project. Finally out of frustration one afternoon after the architects had traveled across the country for their fifth presentation of minor modifications, I blurted out that possession was nine tenths of the law and we better possess the marina soon or we would blow our $15,000,000 lease investment. Time was running out. Jack sensed our frustration. He smiled and said, "Pardner, let's go for it!"

Sam Marshall, our vice president of construction, was out pulling permits the next day. We had already contracted with Smoot Construction on a contingency basis to build the garage. Smoot Construction was a well regarded African American owned construction company that had completed a large portion of the Indianapolis Airport Terminal and we knew we had the right group to fast track our garage.

We teased the public with a nice press release that contained slick pictures of the proposed parking garage. In addition to citing the merits and metrics of the new garage, the press release also leaked out the fact that we were preparing for the potential development of the largest casino boat in the country once the parking garage was completed. We wanted to send a message to both our competitors and the Illinois lawmakers that we were prepared to take on any new entries into the Chicago market that they might elect to approve during their next session of the state legislature. Looking back now, we know the message was not overlooked by Harrah's Entertainment, either.

We broke ground on the parking garage in the fall of 2002 just after the Labor Day holidays as the season for boating was coming to a close in Chicagoland. After relocating the marina boat launching area to the other side of the marina, we took a fast track toward getting the construction completed. We set a completion date for May, 2004.

CHAPTER **20**

WE HAD A marvelous New Years at all three Horseshoe Casinos to end the year 2002 and head into 2003. While Jack Binion was seen in his casinos on a 24/7 basis during the three warmer seasons of the year, he spent virtually all of the winter season on the ski slopes, primarily at his winter home in Vail, Colorado. Unless there was a special event where he was the celebrity or there was a special board meeting or regulatory meeting to attend, Jack was seldom seen by the corporate folks during December through February. He did most of his company business on the telephone during those months and he was always in communications with us. Often he would call from the ski lift, and you could hear the "chuga chuga chuga" of the lift in the background competing with his voice.

With this history, we were surprised to see Jack arrive in the Tinley Park offices the second week in January. Nothing special was going on and the snow at Vail was exceptional, I was told. Jack had an announcement for the corporate bunch. He had decided it was time to leave Illinois and move the corporate headquarters to Las Vegas. Instead of the Mountain coming to Mohammad, he decided it was time for us to be near where he lived full time. He wanted Jon Wolfe and I to identify an appropriate office building that could accommodate our technical requirements. Then he instructed David Carroll to develop a relocation program with a good third party contractor to make the relocation process as painless as possible, recognizing that there would be some pain in a move to a new environment some 1800 miles away in the desert. He felt badly that many of the Illinois based office crew would not be willing to make the move to Las Vegas, but he instructed David to come up with a very generous severance payment for those that did not feel they could accept the transfer.

The idea of moving to Las Vegas was intriguing to me because that is where I grew up, I had aging parents living in Boulder City, and my kids and grand kids all lived in Las Vegas. Certainly Las Vegas was the recognized home of gambling and we could justify the move so that our corporate headquarters would be located in the epicenter of the action. Obviously, the Illinois location had been convenient for our corporate travel to and from our three mid-west and mid-south casinos, all of which operated on the Central Time zone. But, in the end, the best reason for moving the corporate office was the boss. Remember, the boss is not always right, but the boss is the boss.

Jon Wolfe and I scoped out a variety of office facilities during three separate trips to Las Vegas that spring. We finally identified an outstanding complex that was tailor made to our needs. The offices and conference rooms were already built out as if we had designed the facility, and only minor construction was necessary to provide a secure and stand alone technology center and a direct mail operation. We signed the lease on April 1, 2003 and scheduled our occupancy for the last week in June. The location was outstanding. Jack could jog to work from his home in Queensridge and most of the corporate team had purchased their new homes in the Summerlin community, just minutes from the new office. The idea of no more long commutes was quite appealing to all of us.

CHAPTER **21**

WHILE THE NEW Year had started out on a marvelous note, problems surfaced near the end of the first quarter that year. Business at our Bossier City Casino was starting to be negatively impacted by the opening of the Win Star Casino located on the border of Oklahoma and Texas, just ninety miles north of Dallas and Fort Worth. Half the distance from our major feeder market with no taxes to pay, as the Louisiana casinos were required to do (at that time and currently 21.5% of win), the new casino in Oklahoma was able to offer amenities and promotions large enough to attract a large core of customers that heretofore had almost exclusively driven to Shreveport/Bossier for their gambling entertainment. Jack and I headed south to get a read on the problem. We had recently made a change in the marketing leadership and the decision we made for a replacement executive proved to be poor. We summoned David Carroll to join us and instructed him to execute (actually terminate) the new marketing guy. We relocated our corporate database manager, a Southern boy by the name of Todd Chandler into the chief marketing role and moved him down to the Bossier City property quickly to help us take steps to arrest the decline in business. We knew that if we could not get all of our old customers back from Win Star, we'd have to implement some new programs that could steal market share from the remaining business at our closest competitors. We also had to find some

new programs to attract some meaningful new first-time trial business. We knew that the new business might not be as profitable, but
the Horseshoe was driven by market share. Its management team and
employees all worked more effectively on offense and they probably
were not very good at defense. We had too much money invested
in Horseshoe to go on the defense and try to cost-cut ourselves into
the future. By the end of April, we had arrested the bleeding and
recouped our former market share of the Shreveport business, but
absent any unusual shifts in behavior or the economy, it was evident
that the Northwest Louisiana gaming market was flattening out and
probably would remain that way for quite some time. The good news
was we had almost recovered our profit levels of the year before and
at virtually the same margin of efficiency.

Business volumes in the new Hammond Horseshoe continued to
increase monthly, but bad luck plagued us with several of our biggest
customers. One customer in particular reigned from Las Vegas where
he had been banned from several big strip casinos because they just
could not beat him. Jack didn't seem to like the licking we were taking, but he was confident the game was fair and nothing illegal was
taking place. We were committed to staying on against this particular
player and eventually luck turned back around to our side. This player
was dangerous, though, because he came at you with a lot of money
and he only played the safest bets with the lowest house advantage.
He would be back often and we knew it.

About the same time, the Horseshoe in Tunica was experiencing its first real challenge in years. Since its opening in 1995, the
Horseshoe dominated the dollar slot machine market in Mississippi.
With the advent of the new multiple-coin "penny" slot machine that
became popular in the industry in about 2000, most of the other
casinos in Tunica purchased hundreds of these units that seemed to
be the rage. The Horseshoe, however, never found it necessary to
provide the penny-denomination of machines to its patrons. Instead,
the Horseshoe offered a very small number of nickel denomination
machines, but primarily concentrated on the type of customers who

played on dollar and five dollar machines. Jack Binion was very concerned that the gaming operators worldwide were being dragged into the new penny equipment by the machine manufacturers and he considered the ramifications detrimental. Our analysis had already shown that customers who played dollar machines generally made average wagers of around $2.50. On the other hand, people who played the new penny machines generally only averaged wagers of 80 cents per pull. So as the competition scrambled for the new penny slot business, Horseshoe continued to place its emphasis on the dollar customer and offered a few nickel slots to satisfy the few people on the floor who were searching for the cheapest wager machines.

The Horseshoe had 510 rooms in its hotel, but it enjoyed so much high level gaming play that its hotel rooms were always full of great gamblers. Horseshoe also enjoyed so much dollar slot play, that consequently many of our good dollar customers frequently found it difficult to secure hotel accommodations at our casino. It seems that Wally Barr and the marketing team over at the Grand Casino had found our weak spot. Wally was the CEO of Caesars Entertainment, and his company owned three of the nine casinos in Tunica at the time. The Grand was a huge up-scale casino with 1200 hotel rooms and catered to premium customers as we did at the Horseshoe. They also owned the Sheraton Casino and Bally's Casino, which adjoined the Horseshoe. Both of these smaller casinos catered to the lower end of the customer market and the Sheraton was the recipient of hundreds of the new penny machines.

Early in March of 2003, the Grand and Sheraton combined their marketing efforts to attack both the nickel and dollar play of Horseshoe. With 1200 rooms, the Grand was advertising big offers of free rooms to the dollar slot customers of Horseshoe who always seemed to have a tough time booking a room in our hotel. At the same time, the Sheraton made a pitch for the nickel players at the Horseshoe by making big food offers for them at the Sheraton if they would become slot club members at Sheraton and take advantage of the huge array of new penny slot machines. The promotional advertising came out of left field and nobody at Horseshoe saw it coming. Maybe it was complacency over the years, but it happened. We had obviously been getting too much exercise patting ourselves on the back and resting on our laurels and now for the first time we were seeing loyal business decay. It so happened that Jack had just landed in Memphis and saw it for himself firsthand. Driving into the Horseshoe from Memphis International Airport, Jack viewed the multitude of Grand and Sheraton outdoor billboards lining the highway on his way to the Horseshoe from the airport. Their message was making a direct attack on Jack's business. When Jack entered his casino he could tell in his gut that the volume of business was not normal and even the employees appeared a little numb and dumbfounded. I regret that I was not there with him, because I may have been able to slow him down on his next move, but unfortunately I was back in Tinley Park.

The agility of a small company like Horseshoe was usually a wonderful advantage because decisions could be made quickly without a lot of analysis and red tape. Unlike big publicly traded companies where problems have to be carefully analyzed and any material changes to strategies authorized at various levels of the organizational hierarchy, the Horseshoe only had one guy to ask; Jack Binion. That was the good news. The bad news is that sometimes even with Jack Binion's gaming intellect and intestinal fortitude, quick decisions are not always the most profitable. At the time, it did not matter to Jack, though. To him, the Caesars folks were screwing with his family's security and his family's money, and when that happened, he always remembered to take no prisoners.

Jack convened a quick meeting with his general manager, Bob McQueen, and his slot director, Kevin O'Sullivan. Before the meeting was over, Jack had ordered a counter assault. He wanted the dollar slot machines loosened at all entry ways into the casino and he wanted us to advertise double maximum jackpots on all denominations of slot machines of a dollar and higher. For the nickel players, he was giving out free buffets and he did not want to let up until Caesars relented. Jack didn't care if it took a year. He was going to make Wally Barr flinch.

When I heard of his decision I told him I wish he would have let us counter-attack using our database in a more precise manner, but he was convinced that the speedy response he was making would have a greater impact. That's when he hit us with Jackism. He exclaimed, "When some son of a bitch is stealing market share from you, you kick them in the balls quick. When they hunch over, you beat their head in with a ball bat. When they fall down on the ground, you kick them in the ribs. That's about the time when they agree to give your market share back!"

The Grand and Sheraton continued their promotion through May, but as it always happened in the public companies, as they closed their May books, they saw a terrible bottom line for the second quarter approaching. Their assault had cost the Horseshoe some temporary losses in market share, but when Jack kicked in his counter assault, the escalating promotional costs of staying in the marketing war were a disaster to the Caesars bottom line. By the end of May, the war was over. Horseshoe had its entire market share back, but the cost of defending our position was over $10,000,000. Jack told me several months later that, if he had known that he might sell his company sometime soon, he would have used the database instead of reacting as he did. The $10,000,000 reduction in cash flow that quarter in 2003 cost Binion $80,000,000 when it came time to sell his company.

AT THE TINLEY Park offices on June 20, 2003, we bid our farewells to the members of the Chicagoland corporate team who were not going to follow us to Las Vegas. Everyone who was moving west had a week to get there and we planned to start moving into the new Las Vegas office complex on Tuesday, July 1. Following the July 4th holidays, we would officially open the new headquarters office for business on Monday, July 7.

On Thursday, July 3 we were still waiting for most of the executives to arrive in Las Vegas. Some of them were still on the road and others were at their new homes meeting their moving vans. However, I was in my new office pounding in nails and hanging pictures, having already unloaded my banker boxes of files and arranged my bookcases.

As I stood on a small ladder, I turned and saw Jack Binion enter my office along with Jack's financial advisor, Andy Astrachan, and our legal counsel, Dominic Polizzotto. They closed my office door. They had never done that before so I knew something bad must have occurred. The last time the boss closed the door in my office, I was asked to resign, so I really had no idea what was coming next. If they were going to fire me, why did they pay all the money to move me to Vegas? All kinds of odd ideas raced through my head as I stepped down from my ladder.

Jack started with, "I am kind of glad you got off that ladder because I have something to tell you that might have made you fall off. I've decided to sell my company."

I just stood there. Here we were not even open in our new Las Vegas offices for one business day and now we were going to sell the company. What was I going to tell the other executives? What was I going to tell my wife? What was I going to tell the fifty new employees that had left their old jobs and who were scheduled to start working for us the following Monday?

Jack said, "You can't tell them anything! We have to keep this secret until we have contracts signed. You can't even tell your wife."

I reminded Jack of his one of his first *Jackisms*. "Two people can keep a secret if one of them is dead." I told him it was imperative that we let the other senior executives know that very day. We could not go through the Fourth of July holidays trying to keep this quiet. Jack finally agreed and we called a special lunch meeting at Jack's house and rounded up the executive team. It was the right thing to do and Jack confided in the team regarding what was about to transpire. Jack confessed that while he was not actively marketing his company, the idea of selling the Horseshoe had entered his mind, not so much because of the aggravation of defending his reputation at all the recent licensing hearings, but more because no members of his family really wanted to carry on the tradition of the Binion-style gambling business. He also confessed that a short time after the decision to move the corporate headquarters to Las Vegas he was approached by investment bankers representing Ameristar Gaming Corp who wanted to discuss a potential purchase of the Horseshoe. As discussion ensued, apparently Harrah's Entertainment got wind that Jack might entertain an offer to sell his company, and now here in July, we were going to have a bidding contest on what company might buy Horseshoe. It couldn't get any better for Jack and his family.

The idea of selling the company was bittersweet. A sale would mean a very substantial redemption of stock options that all of the executives held in the company. I only owned less than one half of a percent of the Horseshoe equity, but if Jack could sell the company for over a billion dollars, that small percentage of ownership would mean a nice retirement for me. On the other hand, this was the best job I ever had and I hated to see it coming to an end. Worse yet, I hated to see us sell the company to Harrah's. I had never really cared for Harrah's from the first time I turned down a job to work for them at Lake Tahoe in 1973 and my distaste for them carried through the rest of my career. I did not care for their operating techniques in Atlantic City and, since working for Jack Binion, we were trained to show disdain for Harrah's daily and do everything legally possible to relegate them into the number two position wherever we competed with them. The idea of having to cooperate with them for an orderly transition to their ownership was appalling to me and the possibility almost made me nauseous.

On the other hand, I liked the idea of selling to Ameristar. I admired Craig Nielsen, the quadriplegic chief executive officer of his upstart gaming company. Like Horseshoe, their nemesis was also Harrah's and like Horseshoe they were number one in every riverboat market where they competed with Harrah's. As legal documents were prepared for both companies to enter a period of due diligence, I kept my fingers crossed that Ameristar would be the winning bidder.

On July 7, the new Horseshoe office opened for business. By mid-morning, we were called into Jack's office and informed that a coordinated joint public announcement would be made by Horseshoe, along with both Harrah's and Ameristar, to advise the public shareholders and debt holders of the potential sale and the due diligence that would ensue for several weeks. I received permission to tell the corporate staff of what was about to transpire. More importantly, we were now permitted to tell our wives. I excused myself so I could go to my office and inform my bride of the first secret I had ever kept from her.

Then I called my first "all hands" staff meeting in the new office conference room to coincide with the information as it hit the financial news wire. This was the strangest introductory staff meeting

I had ever conducted. It was not easy to make introductions for the first time and then let everybody know we were about to embark on a sale of our company. I passed out a copy of the official press release and then read it for everybody. We explained that the transaction would take some time, perhaps as long as a year. We explained that there was always a chance that a deal may never be agreed upon or materialize in the end, even if we arrived at an agreement. We also explained that when transactions like this finalize, many of the team members on the seller's side are not hired on by the buyer.

I apologized to everybody who had resigned from a good job to take their new position with Horseshoe. I was given authority from Mr. Binion to offer 90 days pay to everybody who was still on the payroll the day the deal closed, and let everybody know that their job was secure at least through the final closing date of the sale, provided they showed up and did their best to help us pass the baton on to the new owner, whoever that may become. I also suggested that anyone who could get their old job back should consider grabbing it. Anybody that decided to return to their previous employer, if they could, would be given a full month's pay from Horseshoe to compensate for the stress and aggravation we caused them.

Jack had also given me permission to offer to pay moving expenses and ninety days pay to anyone who had transferred from Chicagoland to Las Vegas and now decided their futures would be better served by returning to Illinois or Indiana. Strangely enough, nobody wanted to leave our employment. Everybody we had transferred from Illinois elected to stay through the sale. Everyone we had hired on in Las Vegas had no desire to return to their old employer. It truly was a great bunch of employees. It was sad that our time together would be so short.

Data rooms were set up for each prospective buyer to examine relevant Horseshoe documents. We were careful to segregate the information differently for each prospective buyer, because we were still the primary competitor to Harrah's, whereas we had no competing situating with Ameristar. After years of competing toe to toe,

Harrah's knew our properties quite well and therefore most of the diligence efforts they undertook were financial in nature. We were careful not to disclose any granular database information to either prospective buyer, but we were especially careful with Harrah's. If Ameristar won the bid, they would not want Harrah's to have such critical information and if the sale aborted for some reason, we would still be in a heads up battle with Harrah's in three major markets.

The best comment from Jack Binion to come out of the due diligence exercise involved Harrah's. It is well known that Harrah's attempts to fill its executive positions with college MBA's, preferably from the Harvard Business School. As Harrah's officials were examining the roster of all people employed in our company, they questioned Jack as to how many MBA graduates the Horseshoe had on its payroll. Totally dry faced, Jack replied, "We only have one or two MBA's in the entire company. But we do have over sixty CPA's working, just at our Hammond casino alone." The astonished Harrah's executive could not fathom that number of CPA's being required for only one casino. Then Jack told him they were all "Car Parking Attendants." Jack always believed many CPA's working for our customers to provide better service were far more valuable than many MBA's working for the CEO.

Ameristar spent considerable time and resources examining the physical properties of Horseshoe. In fact, to his credit, Craig Nielsen, the Ameristar CEO spent almost ten days himself, touring every nook and cranny of the Horseshoe buildings in addition to personally inspecting each competitor casino in all three markets where Horseshoe operated. I had a lot of respect for Craig. He had a far better understanding of the nuances of each market, in addition to the strengths and weaknesses of the Horseshoe and each of the Horseshoe's competitors, than the CEO of Harrah's. What was amazing though was the fact that Craig Nielsen toured over twenty casinos in three geographical locations, and he did it in his specially equipped van and wheelchair. Jack assigned me to accompany Craig on this long tour, and what at first I considered a real chore turned out to be an honor.

Furthermore, I finally understood why compliance with the American with Disabilities Act is a moral obligation and not just something a business does to avoid a fine. While every casino we inspected was technically ADA compliant, it was a major inconvenience trying to navigate Mr. Nielsen's wheelchair through the narrow aisle ways and tiny elevators of almost every Riverboat casino we visited. Craig liked the Horseshoe, because our aisle ways and elevators were very spacious.

Craig Nielsen kept strange hours, though. His executives told me stories about how he would hold staff meetings next to his bed at midnight. Several people I knew who interviewed for jobs, did so at his bedside at two o'clock in the morning in his Las Vegas home. Craig seemed to like me and he invited me to stay on with Ameristar when he bought Horseshoe. Apparently his conversation led him to believe I was already on his payroll, because he started calling me nightly around midnight, to check in and see how the due diligence process was going. He would wake me up almost every night and ask me questions that he should have been asking his own people. I couldn't tell him how diligence was going from his company's stand-point. I had no idea.

One day I called his vice president of operations, a wonderful lady named Angie. She had worked with Craig in his Jackpot, Nevada casinos for many years and had apparently also been the person who pulled him from the wreckage of a car in a terrible accident that para-lyzed him. I told her that Craig had been calling me every evening around midnight and was waking me and my wife up from our sleep. Angie told me that this was normal. In fact she said to me, "Heck, the boss calls me three or four times a night after midnight, so don't feel bad."

To which I replied, "Yes, but you're on his payroll. I am not!" Nonetheless, I liked Craig and respected what he had built under some very adverse circumstances. I was not anxious to work for him, but I still wanted him to win the bid.

CHAPTER **23**

JACK BINION, ALONG with his financial and legal team, had made it clear that the best "first" bid would win the rights to purchase his three Horseshoe casinos. They also made it clear that the process was not going to auction. Each pursing company would have an opportunity to make only one sealed bid. Jack said privately that he was not going to accept any offer under $1.2 billion dollars, which was roughly 6.5 times the Horseshoe Company's trailing twelve month cash flow. Jack's three casinos were virtually brand new. All of the 1000 hotel rooms and suites had been renovated the year before and the kitchens, restaurants and casinos were all meticulously maintained. Jack Binion was also a believer in replacing slot machines on a frequent basis and none of his machines were more than four years old in any of his casinos and every one of them was now coinless. Therefore, in his mind, Jack knew the successful buyer would have very little capital to invest in renovations and thus the condition of the Horseshoe demanded a premium.

The night before the bids were due, Craig Nielsen had dinner with Jack and me in the Steakhouse in Tunica. Craig invited us up to his suite following dinner, at which he expressed a sincere hope that he would become the buyer of the Horseshoe. He told Jack that he was going to make a significant offer for the Horseshoe the following day, and he hoped that if he was close, Jack would give him an opportunity to improve his bid. Jack informed him that the rules remained as they were set on day one. "Sorry, Craig," Jack told him, "have your guys give me your best shot in the morning. The highest bid wins it. No further negotiations on the base price after that." Craig understood and said he would tell his guys.

Jack and I flew back to Las Vegas the next morning to await the bids that were due. As promised, Ameristar's bid came in that afternoon at an amazing $1.25 billion dollars, almost $25,000,000 more than Jack was expecting. An hour later, the Harrah's bid arrived. $1.45 billion dollars! Harrah's was offering almost $220,000,000 more for Horseshoe than Ameristar and it wasn't even close. I still disliked the idea of Harrah's taking over Horseshoe, but I was already counting my retirement money. At this price, after debt and closing costs were paid off, the remaining equity would amount to a billion dollars. A purchase agreement was executed in late September, 2003 with Harrah's and the transition process began. With potential anti-trust issues to overcome in Chicagoland, it was expected that the closing might take as long as nine months. Both sides were anxious to keep the momentum of Horseshoe's market share growth. Harrah's wanted to see their potential purchase improve in value even while they waited to close the deal and Jack wanted to be certain we did not lose any value in case the deal fell apart for any reason. Harrah's was the biggest gaming company in the world and it was not likely the deal would fall apart, but they still required financing, shareholder approval, regulatory approval in three states and FTC approval from the Federal Government.

Jack and his financial advisors were shrewd, but so was the buyer. Harrah's not only agreed to pay Horseshoe $1.45 billion dollars for our company, but they also agreed to let us keep any excess cash we accumulated from the date of the sales agreement until we closed. If we could maintain our momentum of the previous twelve months going forward, we could generate another $5,000,000 per month for each month it took to close the deal. Jack called me in and told me to go to the whip on the back stretch. For every extra million dollars we could generate, Jack would throw $100,000 of the extra money into a pot to be distributed at the end of each 90 day quarter among the senior executives in the corporate office and the executive teams at each of the three casinos. This extra bonus would continue until the company was sold. Best of all, this extra bonus would be on top of the regular annual incentive bonus plan that was in place for our entire executive group. When Harrah's finally closed the purchase of the Horseshoe Company on July 1, 2004 the Horseshoe team had generated another $50,000,000 in cash, making the total deal worth over $1.5 billion dollars. Maintaining our momentum even in the face of the sale meant a bigger sales price for us and a transparent and seamless transition for Harrah's. The new buyer never skipped a beat. At that time in 2004, the purchase of the Horseshoe Company by Harrah's was the largest single acquisition by a gaming company, and started the rapid consolidation of six major casino companies into three giants; Harrah's with Caesars; MGM with Mirage; and Penn National with Argosy.

Jack Binion was a unique boss. His Horseshoe gaming Holding Corporation was a private company, but he distributed phantom ownership in the form of share appreciation rights to every member of management right down to the lowest line supervisor at every property. He made everybody feel like an owner. Unlike most big public corporations that bestow equity grants with 80% of the grants going to the top executives in the company and the remaining shares distributed to the lower level management people, Binion did it the opposite. While very generous to his top executives, he spread the perception of ownership down through all the management ranks, where every manager felt the success of winning and the pain of losing in a very meaningful way. When the company was finally sold, the 400 members of management cashed out over $60,000,000 and over 80% of this money was distributed to management supervisors that included pit bosses, housekeeping managers, sous chefs and stewarding supervisors. The senior corporate executive team cashed in $12,000,000 from their end of the stock sales. Between incentives paid for change of control, normal bonuses paid for meeting budgeted plans and the incentive bonus put in place for going to the whip, July 1, 2004 was a grand payday for all.

The sale of the Horseshoe marked the end of an iconic gaming era. Jack Binion's management style is a textbook for how a casino should be operated. It is a college primer for marketing and a human resources manual for how to treat employees at every level in a casino or hospitality operation.

Jack Binion lived every day for the gambling business. It was ingrained in him to work his casinos 24/7, because except for the ski slopes of Vale, Colorado, it was just too damn fun to be away from his "gambling joints." To say it was no work and all play may be stretching it a bit....... but it certainly made Jack a Rich Boy.

The End.......... NO!

CHAPTER **24**

YES, THIS IS the logical conclusion of my book, but not yet the end of my story. My six years with Jack Binion and his team provided me some of the most humorous memories of my career and some must be published for the record book because they were always funny when Jack was involved.

Jack was the consummate story teller. While he was a shy individual and somewhat uncomfortable with public speaking engagements, he was quite the opposite in small groups. Whether it was a small group of employees, a round table of investment bankers, or dinner with a group of high rolling gamblers, Jack Binion could mesmerize his audiences. Interestingly, many of his stories involved the family patriarch, his father Benny Binion. Jack never referred to his father as "Dad". Instead, It was always "Benny Binion did this or Benny Binion did that!"

The funniest story about Benny Binion originated from an illegal crap game that Benny was operating out of a hotel room down in either Dallas or Galveston. Jack was just a little boy when this incident took place, but hearing Jack tell the story, you would believe he was in the room when it happened. Apparently Benny Binion stationed a "lookout" in the hallway of the hotel in case any heat might come during the game. The lookout advised Benny Binion that the noise from the crap game was audible in the hallway and might present a problem if some *goody two shoes* walked down the hallway. Anyway,

Benny agreed and dispatched the fellow over to the electronics store across the street from the hotel to purchase a small radio. Benny would plug in the radio and set it in the hotel room entry hallway with music playing to drown out the sounds form the crap game.

As the story goes, when the lookout brought the radio back to Benny and they plugged it in, the radio was defective and would not work. Benny sent the fellow back across the street to exchange it for a good radio or get a refund. When the lookout told the electronic store owner the problem, the proprietor pointed to a sign on the wall that said "No refunds or exchanges." The owner declared, "Can't you read? I have a policy. No refunds." The lookout tells the shop owner that Benny is not going to be happy with that answer. The shop owner repeats his sentence again. "Can't you read? I have a policy. Tell Benny No refunds. Period! That's my Policy"

The lookout returns to the hotel room and tells Benny what transpired at the electronics shop. Enraged, Benny takes off himself to get a refund. When Benny Binion confronts the store owner over the defective radio, the owner stands firm and says to Benny, "You could have saved a trip over here. Didn't your flunky tell you that I have a policy? No refunds period."

With that, Benny Binion winds up like baseball great, Randy Johnson, and throws the defective radio against the display wall behind the owner, shattering all kinds of electronic appliances. Then Benny grabs his Smith and Wesson revolver and points it at the owner, yelling, "and I also have a policy. Don't ever let anybody screw me. That's my policy. Period!"

And with that Benny shot up another six appliances on the back counter before running out of bullets and exiting the store with a brand new radio in hand. This one worked well and the crap game went on as planned.

Jack also had some of the most unusual tales of customers, many of whom were notorious characters in their own right. We constantly encouraged Jack to write a book about these people, but he always said he couldn't write about these people until after he died himself.

For that very reason, I will not recite any of these stories, although Jack was always careful to avoid using any real names. It seemed most of these characters all had nicknames such as "Slim, Hammer or Wingy" and it also seemed that most of them were either connected or running from the law. But they were all wonderful gamblers and obviously a lot of fun to be around. That is of course, unless you are applying for a gaming license in another state.

The list of "Jackisms" grew over the six years I was working for Jack Binion. Some of them evolved from the television commercials that were produced in which Jack played the leading character. And he was good at it, too. You felt you were right there talking with him when you watched him on your TV set. The best "Jackism" to come out of a commercial was one where he bragged about his buffet restaurant in Tunica, Mississippi. While the Horseshoe Comps were the most liberal in the industry, our competitors also did provide considerable complimentary services and food to their players, as well. So in this particular television commercial, Jack acknowledges: "Sure, you can get comps at the competition.....but then you have to eat there."

As I mentioned in an earlier chapter, Jack didn't own a company plane and he didn't believe it was a good use of company money. However, on occasion, a group of our corporate team had to attend a common meeting such as the annual budgeting sessions with property management. If it made sense, we would charter a small jet. We happened to have our insurance agent flying with us to Shreveport from Chicago one day, when Jack and five of our key executives were on the plane together. The insurance agent commented to Jack that it was probably a bad idea to have the entire team in one airplane and maybe we should be taking two planes just in case there was an airplane crash. Without smiling, Jack replied, "What if the plane goes down? If it does, it will be somebody else's f---ing problem."

On September 10, 2001 we charted a small jet to shuttle our eight corporate executives, including Jack Binion and his daughter, Perri Howard, from Chicago to our two Southern casinos in order to finalize the 2002 business plans and budgets. Our first stop was Shreveport, where we planned to meet with the property management team the next morning. While I was shaving and preparing for the long day of budget talks, I received a phone call from my wife in Chicago. She said, "Turn on the TV quick! Two airplanes have slammed into the World Trade Center in New York City."

Needless to say, the budget meetings were postponed so we could all watch the tragedy of that day unfold before our eyes on the television set in the Bossier City Conference room. The third plane crashed into the Pentagon and we all were wondering when the mayhem was going to stop. War had been declared on us and we had no idea who or where the enemy was. When the fourth plane crashed in Pennsylvania, Jack pointed out that we were probably in the safest place in the country if the enemy was going to continue to attack. The enemy had certainly never even heard of Bossier City. About the same time, a news alert came over the television set. The Secret Service had decided to divert President George W. Bush in *Air Force One* to Barksdale Air Force Base. You guessed it. Barksdale Air Base is located just three miles from the Horseshoe Casino in Bossier City. Now the enemy knew where we were.

All private and commercial planes were grounded indefinitely and now we were stuck in Bossier City with no idea when we could leave. On September 12, we went ahead and finalized our budgeting and business planning, trying to factor in what we thought the impact of this horrific event would have on our business. Since our bonuses were calculated on profits, Jack was not going to let us lower our targets, but he acknowledged that "9/11" was certainly a game changer and would have some major impact of the economy. He just hoped gaming would not be hit as hard as other industries.

The stock exchanges in New York did not open after the twin towers collapsed so we had no idea how to gauge the expected decline in business. The stock market closed for ten business days and when it reopened the Dow Jones index had declined 1370 points from the close on September 10, a loss of over 14%. Using teleconference equipment, we finished the planning process with the property team at our Mississippi property right from the Bossier City conference room. Anxious to get home to our families in Chicago who were all worried about our safety and their own, we attempted to find a couple rental cars. By September 13, every rental car company was sold out so we looked for a limousine or even a motor home to rent. We figured we could get home to Chicago in eighteen hours driving around the clock. If we could rent a motor home with a driver, we could play poker all the way back. We finally located one rental car so we grabbed it.

Our pilots told us they thought we might be able to take off on September 15, so several of us decided to wait it out, and we let the guys with children at home take off in the rental car. Lo and behold, on September 15, we were given the green light to fly our plane. Because Jack Binion was so revered in the Shreveport Airport, the tower gave us permission to be the first aircraft in the air. Ironically, we landed in Des Plaines airport at the exact time as the five guys reached Chicagoland in their rental car. We were all happy to be home, still awe struck by the devastation that we had seen occur in real time. We also knew that homeland security was going to be viewed differently from that day forward.

JACK WAS VERY protective of his executives, some of whom were "naughty boys" from time to time. One guy in particular (I will not use his name) was a great general manager who worked in one of our joints. Through our company whistleblower hotline, it was alleged that this guy might be doing something nefarious that could get the company in some hot water or at least a good law suit. David Carroll, our vice president of human resources, brought the matter to me and we decided it was something Jack should know about.

The most important Jackism of all was "The law of no surprises." Jack acknowledged that mistakes are made and things do not always go as planned. Sometimes bad things happen and in this day and age, the media can bury a company's good will because of one simple mistake. Therefore Jack was adamant that we always make him aware of anything happening that might cause problems. He did not want to hear about a problem from a regulator or the press.

So we take the serious allegations of policy violations by this general manager to Jack, advising him that we were obliged to investigate the matter and consider it serious until it could be proven otherwise. We also knew that this particular general manager was one of Jack's favorite executives and one whom he had trusted for many years. Nonetheless, he agreed to allow us to proceed with a covert investigation to determine if there was any truth to the allegations. David

Carroll recommended using a private detective that had done some work for us beforehand and Jack approved the idea. As we left the office, I overheard Jack dialing up the general manager in question. I just knew he was warning the guy that we were on to him and that he should keep his hands clean for a few weeks. Jack was willing to spend the money on the private eye to satisfy David's and my concerns about policy infringement, but he couldn't afford to lose his special general manager. I telephoned David and instructed him to cancel the detective. We would just be wasting our money because our cover had been blown. Years later after we sold the company, with a great deal of jocularity, Jack admitted to all of us that he did tip off the executive in question, confirming what we suspected all along.

While usually most of Jack's senior executives were strategic managers with a global perspective, every once in a while some of them would get mired down in minutia. The best example was the selection of a toilet seat. It all started with a minor renovation of the concierge lounge in the pavilion of our Indiana casino. There was a small unisex bathroom in the facility that was probably six by eight feet in dimension. The general manager decided that a luxury facelift in this restroom was needed. There was consensus on the wall paper, granite counter tops and general fixtures, but it almost took an act of Congress to make a determination on the color and style of the toilet seat cover. Jack called me into his office and told me he thought the toilet seat dispute was a symptom of a deeper rooted problem with the executive team. Apparently two of the three executives involved had pulled Jack aside on his last visit to the property to suggest that it may be time for each of them to consider moving on. In other words, there wasn't enough room in Dodge (or Hammond, in this case) for the two of them to exist. Jack told me to "solve the problem." Jack knew the executive team at Hammond would probably never be drinking buddies. Each of them was a superstar in his own right (and own mind), but for the Hammond casino to succeed and transform quickly, Jack needed all of their talents working together. I contacted the guys, one at a time and told them about our concerns. Then I told them I wanted them to have dinner at my townhouse in Orland Park, where we would hash out their disagreement after a nice dinner and several bottles of wine. I summoned all three of them via limousine, and by the end of the dinner (and with a little help from the Napa Valley) we had consensus to cooperate on future business matters even if the three guys did not particularly like each other personally. And I solved the toilet seat issue myself. We installed a white colored Kohler model.

Another interesting executive on staff was one of our property marketing vice presidents, then stationed in Bossier City at the time of his major blunder. The Horseshoe company had just completed the purchase of the Empress casinos and we held our first off-site management retreat in San Diego with all the new management people from the two Empress casinos invited to attend, along with the new president, Joe Canfora. Each member of management made a presentation on their thoughts for the future of Horseshoe. When it came to the Bossier City presentation, this marketing guru suggested that the "Horseshoe" name may have run its useful course and it might make sense to consider changing the name of the Horseshoe company to something more modern. "After all," he concluded, "we all know that the original Horseshoe was a sawdust joint in downtown Las Vegas whereas the newer Horseshoe Riverboats are more modern and luxurious, and therefore deserve a better name to reflect the quality of say the Mirage or Caesars Palace." The whole place turned silent and our eyes all turned to look at Jack's face. You could have heard a pin drop for about three minutes straight. The idea was tantamount to passing gas in church, but the marketing guy maintained his position. Imagine how much higher a price Jack could have sold his company to Harrah's for had he actually changed the name of Horseshoe to the *"Whatever Casino"*?

This same marketing guy (and I won't mention his real name either, because he is still a friend of mine) was about as unconventional as any I have ever witnessed. He was more like a contestant in the

Ultimate Fighting Circuit. If you were in a fist fight, you wanted him in your corner. He was a good guerilla marketer and, with Jack Binion's position that you maintain market share at all costs, this guy could take to the whip and punish a competitor's assault on Horseshoe. So you see why we put up with him. His personality was rougher than a stucco bathtub, but he was effective on most accounts.

He did make some memorable first impressions, too. We had hired a new advertising agency from Chicago, and several members of the new agency were in Bossier City for an introductory meeting. Following dinner the first evening, they were invited over to this executive's home for some cocktails and entertainment. What the new advertising team did not expect was a tour of this executive's home, especially the "Grand Boudoir", complete with a Cheetah skin bedspread on the giant bed and a commercial fire extinguisher on the night stand. He was quick to point out that his "Little Erotica" often got mighty hot and the fire extinguisher was there just in case things got out of hand. He then serenaded the new Chicago crew with a very bad guitar concert. Quite unconventional you will agree, and the females from the advertising agency never again returned to Bossier City.

The Horseshoe executive team worked hard together and often played hard together. You are never too old to learn and I was fortunate to learn some new tricks working with these guys. David Carroll, our human resources executive, became my role model for what a good HR Executive should be like. He was my first official contact at Horseshoe after Jack Binion, and we became good friends. Gary Border, our vice president of marketing was the company wine sommelier in addition to being an outstanding marketer. Gary was my greatest mentor with the Binion family when I first joined the Horseshoe and he also filled the role of partner and friend. Kirk Saylor, my other half of the odd couple, was my partner, my friend and for a while my roommate. The keenest relationship I developed was with the youngest executive on the team, a portly guy named Jon Wolfe. Twenty years my junior, this guy became my immediate role model for how to deploy business technology from an entrepreneur's point of view. Jon became a partner and friend almost immediately after I joined the company. I had been blessed over my career to have worked with some great technology people, but none of them held a candle to Jon Wolfe. Jon understands how the business works in every single department of a casino resort and was able to quickly assess and set specifications for solutions that enabled the business to operate quicker and more efficiently. He didn't design systems just to computerize a process, as is frequently done in our industry; instead, he developed applications that put simple tools in the hands of the front line service employees who were charged with the responsibility of taking care of our customers. Jon is one of my very few colleagues I can say fills the position of role model, mentor, partner and friend.

When the Horseshoe company was sold to Harrah's, a few of the guys elected to stay on with the buyer. Several others grabbed employment opportunities in other casino companies. The rest of us decided to form a gaming consulting company and the first person I wanted to go into business with was Jon Wolfe. Along with Dominic Polizzotto, the Horseshoe general counsel, we formed a group called House Advantage L.L.C. and we prospered from our inception. Dominic eventually left us to become the manager of the Binion family office. When I finally decided to retire, I tendered my share of ownership to Jon Wolfe who has developed our consulting company into a major casino technology and business solutions provider and is serving some of the biggest names in gaming today.

The decision to retire was difficult. But after 45 years of "all play and no work," I found myself finally losing the passion to devote the number of hours it takes to really excel and be effective in our type of business. I was lamenting the fact that over half of the places I had worked had been blown up or torn down to make way for newer and more luxurious facilities. The Dunes Hotel was blown up to make way for the Bellagio Resort. The Sands was imploded to make way for the Venetian Hotel. The Castaways was bulldozed to make space for the Mirage Casino. The Desert Inn was knocked down to make room for the Wynn Resort. The Frontier was demolished to make way for the planned New York Plaza (the recession put this resort development on hold after the Frontier came tumbling down).

While still standing, the MGM in Reno had changed hands five times and was closed for business when I started writing this book. The Claridge Casino Hotel in Atlantic City was downsized and added to Bally's as a spare hotel tower. The Trump's Castle, which became Trump Marina after I left it, is now the Golden Nugget.

With all this behind me, it was time to get out of the full time gaming management business. I have not yet become as obsolete as the buildings I worked in, but I was starting to feel that way. It was a great run and, if I had it to do all over again, I would take the same course. To anybody considering a career in the gaming industry, the stars are the limit. It is everyday fun. In reality, it actually requires a lot of perseverance and work. But if you love the business like I did, it just doesn't seem like work. After all, that is what makes life worth living and it just doesn't get any better than this.

Thanks for reading my story to the end.

Sincerely,
Roger P. Wagner

Afterword

I CONSIDERED MY time at Horseshoe as the official end of my career. After all, you can only be "Born Again" once. The sale of the Horseshoe Corporation to Harrah's concluded on July 1, 2004. Shortly after the sale, Jon Wolfe, Dominic Polizzotto and I formed House Advantage LLC and began a period of providing consulting services to a wide array of casino clients. In April, 2005 we signed a deal with a Colony Capital subsidiary, Resorts International Holdings to help them undertake the transition of merging four casinos they had purchased from Harrah's under a single umbrella with two other casino they owned. Upon completion of our ninety day consulting deal, we were offered the opportunity to join the Colony Organization as executives to oversee the assimilation of the six casinos. Jon Wolfe signed on as the Company's first Chief Technology officer and I became the Chief Operating Officer. Dominic Polizzotto decided to turn down the offer of General Counsel; and went back to work for the Binion Family.

Colony Capital had purchased four of the orphan casinos in the Harrah's portfolio of assets. Now with hindsight, they had paid too much for them and they had failed to protect the customer data bases of the four individual casinos, instead letting the seller keep the data bases to themselves. It proved to be a grave mistake. It was always Jack Binion's axiom to "sell to a fool smarter than yourself". Harrah's sale of these four casinos appeared to be the case with with the Colony purchase. Then to repeat another *Jackism*, "In the valley of the blind the one-eyed guy is King", we found that this old saying applied to much of the management Colony had put in place to operate their four newly acquired casinos. While they were all nice people and obviously good executives in different venues at different times, some of them were out of place in the geographical realm we found the company in when we got there. In eighteen months, we were successful in engineering a turn around to the point that we were able to recover market share in all but one casino and even improve market share in our East Chicago asset over what Harrah's had achieved before the sale to Colony. In April, 2007 Colony announced a deal to sell its Chicagoland Casino for $675 million dollars, reaping a $250 million dollar profit in less than two years. When the sale was consummated on September 17, 2007, Jon Wolfe and I exited the company redeeming our shares of stock for a tidy sum of money. We were lucky to leave when we did. In early 2007, Pennsylvania opened gaming in their state and when the recession accelerated the decline in business volumes in 2008, the Colony subsidiary became worthless and fell behind on its interest payments as did its two sister subsidiaries, Resorts Atlantic City Casino and the Las Vegas Hilton casino. Luck and fate got me into the business at the right time and luck and fate got me out in the nick of time.

The next two years Jon Wolfe and I rejoined Jack Binion to look for investment opportunities during the recession. Jack was looking for the proverbial "Birds nest on the ground", which we never did find. We took a hard fought run at winning the gaming license for Sumner County, Kansas but lost out to our old nemesis, Harrah's. When Harrah's decided not to move forward with their Kansas casino development, the Binion group was solicited again to make a proposal in round two. Jack declined. He figured the process had been rigged during round one and it no doubt would be politically rigged again in round two. After a $4 million dollar failed effort, he was not about to try it again. On January 1, 2010, we closed down our development efforts. At this writing, I currently serve on the Board of Directors of a small publicly traded gaming company, which still allows me to keep my finger in the business without having to devote full time to the effort.

CPSIA information can be obtained at www.ICGtesting.com
Printed in the USA
BVOW021128101111

275747BV00001B/5/P